Structural change in the world economy

Edited by Allan Webster and
John H. Dunning

ROUTLEDGE
London and New York

First published 1990 by Routledge
11 New Fetter Lane, London EC4P 4EE
29 West 35th Street, New York, NY 10001

© 1990 Allan Webster and John H. Dunning

Typeset by Thomson Press (India) Ltd, New Delhi
Printed and bound in Great Britain by
Biddles Ltd, Guildford and King's Lynn

British Library Cataloguing in Publication Data

Structural change in the world economy
  I. Webster, Allan, *1955-* II. Dunning, John H. *1927-* 330

  ISBN 0-415-02420-X

Library of Congress Cataloging-in-Publication Data

Structural change in the world economy/edited by Allan
  Webster and John H. Dunning.
      p. cm.
    Bibliography: p.
    Includes index.
    ISBN 0-415-02420-X
    1. International economic relations. 2. Industry and
state-History. 3. Capitalism–History. 4. Economic
history. I. Webster, Allan, 1955- . II. Dunning, John H.

HF 1359.S77 1989   89-5957
337–dc 19   CIP

Contents

List of tables   vii

List of figures   x

List of contributors   xi

List of abbreviations   xiii

Part One–The context of structural change

1 Introduction   3
  John H. Dunning and Allan Webster

2 UK manufacturing industry: structural change and
  competitiveness – a lesson for other countries?   12
  John Reynolds

3 Historical perspectives on structural change and
  economic decline   33
  Stephen Nicholas

Part Two – Causes of change in the world economy

4 Competition, innovation, and industrial performance   49
  Kirsty S. Hughes

5 The role of services in global structural change   67
  H. Peter Gray

6 The growing internationalization of industry: a
  comparison of the changing structure of company
  activity in the major industrialized countries   91
  John Cantwell

Contents

7 **Intra-industry foreign direct investment: a study of
recent evidence**   **114**
Jeremy Clegg

8 **Restructuring among the largest firms: changing
geographical and industrial diversification, 1977–82**   **143**
Robert D. Pearce

Part Three – Policy and structural change

  9 **Japanese manufacturing investment and the
restructuring of the United Kingdom economy**   **167**
John H. Dunning

10 **Trade liberalization and specialization in manufactured
goods**   **183**
Chris Milner

11 **Voluntary export restraints and lobbying: another
example of the non-equivalence of equivalent
restrictions**   **211**
David Greenaway

12 **Skills in international trade policy**   **221**
Allan Webster

Index   **237**

Tables

		Page
2.1	Industrial employment in OECD countries	13
2.2	The structure of national output, 1975–85	16
2.3	Gross fixed investment in the G7 countries	18
2.4	Rates of return before interest and tax at current replacement cost	19
2.5	Output per person per hour in manufacturing	20
2.6	Measures of UK competitiveness in manufacturing	22
2.7	Changes in employment in different manufacturing sectors	24
2.8	Output trends of manufacturing industries, 1975–85	25
2.9	Trade performance of UK manufacturing industries, 1975–85	26
4.1	GDP per head of population	51
4.2	Productivity and unit labour costs in manufacturing industry	51
4.3	Annual average growth of manufacturing industry, 1972–81	52
4.4	Importance of high R&D industries in total manufacturing output and exports	52
4.5	Trade balance of manufacturing by technology group, 1970–84	53
4.6	Export market shares of manufacturing by technology group	53
4.7	Import penetration of manufacturing industry by technology group	53
4.8	Export/import ratios of the high-technology groups	54
4.9	Export/import ratios of the medium-technology groups	55
4.10	Gross expenditure on R&D (GERD): constant 1975 prices	56
4.11	R&D in the OECD area	56

Tables

4.12 Gross expenditure on R&D as a percentage of
      GDP   57
4.13 Funding of R&D   57
4.14 Government R&D funding   58
4.15 Business enterprise R&D – rate of growth   58
4.16 Proportions of industries' R&D 1981   59
4.17 Distribution of manufactuing R&D within
      countries, 1983   60

5.1   Sectoral shares of GDP for five developed nations,
      1960–84   71
5.2   Selected components of service activities, 1970 and
      1983   73
5.3   Estimates of US service balance of payments,
      1982–4   74
5.4   The international net worth of the United States   81
5.5   Outstanding financial assets of non-Americans in
      US financial markets: end-of-year data   82
5.A.1 Employment in services in the United Kingdom   86
5.A.2 Employment in services in the United States   87

6.1   The measure of the general trend towards
      internationalization over the period 1974–82   105
6.2   The proportional change in the foreign production
      ratio of national groups of firms over the period
      1974–82   106
6.3   The proportional change in the degree of
      internationalization over the period 1974–82   108
6.4   The estimated contribution of ownership
      advantages to the proportional change in the
      degree of internationalization over the period
      1974–82   109
6.5   The estimated contribution of location advantages
      to the proportional change in the degree of
      internationalization over the period 1974–82   111
6.6   The estimated contribution of the catching-up effect
      to the proportional change in the degree of
      internationalization over the period 1974–82   112

7.1   Estimates of intra-industry foreign direct
      investment for the USA, 1980   128
7.2   Estimates of intra-industry foreign direct
      investment for the UK, 1974–81   131
7.3   Estimates of intra-industry foreign direct
      investment for the Federal Republic of Germany,
      1976–85   134

7.A   Concordance of the estimates of intra-industry foreign direct investment between the USA, UK and the FRG, 1980–1   138

8.1   Regressions with CIDR as dependent variable   148
8.2   Regressions with COPR as dependent variable   155
8.3   Regressions with CPER as dependent variable   158
8.4   Regressions with CIDR as dependent and COPR as independent variable   161

10.1   Average levels of intra-industry at the third digit level in the UK   184
10.2   Cross-country comparisons of average levels of intra-industry at the third digit level, 1980   185
10.3   Average levels of intra-industry trade for country types, 1978   186
10.4   A schema of possible effects of trade liberalization on trade and specialization indices   190
10.5   Tariffs on manufactured imports in the UK, 1967–85   194
10.6   Industry indices of share of intra-industry trade in total trade, 1970–84   196
10.7   Industry indices of intra-industry specialization, 1970–84   196
10.8   Industry indices of intra-industry specialization, 1970–84   197
10.9   Changes in trade and specialization indices: UK manufacturing industries, 1970–84   198
10.10   Consistency of observed changes in trade and specialization indices with alternative hypotheses   200

Figures

11.1   The market conditions for importables in a small
       open economy   214
11.2   Market structure, volume, and ratio VERs   216
11.3   Demand shifts, volume and ratio VERs   217
12.1   Quality and a human capital subsidy   226
12.2   Human capital subsidies as a strategic policy   227
12.3   The basic Brander and Spencer case   229

x

Contributors

John Cantwell is Lecturer in Economics at the University of Reading and has also been Visiting Professor at the University of Rom 'La Sapienza'. He is the author of *Technological Innovation and Multinational Corporations* (1989) and has published a variety of research papers. He has acted as a consultant to international organizations including the World Bank, the OECD, and the United Nations Centre on Transnational Corporations.

Jeremy Clegg is Lecturer in Business Economics in the School of Management, University of Bath, with previous appointments at the University of Reading, University College of Swansea, and the University of Exeter. His research interests lie in the economics of international business and the multinational enterprise. He is the author of *Multi-national Enterprise and World Competition: A Comparative Study of the USA, Japan, the UK, Sweden and West Germany* (1987).

John Dunning is ICI Research Professor in International Business at the University of Reading, and State of New Jersey Professor of International Business at Rutgers University, in the USA. He has written or edited over thirty books and reports on international investment and business over the past thirty years. He is also Chairman of Economists Advisory Group, a London-based consultancy company.

Peter Gray is Professor of Economics and Finance/Management at Rensselaer Polytechnic Institute in the USA. He has been a professor at Wayne State University; Thammasat University, Bangkok, Thailand; and Rutgers, the State University of New Jersey. He has written seven books and edited five, and has published about ninety articles and papers. He has been a consultant for the World Bank, the International Labour Organization, and the International Monetary Fund.

Contributors

David Greenaway is Professor of Economics at the University of Nottingham. He has published articles in a number of journals including the *Economic Journal, European Economic Review, Kyklos*, and *Weltwirtschaftliches Archiv*. He is the author, co-author, editor, and co-editor of several books.

Kirsty Hughes is a Lecturer in Economics at the University of Manchester. Prior to this appointment she was a Lecturer at the University of East Anglia. She took her first degree at Cambridge and her PhD at Bristol.

Chris Milner is Senior Lecturer in Economics at Loughborough University. He has published articles in a number of journals including the *Economic Journal, European Economic Review*, and *Weltwirtschaftliches Archiv*. He is editor of *International Money and Political Economy* (1986) and is co-author (with David Greenaway) of *The Economics of Intra-industry Trade* (1986).

Stephen Nicholas is Senior Lecturer in Economics at the University of New South Wales, Australia. A graduate of Syracuse University and the University of Iowa, he has published articles on the British Industrial Revolution, and twentieth century economic history and the emergence of the multinational enterprise, in such journals as *Oxford Economic Papers, Journal of Economic History*, and *Economic History Review*. He was editor and principal author of *Convict Workers: Reinterpreting Australia's Past* (1988).

Robert Pearce is Senior Research Fellow in the Department of Economics at the University of Reading. He has published widely on the subject of international business. His current research interests include the industrial diversification of large firms and the decentralization of R&D by multinationals.

John Reynolds is the Senior Economist and Vice-President for Prudential-Bache Capital Funding Ltd in London. Before assuming this position in 1986 he was employed as a management consultant.

Allan Webster is Lecturer in Economics at the University of Reading. He has published articles in *Applied Economics* and the *Journal of Economic Studies*.

Abbreviations

ACOST	Advisory Council on Science and Technology (UK)
EEC	European Economic Community
FDI	foreign direct investment
FPR	foreign production ratio
GATT	General Agreement on Tariffs and Trade
IIT	intra-industry trade
LDCs	less developed countries
MITI	Ministry of International Trade and Industry (Japan)
MNEs	multinational enterprises
NICs	newly industrializing countries
OECD	Organization for Economic Co-operation and Development
R&D	research and development
SSQs	source-specific quotas
UNCTAD	United Nations conference on Trade and Development
UNCTC	United Nations Centre on Transnational Corporations
VER	voluntary export restraint

Part One

The context of structural change

Chapter One

Introduction

John H. Dunning and Allan Webster

The 'structure' of an economy is a very broad concept. For example, it can encompass institutional factors, underlying social conditions, diverse consumer preferences, resource endowments, and cultural elements, as well as the particular mix of production of goods and services. No single volume can hope to produce an exhaustive discussion of all aspects of change in such structures. We have, here, attempted to limit the task by abstracting from those influences that are likely to be predominantly national in their nature. Thus, for example, institutional, cultural, and social factors which tend to be specific to the individual economy are largely ignored by this book. This is not because the authors or editors consider them unworthy of attention but reflects our attempt to draw inferences and conclusions that are valid across national boundaries.

A second feature of our emphasis on the international context is that this book is primarily concerned with industrial change and industrial policy for open economies. In short, the focus is upon the two-way interaction between changing national economies and changing world conditions. Moreover, the book has concentrated upon such changes from the viewpoint of developed market economies. Economic development is, of course, a change in the structure of the economy concerned (typically from agricultural to manufacturing output) but is one that is extensively covered elsewhere. Similarly, developments in East–West economic relations is a topic more suited to separate consideration.

A central theme of this book is the interdependence of different economies and, in particular, that of the world's leading capitalist nations. It is precisely because interdependence is both important and growing in significance that structural change is increasingly effected through the 'world economy'. The growth of world trade, the expansion of capital flows between economies, and the development of firms producing in more than one country are all elements that lead one increasingly to consider changes in production in an international context.

The UK, with her traditional reliance upon international trade, has been more interdependent than many other countries. It may be argued, moreover, that her position as the world's first industrial nation has led her to experience the pressure for change to a greater extent than other nations. Certainly, as problems associated with industrial decline and structural change are frequently dubbed the 'British disease', the UK would seem to be an appropriate place to start our consideration. The relevance of the British experience, particularly in the light of the performance of the US economy in the 1980s, should not be lost on the reader.

In Chapter 2, therefore, John Reynolds sets out the recent experience of British manufacturing industry. The principal symptoms of the 'disease' are discussed as the relative decline of the share of manufacturing in gross domestic product (GDP), a contraction of manufacturing employment, and a declining trade balance in manufactures. Note, however, that the evidence of more recent growth in manufacturing output suggests an element of transitional problems in response to structural change within the manufacturing sector. However, the shift from manufacturing to the service sector raises the possibility of a more permanent decline in the relative significance of manufacturing. This point is discussed further by H. Peter Gray in Chapter 5.

Reynolds also outlines a number of reasons for the decline of the UK manufacturing sector. Clearly, the effects of North Sea oil combined with restrictive macro-economic policy induced a greater 'shake-out' than would otherwise have occurred (an issue which is further explored by Nicholas in Chapter 3). Amongst the longer term factors which Reynolds uses to explain the decline of UK manufacturing are low investment and low labour productivity. These are likely to be closely related to the other main reason he offers for decline – the poor performance of industries that are not intensive in research and development (an issue which Hughes also discusses in Chapter 4).

Stephen Nicholas, in Chapter 3, develops the theme of structural adjustment problems in response to windfall resource gains. Analysis of such effects for a modern, developed economy has already been developed by authors such as Neary and Corden (1982). In short, the main argument is that a natural resource windfall must inevitably produce a contraction in the remainder of the tradeables sector – manufacturing. Economists have tended to see this as a problem peculiar to the twentieth century, particularly in the case of Dutch gas deposits and British oil deposits.

The contribution of Nicholas is to draw our attention to the point that these types of effects can be observed with some frequency throughout history. The experience of sixteenth-century Spain, where the windfall effect of gold and silver from foreign conquests to a large extent eradicated Spanish industry through inflationary pressures, is particularly instructive. Similarly, his discussion of the effects of a booming coal sector in the late nineteenth and early twentieth centuries shows that North Sea oil is not the first instance where manufacturing has been squeezed by natural resource booms in Britain.

The consequences of this for the economic analysis of structural adjustment problems is clear – booming sector effects upon manu-facturing industry are not merely features of highly developed modern economies but are part of the inevitable adjustment process to booms in natural resources. Moreover, Nicholas's discussion of sixteenth-century Spain casts some light on a further issue. Econo-mists have tended to presume that, as the once booming natural resource approaches exhaustion, the adjustment process will reverse itself, thereby leading to a resurgence of manufacturing. However, the Spanish experience suggests that this is far from certain – it may be more difficult to re-create manufacturing sectors than it is to allow them to decline.

Thus, Reynolds in Chapter 2 sets out the main reasons for change and decline in a manufacturing sector. Nicholas, in Chapter 3, draws our attention to the evidence of history that such changes are an inevitable feature of economic life. Section 2 of the book, therefore, seeks to examine in more detail the underlying reasons why such changes occur, with particular reference to recent changes in the world economy.

An obvious point to start this examination is with technical change and innovation. Kirsty Hughes, in Chapter 4, analyzes the role of innovation in the changing structure of four economies – the USA, the UK, Japan, and West Germany. To some extent, as she notes, it is difficult to separate cause and effect here, as innovation tends to be associated with high growth, which has positive implications for innovation. None the less, research and development can be linked to two key factors – productivity growth and trade performance.

As Hughes shows, Japan has tended to outperform the UK, USA, and Germany in terms of trade performance. It is unlikely to be purely coincidental that, for the period considered, Japan increased gross expenditure on R & D in both absolute and relative terms more rapidly than any of the other countries considered. The USA remains, in proportion to GDP, the world's largest spender on R & D but has tended to deteriorate relatively in terms of economic performance.

The UK, in contrast, exhibits strong relative decline in both trade and R&D performance.

Thus, the evidence suggests a clear link between R&D and economic performance which we should, perhaps, not find surprising. However, it remains to explain why countries differ in their ability to innovate. Hughes offers a number of complementary explanations. Levels of domestic aggregate demand can provide a stimulus to innovation. To an extent 'success-breeds-success' factors can be important and, over short planning horizons, can lead to under-investment in innovation. It is unlikely, however, that expenditure on military R&D 'crowds out' commercial spending in any simple fashion. Lastly, she considers possible future developments, particularly in the light of increases in co-operative R&D and the increased importance of multinational enterprises.

In Chapter 5 Peter Gray analyzes the growing contribution of services to the GNP of most countries; and their rising share in international trade. After delineating the particular characteristics of services (as compared with goods), Gray examines the impact of the new knowledge-intensive technologies on the international division of labour; and especially the extent to which the resulting structural changes favour the developed or developing countries. He is generally optimistic about the prospects for North–North trade in services, particularly within Europe after 1992, but is less sanguine about North–South trade and fears that its growth may be inhibited by non-tariff barriers imposed by developing countries.

The author next considers some of the implications of increased trade in services. He suggests that the easier cross-hauling of financial services, while leading to more integration of financial markets, might do so only at the cost of financial volatility. He argues that the new service-related technologies will lead to more centralization of decision-taking within multinational corporations; and that, in general, the telematics revolution may lead to more rather than less inequality of income distribution between developed and developing countries.

The final section of Chapter 6 presents the intrusion hypothesis, which suggests that services intrude to a greater degree, and more irreversibly, into the structure of domestic economies than do goods; and where foreign-owned will tend to reduce national economic autonomy. Thus, while greater openness in trade and investment in services may bring greater allocative efficiency between countries, the same openness may require some relinquishment of natural sovereignty and lead to more economic instability. In Peter Gray's own words 'nations must see the growth in the freedom of trade in services in terms of the potential for economic growth ... against the possibility of greater volatility in economic performance in times of turbulence'.

Changes which tend to have effects in a somewhat aggregate fashion, such as natural resource effects, innovation, and the growth of services, are not the only likely sources of structural change in the world economy. In particular, changes in the nature of firms and in the way that firms behave are likely to have profound consequences for the world economy. This is particularly true when the firms are themselves, in some sense, international. Part II, therefore, continues with a series of three chapters concerned both with developments in the internationalization of firms and with changes in the behaviour of multinational enterprises (MNEs).

John Cantwell provides the first of these in Chapter 6. He discusses four main reasons leading to the internationalization of firms – ownership advantages, locational advantages, 'catch-up' factors and a general trend towards internationalization (through, for example, reduced transport and communication costs). The chapter assesses the significance of each of these factors in changes in the internationalization of firms for the period 1974–82.

He finds that there was a significant tendency for internationalization of firms to increase for manufacturing industry generally. This tendency towards increased multinational activity is, perhaps, somewhat less than might have been expected, due in no small part to a decline in the significance of foreign production for US firms and the dominant role of US firms in multinational production. Thus, the main part of the increased internationalization of the world's manufacturing firms has been provided by substantial increases in the internationalization of European and Japanese firms.

Of the factors comprising these aggregate effects, Cantwell finds evidence of strongly increased ownership advantages of non-US firms and of a shift in locational advantage from Europe and Japan to the United States. The catch-up effect is found to be significant only for Japanese firms. Thus, the main picture that emerges is one of continuing increases in the internationalization of the world's manufacturing firms but, in recent years, an increased tendency for non-US firms to develop international activity which is increasingly located in the US.

Jeremy Clegg (Chapter 7) considers a change in the nature of multinational activity from inter-industry foreign direct investment (FDI) to intra-industry. As he notes, this parallels the literature on international trade, in which intra-industry trade has been argued to be a significant and growing feature. Traditional theories of the MNE have tended to emphasize inter-industry aspects, with a one-way flow of FDI from the source to host country. Clegg produces evidence of substantial intra-industry flows of FDI for a number of countries, using the maximum available degree of industrial and geographical disaggregation.

He offers three principal explanations for this increased tendency for FDI to be a two-way process within the same industry. First, he argues that increased differentiation (both horizontally and vertically) has meant that ownership advantages have become more specific. As these advantages increasingly apply to a particular sub-set of activities within an industry, intra-industry FDI is an inevitable consequence. Second, increased economies of scope have tended to lead to within-firm specialization and, therefore, increased geographical diversification. Last, he argues that oligopolistic rivalry has led firms to engage in strategic FDI, thereby encouraging rivals to 'invade' each others' domestic markets. His broad conclusions are that firm-specific economies and government policy best explain the continued expansion of intra-industry foreign direct investment, together with the tendency towards increased intra-firm and intra-industry trade.

Robert Pearce develops the theme of the increased diversification of the MNE in Chapter 8. An important point of this paper is to note that the existence of the multinational enterprise necessarily implies that structural adjustment will be, to some extent, within-firm adjustment. Thus, changes in the world economy that affect industrial production also lead large, multinational firms to adjust the industrial and geographical composition of their production. Pearce considers exactly these effects on the diversification of multinational activity.

Using the period 1977–82 he finds a significant tendency to increased industrial diversification amongst large multinational firms. He finds that growth in the main activity of the firm is negatively related to industrial diversification – in short, a principal motivation is constrained demand in the main activity. The size of the firm is shown not to be a significant feature of this process. He also finds, like Cantwell in Chapter 6, a significant tendency for these firms to become increasingly internationalized. Again, this can be explained by slow growth – in this case, of the domestic market. Thus, domestic demand-constraints are a key factor in persuading firms to diversify geographically their activity. Finally, he looks at the relationship between this industrial and geographical trend to diversification and finds that the two elements are largely determined independently.

Pearce, therefore, concludes our consideration of the main under-lying causes of changes in the location and nature of the world's industrial production. Section III, which comprises the last four chapters of the book, turns our attention to the impact of government policy upon structural change. Clearly, as we argued earlier, structural change is an inevitable feature of the economic interdependence of nations. Therefore, policies which impact upon this interdependence – particularly policy directed at trade and at multinational production – are likely to have consequences for the process of change.

The third set of contributions to this volume consider some of the implications of structural change for government policy. In Chapter 9, John Dunning argues that the current wave of Japanese direct investment in British manufacturing industry is necessitating some modification to existing UK micro-economic policy if the full benefits of such investment are to be realized. In particular, he stresses the need for a holistic approach towards economic restructuring which will help the UK develop strong indigenous supply capabilities in those industries in which it is perceived to have a dynamic comparative advantage. He contends that, because of the high transaction costs involved, the market alone cannot ensure the socially desirable restructuring of resources, or generate the supply capabilities (especially human capital and innovations) necessary to promote UK competitiveness in international industries.

Dunning asserts that, without more co-operation between Government and industry, and a realization that governments, like firms, are competing with each other for resources and markets, there is a danger that the UK might becomes a manufacturing satellite for Japanese multinationals seeking to exploit the European market. The alternative, and a much more promising scenario, is that the Japanese affiliates will increasingly steer their high-value-added activities to the UK, which could then become a regional centre for the research and development laboratories of Japanese firms. At the same time, stimulated by the Japanese presence, UK multinationals might themselves become more internationally competitive. However, Dunning cautions that, for this to happen, the Japanese market may have to become more open to the product of UK companies than it is now – a subject which has its own policy implications for both the Japanese Government and for UK–Japanese economic relationships.

Chris Milner considers the impact of post-war trade liberalization in Chapter 10. He examines the consequences of liberalization for both intra-industry and inter-industry trade. In theoretical terms, he argues, tariff liberalization should stimulate both forms of trade relative to production. However, the particular manner in which liberalization has been achieved is likely to have favoured an increasing share of intra-industry trade in total trade. This is principally because GATT has encouraged symmetric tariff reductions – in short, reductions in the tariff on a particular commodity by one country have tended to be matched by reductions in the tariff on the same commodity by others.

To examine this contention he looks at three periods of tariff liberalization – the Kennedy round, EEC transition, and the Tokyo round – and the effects on UK trade. He finds that the post-Kennedy-round period was characterized by increases in intra-industry trade with net exports declining in nominal terms for a substantial number of industries. The position for the EEC accession years is somewhat similar, in that the share of intra-industry trade in gross trade was increased for almost 60 per cent of the sampled industries. For the post-Tokyo-round period, however, increases in intra- and inter-industry trade were approximately matched.

Thus, the tentative conclusion must be that tariff liberalization, in general, tends to stimulate both forms of trade but there is some evidence to suppose that reductions which are reciprocal by industry tend to stimulate intra-industry trade more. Last, Milner considers the issue of structural adjustment to liberalization and argues that adjustment costs are likely to be less in the case of intra-industry trade. This is chiefly because the adjustment within an industry is likely to be less costly than one between dissimilar activities.

In Chapter 11, David Greenaway examines a central feature of the 'new protectionism' that has characterized many developed countries' responses to problems of adjusting to structural change – the voluntary export restraint (VER). He argues that there are a number of reasons why such measures have become prevalent – not least because, unlike a subsidy, costs are not in an explicit form (to the exchequer) but are 'hidden' in the extra costs to consumers as rent is extracted by exporters.

Moreover, Greenaway examines two types of VER – a volume VER and a ratio VER. He shows that the specific type of VER used is likely to depend upon market structure. In particular, ratio VERs are likely to be preferred by domestic industries that are highly concentrated. This is because they more effectively inhibit marginal competition and, therefore, enhance monopoly power. Thus, the response of governments to adjustment pressures is to some extent likely to be determined by domestic market structure – at least with regard to the type of measure employed.

Allan Webster, in Chapter 12, considers the role of skill subsidies in international trade policy. For a conventional comparative-advantage/factor-proportions trade model the consequence of such a policy by one country is quite clear – it would tend to shift comparative advantage in favour of domestic industries that use skills intensively. However, the consequences for trade patterns where international trade is not based on competitive industries or upon homogeneous products are not so clear. This chapter examines the effect of a human capital subsidy for two different 'imperfect' competition trade models.

The models examined are those of international duopoly and of perfect competition in a vertically differentiated good. The policy, as with any other intervention in trade, is most likely to be welfare-improving if it directly tackles a market imperfection or distortion of some form. It is argued that the market for human capital is likely to exhibit such imperfections. In both models it is shown that there are grounds for supposing that such an intervention will perform better than other comparable interventions in markets for tradeables. Moreover, in one of the models it is shown that skill subsidies perform well when adopted by more than one country. The possibility that skill subsidies may be a desirable multilateral intervention is, therefore, speculatively raised.

Chapter Two

UK Manufacturing industry: structural change and competitiveness – a lesson for other countries?

John Reynolds

Introduction

The manufacturing sector has traditionally played a vital role in Britain has earned her living by importing raw materials and exporting employment opportunities. Ever since the Industrial Revolution, Britain has earned her living by importing raw materials and exporting manufactured goods. Britain's dependence on imported food and raw materials, including, until recently, energy, was highlighted by the 'Export or Die' slogan of the early post-war period. Whilst manufacturing industry still plays an important role in the national economy, that role has clearly diminished, however, over the past twenty-five years – as large chunks of the old traditional industries of steel, shipbuilding, textiles, and metal manufacture have found it difficult to keep pace with international competitiveness. Manufacturing represented just under a quarter, 24.3 per cent, of all activity (GDP) in 1986 against 36.5 per cent in 1960. By comparison, the share of services (broadly defined) rose from 45.0 per cent to 55.5 per cent over the same period.

Although all advanced industrial countries have seen manufacturing decline in relative importance as a share of their GDP, it is significant that following the world-wide recession of 1973 only the United Kingdom has experienced a sustained absolute fall in manufacturing production. The most evident consequences of Britain's relatively poor industrial record over this period have been a sharp reduction in industrial employment and a decline in the trade balance in manufacturing, which in 1983 fell into deficit for the first time since the Industrial Revolution. It is this absolute decline in industrial employment, particularly in the manufacturing industry, which is a worrying feature of the UK economy and which, as Thirwall (1982) remarked, warrants the description 'de-industrialization'.[1]

Table 2.1 gives the numbers employed in industry in the OECD

Table 2.1 Industrial employment in OECD countries (in thousands)

	1966	1973	1979	1981	1985
United Kingdom	11,559	10,482	9,711	8,601	7,790
Canada	2,438	2,685	3,002	3,112	2,883
United States	26,278	28,225	30,918	30,191	30,047
Japan	15,800	19,570	19,140	19,700	20,250
Australia	1,805	2,042	1,895	1,950	1,846
New Zealand	401	412	424	411	430
Austria	1,312	1,352	1,295	1,272	1,174
Belgium	1,592	1,512	1,306	1,199	1,070
Denmark	824	806	793	695	709
Finland	707	769	779	821	775
France	7,705	8,241	7,725	7,459	6,681
Germany	12,656	12,554	11,289	11,121	10,250
Greece	709	881	994	1,023	981
Ireland	293	335	365	363	305
Italy	7,063	7,454	7,583	7,647	6,896
Luxembourg	63	67	60	59	53
The Netherlands	1,836	1,706	1,567	1,498	1,347
Norway	531	560	564	575	560
Portugal	1,074	1,137	1,350	1,450	1,422
Spain	4,069	4,632	4,266	3,878	3,381
Sweden	1,556	1,427	1,360	1,323	1,284
Switzerland	1,440	1,469	1,230	1,267	1,196

Source: Labour Force Statistics, OECD, Paris

countries since 1966, the time of peak industrial employment in the UK. In countries such as Canada, the United States, and Japan – all major competitors of the UK – industrial employment has risen over the ensuing twenty-year period. However, eleven other countries, in addition to the UK, have experienced an absolute decline in industrial employment. For these other countries, most of the decline in employment has been confined to the period since 1981, making accusations of de-industrialization a relatively recent phenomenon. In no other country, however, has the decline since 1966 been so pronounced. In the UK there has been a loss of almost four million jobs in industry (of which three million were in manufacturing). The decrease was particularly rapid in the recession of 1980–1, where output fell by 14.2 per cent and manufacturing employment by 14.3 per cent; none the less, this absolute decline has been sustained over the period since 1966.

The decline in the UK's manufacturing sector has had severe regional repercussions. Northern Ireland, Scotland, the North of England and, more recently, the West Midlands have experienced the largest losses in terms of industrial capacity and employment. Effectively, the 1980–1 recession eliminated about 15 per cent of manufacturing capacity. The House of Lords Select Committee Report on Overseas Trade (1985) expressed concern over the decline of manufacturing, and in particular its implications for the UK's trade position. It viewed the shrinkage of Britain's manufacturing base as posing severe problems for the UK economy. This would be revealed as oil production in the North Sea – and the associated trade surplus in oil – started to dwindle. The principal recommendation was for a radical change in the national attitude towards trade and manufacturing 'if we [Britain] are to avoid a major social and economic crisis in our nation's affairs in the foreseeable future'.

The rapid fall in oil prices in the first half of 1986 added urgency to the debate. In 1986 the value of the UK's oil surplus fell by £4 billion to £4.1 billion, putting pressure on non-oil trade performance to prevent a serious deterioration in the UK's balance of payments. Both a lower oil price and a weaker currency provided an opportunity for manufacturing industry to make up some of the lost ground. Greater profitability and an improved share of national output over the past two years have injected hope into the manufacturing sector.

The British Government has hoped that the slimline, more profitable core of manufacturing industry that remains will provide a springboard for greater industrial success. Improved profitability, strong company balance sheets, and generally low gearing have led some, including former Industry Minister John Butcher, to regard Britain as being within each of a dramatic, sustained turnaround in its industrial performance. However, although manufacturing output has picked up substantially from its nadir in 1981, the improvement has not been sufficient to offset the rising tide of imported manufactured goods or completely arrest the declining trend in manufacturing employment.

The experience of the UK manufacturing sector, therefore, provides a particularly striking example of the effects of changes in the structure of international comparative advantage over the past quarter century. The purpose of this paper is to examine some of the consequences and explanations behind Britain's relatively poor industrial record over this period, with a view to providing an insight into Britain's manufacturing prospects.

Changing structure of the UK economy – causes of manufacturing decline

It has been well documented (see Cherney 1981, and Maddison 1979) that a shift towards service-type activities is a natural outcome of the development process. First, there are resource shifts from agriculture to industry and then from industry to service-type activities, in accordance with differences in the income elasticity of demand for products as income rises, and with differences in the sectoral rate of growth of labour productivity.

The theory of international trade takes as its starting point the concept of comparative advantage in natural resources, human resources, and capital. In the long run, international specialization according to comparative advantage largely determines a country's pattern of trade. As specialization develops within particular industries, it gives rise to the phenomenon of intra-industry trade. As a result of this process, trading has become more important for most developed countries. Britain, once proudly known as the 'workshop of the world', the first industrial nation, has seen its relative trading position decline over a very long period of time, as other countries have developed their manufacturing industries and exploited their comparative advantage. However, the position of the UK has been eroded further than either the spread of industrialization or specialization would lead one to expect, and, for the larger part of this century, the UK has grown more slowly than her major competitors.

The structural pattern of an economy is therefore changing all the time. In particular, it has changed considerably in the UK in the past ten years (Table 2.2), partly because of the emergence of oil production, but partly also because industries that previously constituted the mainstay of the UK economy – like steel, shipbuilding, textiles, and metal manufacture – have declined in importance, whilst others – for example, electronics and chemicals – have become the driving force of industry, and certain types of service have grown out of all proportion to the national economy as a whole. This point is illustrated by the fact that in the ten years to 1983 manufacturing output fell by 15 per cent, while at the same time the output of all services increased quite markedly and one section – banking, financial business and professional services, insurance, and leasing – grew by some 70 per cent.

The importance of a competitive manufacturing sector in the UK and the need to continue reversing its relative decline are generally accepted. It is widely documented (see Thirlwall 1982) that manufacturing possesses certain growth-inducing characteristics that other sectors of the economy do not have. With many domestic service activities owing much to a buoyant manufacturing sector and many services being less tradable, the extent to which the international earnings of services can replace manufacturers as a source of foreign exchange is limited. As Smith (1986) points out, the means by which this end can be achieved are a matter of controversy, reflecting differing views on the causes of the decline and differing inter-

15

Table 2.2 The structure of national output, 1975–85

	Contribution to GDP, parts in 1,000		
	1975	1980	1985
Agriculture	26	21	18
Industry	412	433	424
Oil and gas extraction	[a]	44	62
Other energy and water	53	57	50
Manufacturing	292	270	251
Construction	67	62	61
Transport and communication	82	71	69
Distribution, hotels and catering	126	124	132
Financial and business services[b]	70	75	84
Public services[c]	172	162	156
Other services	53	54	59
Total GDP[bd]	1,000	1,000	1,000

Source: UK national accounts 1986

[a] Less than 0.5
[b] Net, after adjustment for financial service
[c] Public administration, defence, education, and health
[d] Includes ownership of dwellings

Source: UK national accounts 1986

pretations of the changes in manufacturing which have occurred since the 1980–1 recession.

A multiplicity of causes have been advanced to explain the decline of UK manufacturing industry and the deterioration of the balance of trade of manufacturers over the past decade. It has been argued, for example, that with the emergence of the UK as an oil exporter, a relative decline in the share of manufacturing in the UK's GDP and a deterioration in the balance of trade of manufactured goods were inevitable (see Neary and Corden 1982). The oil surplus, combined with the traditional surplus on invisibles, bolstered the exchange rate to a level which made it difficult for manufacturers to compete. It is clear, however, that Government strategy in 1979–80 did little to accommodate the effect of oil. Through the implementation of the Medium-Term Financial Strategy it pushed interest rates up, thereby reducing domestic demand and encouraging further capital inflows. For example, Goodhart and Temperton (1983) suggest that the Medium-Term Financial Strategy explains perhaps two-thirds of the rise in the exchange rate between 1979 and 1981, compared with one-third explained by oil price increases and the discovery of additional oil reserves. The rise in the exchange rate between 1979 and 1980 contributed to a J-curve effect, which initially improved the manufacturing balance before its plunge into deficit in 1983. Hence, the recession of 1980–1 and the rationalization of industrial capacity were hardly an inevitable consequence of North Sea oil but in large part a reflection of a radical change in industrial and economic policy aimed at improving the efficiency of both product and labour markets, with a view to enhancing industrial productivity and fostering change. In this context the 'shake-out' that occurred in manufacturing industry in the early 1980s can be viewed as the (necessary) first stage of a rationalization and restructuring process which recognized that much of Britain's slow growth and lack of international competitiveness pre-dated the oil-surplus days and was to be found in low productivity, low investment, poor product quality and design, as well as other specific cultural factors.

Over the past few years, improvements in industrial output and productivity in the UK have enabled manufacturers to achieve a slightly increased share of both national output and UK exports' share of world trade. However, with the considerable oil price decline since 1985, the urgency for a continued improvement in the UK's industrial performance to prevent an alarming deterioration in the UK's balance of payments position, has increased. Much depends on the extent to which all the longer term manufacturing 'ills' have been truly cured.

Investment

The UK's relatively poor rate of growth of gross investment has commonly been blamed for her slower overall economic growth. This is because of a clear but imperfect link between investment, particularly in manufacturing, and growth. In 'normal' (non-recessionary) times, there is a strong positive correlation between manufacturing output growth and manufacturing productivity growth on the one hand (Verdoorn's Law), and between manufacturing output growth and productivity growth outside manufacturing on the other. The latter link arises because many non-manufacturing activities are characterized by diminishing returns or by surplus labour or both. Thus, whenever industrial output and employment expand, labour resources are drawn from these other sectors, which raises the average product on these sectors either because output is not affected at all or because the less productive marginal man is absorbed. In addition, the expansion of industry will automatically generate an increase in the stock of capital employed in industry. Thus, industrial expansion generates resources, while hardly diminishing the output of the other sectors, in a way that other sectors, by their very nature, would find

17

it hard to emulate.[2] The essential ingredient required in the process of sustaining growth in manufacturing output is investment in capital equipment, which incorporates increasing levels of technical sophistication and hence permits increases in productivity to take place. Without an expansion of productive capacity (through investment), there is a limit to which the pace of output growth can be sustained without a significant injection of inflationary pressure and a deterioration in the trade balance of an economy.

Table 2.3 reveals that, during the past fifteen years, the UK's gross investment has been closer to, though still lower than, those of its main competitors – except Japan, where investment is still far greater. At first sight it would appear that blaming low investment in the UK for her slower economic growth has become less relevant. However, it still appears that investment in manufacturing has been significantly lower. Manufacturing investment fell dramatically in 1980 and has since recovered barely half of that decline.[3]

Various reasons have been given for the UK's generally lower rate of investment. Perhaps the most important factors cited by industrialists for constraint on investment in the past have been the lack of certainty firms place in the future, uncertainty as to changes in policy of successive governments, the lower profitability of British industry, high capital taxation, and the high cost of capital. However, since the Conservative Party came to power in 1979, many of these constraining factors would appear to have been reduced.

Bank of England researchers have charted the course of profitability since the early 1960s in a series of special articles in the *Quarterly Bulletin*. The results show that real, pre-tax rates of return on trading assets declined significantly, reaching very low levels indeed by the end of the 1970s, before recovering quite strongly since 1981.

Table 2.4 shows that rates of return on capital employed of UK manufacturing companies has recovered to levels last seen in the early 1970s.

Table 2.3 Gross fixed investment in the G7 countries (in percentages of GNP)

	USA	Japan	Germany	France[a]	UK[a]	Italy[a]	Canada
1965	16.4	18.0	27.0	23.0	20.0	28.0	17.0
1970	15.5	27.0	25.7	23.0	21.0	30.0	16.0
1975	14.7	23.0	21.6	23.0	20.0	25.0	17.0
1980	16.2	22.0	22.6	22.0	18.0	24.0	20.0
1985	17.4	23.0	20.0	20.0	18.0	22.0	18.0

[a] As percentage of GDP

Source: OECD databank, datastream

Table 2.4 Rates of return before interest and tax at current replacement cost

	All industrial and commercial companies		Manufacturing companies	
	Gross[a]	Net[b]	Gross[a]	Net[b]
1960	11.4	13.1	12.0	14.5
1970	8.9	8.9	7.9	8.0
1972	9.3	9.5	8.0	8.1
1974	6.3	5.2	5.2	4.0
1976	5.9	4.4	4.6	2.9
1978	8.4	7.9	6.5	5.9
1980	7.4	6.4	4.7	3.1
1982	8.1	7.5	5.7	3.6
1984	10.2	10.7	5.7	4.8
1986	9.7	10.0	7.1	7.2

Basis of estimates:

Profits
[a] Gross operating surplus on UK operations, i.e. gross trading profits less stock appreciation plus rent received
[b] Net operating surplus on UK operations, i.e. gross operating surplus less consumption at current replacement cost.

Capital employed
[a] Gross capital stock of fixed assets (excluding land) at current replacement cost, plus book value of stocks, in the UK.
[b] Net capital stock of fixed assets (excluding land) at current replacement cost, plus book value of stocks, in the UK.

Source: British Business, 9 October 1987, p. 33

Manufacturers' profitably received a strong boost in 1985 and 1986 from the widening of profit margins arising from a substantial slowdown in the rate of increase in fuel and raw material costs. The combination of a period of rising profitability throughout the 1980s and subdued capital spending has given rise to a substantial accumulation of financial assets which has left UK manufacturing companies' balance sheets looking stronger than they have done for years. With the restraint of low profitability removed, British companies now have the funds available for a renewed phase of capital investment. Whether or not companies choose to invest is likely to hold a significant key to the future success of the UK manufacturing industry.

Competitiveness

Another factor often blamed for Britain's relative industrial decline has been her failure, at least until recently, to match levels and rates of growth of productivity achieved by other industrialized economies. Jones (1976) recorded the fall of British industry from near the top of the European average 'league tables' in the 1950s to bottom place

Table 2.5 Output per person per hour in manufacturing (index 1980 = 100)

	USA	Canada	Japan	France	Germany	Italy	UK
1975	87	87	73 .	76	85	79	93
1976	92	91	80	85	91	86	98
1977	94	94	84	88	94	85	99
1978	95	98	91	92	96	88	101
1979	98	100	97	99	100	96	101
1980	100	100	100	100	100	100	100
1981	103	101	100	101	102	104	105
1982	108	100	100	105	105	104	110
1983	114	107	103	110	110	106	119
1984	119	126	112	114	113	112	124
1985	124	130	116	117	119	115	124
1986	128	130	116	120	120	116	132

Source: NIER table, November 1987

of the countries studied, when Italian performance overtook the British in the early 1970s (other EEC countries having gone ahead of Britain by the mid-1960s). Not only was Britain's absolute level of productivity disappointing in comparison with other countries over the period examined, but her rate of growth also failed to match rates recorded elsewhere. Throughout the 1960s and early 1970s Britain was therefore falling further behind.[4]

Table 2.5 extracts information since 1975 on the growth performance in productivity for the seven largest (in terms of GDP) OECD countries. Output per person per hour has recently shown a dramatic improvement in the UK. Throughout the present decade, the advance in these terms has been the fastest among the seven largest OEDC countries.

This dramatic recovery in productivity in the UK has received a great deal of attention (see Mendis and Muellbauer 1984, and Muellbauer 1986). Five main hypotheses have been advanced.[5] The first focuses on the rise in unemployment and the weakening of trade unions through government legislation since 1979. This has enabled the introduction of more flexible work practices and has also resulted in less resistance to the introduction of new technology. This 'industrial-relations' hypothesis may be consistent with a permanently higher rate of growth of productivity.

The second hypothesis, labelled the 'microchip' hypothesis, is that there is currently a wave of innovation of new technology, for example through the spread of computer-controlled machine tools and through computer-aided design, which promises a higher rate of productivity growth for some years to come. The third, which

Muellbauer calls the 'shedding of the below-average' hypothesis, is that the improvement in the average quality of workers, management, and plant, from the shedding of less productive resources, is responsible for the improvement in productivity growth. This is a once-and-for-all effect. Fourth, there is the 'capital scrapping and utilization' hypothesis. This suggests that after a period of above-average scrapping and below-average capital utilization in 1973–80, especially after the 1979–80 shake-out, scrapping fell from 1981 and utilization improved, allowing growth in output per head to resume the sorts of growth rates experienced before 1973. Finally, there is the 'labour-utilization' hypothesis. This notes the initial decline in output per head with the collapse of output in 1979–80. Given the adjustment costs, the shedding of labour at first lagged behind but in the end caught up, as output stabilized at a level some 16 per cent lower. In the catching-up phase, declining employment with stabilizing output resulted in a short-term increase in output per head.

However, this rather encouraging picture needs qualification. Despite a better productivity performance in the UK in recent years, it must be emphasized that the UK's level of productivity (i.e. in absolute terms) is still significantly below those of many of our major competitors (see Ray 1987). This has been borne out by a series of studies comparing the performance at the plante level within different countries. (See Pratten 1975, and, more recently, *Financial Times* February, 1983.)

Improved productivity by itself, therefore, is not the complete recipe for success. Other price factors such as labour costs and the exchange rate – and non-price factors like quality and marketing – are very important competitiveness factors governing a country's ability to respond to world demand for her products. For example, a relatively low level of productivity is not necessarily of itself a problem since its potential consequences for international cost-competitiveness can, in principle, be offset by periodic devaluation or depreciation of the currency.

Table 2.6 shows various measures of competitiveness. The one most commonly used is normalized unit labour costs rather than relative prices, because prices can change when profit margins are cut and hence they do not necessarily reflect the underlying ability to compete from the point of view of the seller. The costs are 'normalized' to remove the effects of variations which occur over the period of each country's economic cycle. The lower ones relative unit labour costs the greater ones competitiveness. However, non-labour costs also contribute to competitiveness. Indeed, it is widely thought that the cutting of overheads has been a major feature in

Table 2.6 Measures of UK competitiveness in manufacturing
(index 1980 = 100)

	IMF index of relative unit labour costs[a]		Relative export prices[a]	Relative profitability of exports
	Actual	*Normalized*		
1970	73.2	75.2	80.1	103.4
1971	75.3	78.4	81.9	98.8
1972	73.4	77.4	82.0	98.4
1973	65.3	69.2	75.5	101.3
1974	65.2	69.9	74.2	101.3
1975	70.1	74.8	77.9	103.5
1976	63.9	68.2	75.5	104.7
1977	63.3	66.7	79.7	106.4
1978	68.6	71.7	84.5	106.5
1979	81.0	82.7	90.4	102.5
1980	100.0	100.0	100.0	100.0
1981	99.7	104.7	98.1	100.5
1982	93.3	101.0	92.2	101.8
1983	85.2	96.0	89.2	105.0
1984	84.7	95.7	87.6	107.8
1985	87.8	101.1	89.7	109.7

[a] Downward movements indicating greater competitiveness

Source: Economic Trends, Annual Supplement 1987, p. 122

improving the competitiveness of British manufacturing industry in recent years.[6]

It is clear that UK manufacturing competitiveness improved in the mid-1970s after the first oil crisis but then worsened markedly up to 1981, since when it has again improved. Breaking relative unit labour costs down into their constituent parts – wage costs, productivity, and the exchange rate – explains what has happened in the UK.

Labour costs themselves are composed of wage and non-wage elements. Non-wage labour costs (national insurance and pension contributions) have been rising in recent years in the UK, but they are still considerably lower than in West Germany, France, and Italy (see Ray 1987). What stands out is the way in which wage costs have risen in the UK compared with foreign countries. Over the period 1974–84 they have risen 260 per cent compared to 70 per cent in West Germany and 110 per cent in the USA. This rise has not been offset by a more rapid rise in productivity. Indeed, relative productivity fell between 1974 and 1984, with the result that unit labour costs have risen more rapidly than in all other G7 countries, except Italy. Recently, this trend has been reversed, as sharp improvements in the UK's productivity have brought down our relative unit labour costs. However, given that much of the recent improvement in productivity has been due to favourable one-off effects and that average earnings in the UK are currently above 8 per cent, the underlying picture is not quite so encouraging.

Most improvements in competitiveness in the 1970s and, again, since 1981, have therefore been obtained largely through the exchange rate. The disadvantage of relying purely on exchange rate adjustment is that it does not 'solve' the underlying cause of poor competitiveness; indeed it may contribute to sustaining it. The experience of the late 1960s and the decade of the 1970s suggests that currency devaluation or depreciation led, via higher import prices and real wage resistance, to higher domestic inflation within a relatively short time. Any international price advantages were therefore rapidly eroded. Some commentators believe that the devaluation or depreciation could have aggravated the problem of low productivity by engendering managerial complacency. In particular, it may have diverted managers' attention away from the need to make progress in important aspects of non-price factors such as the quality of the product, good design, prompt delivery, reliability in use, etc. These are achieving increasing recognition as factors which contributed to the success of, for example, German and especially Japanese manufacturing industry, many of whose products are sold at premium prices.[7]

The experience of particular industries

In considering the prospects for various parts of manufacturing industry it is useful to look beyond the overall picture and try to highlight the experience of particular activities. While it is acknowledged that past history is not necessarily the best guide to the future, it does provide us with an unavoidable starting point. An examination beyond the overall growth of the manufacturing sector reveals wide variations from one industry to another.

Tables 2.7, 2.8, and 2.9 indicate changes in employment, output, and trade performance of all manufacturing industries between 1975 and 1985.[8]

One factor often cited as the cause of poor industrial dynamism in the past has been the relatively small amount spent by British industry on civil research and development. This message was put forward by the House of Lords Committee Report (1983). Data in Tables 2.7, 2.8, and 2.9 have therefore been aggregated to show the marked differences in the performance of high-, medium-, and low-technology industries, defined according to the level of research intensity,[9] which was first adopted by Dunning and Pearce (1985). Although the categories into which the industry is grouped for the

Table 2.7 Changes in employment in different manufacturing sectors (in percentages)

SIC 1980		1975–85	1980–85	(1979–81)
	High research intensity			
25–26	Chemicals and man-made fibres	−20.0	−17.8	(−12.2)
33–34, 37	Office machinery, electrical engineering, and instruments	−19.6	−16.7	(−9.6)
35	Motor vehicles and parts	−42.0	−38.8	(−22.0)
	Total	−25.2	−22.3	(−13.3)
	Medium research intensity			
21–24	Metal manufacturing, ore, and other mineral extraction	−41.0	−30.9	(−21.6)
31	Metal goods n.e.s	−39.2	−33.7	(−18.9)
32	Mechanical engineering	−28.7	−25.6	(−12.6)
36	Other transport equipment	−30.3	−23.7	(−7.3)
	Total	−34.4	−28.2	(−15.5)
	Low research intensity			
41, 42	Food, drink, and tobacco	−21.6	−18.7	(−6.8)
43–45	Textiles, leather, footwear, and clothing	−37.5	−23.5	(−23.2)
46, 48–49	Timber, wooden furniture, rubber, plastic, etc.	−21.2	−14.4	(−15.4)
47	Paper products, printing, and publishing	−13.1	−10.7	(−5.9)
	Total	−24.8	−17.4	(−13.5)
	Total manufacturing	−28.5	−22.7	(−14.2)

Source: Department of Employment, Runcorn, Cheshire

employment data is at a slightly higher aggregate level than that for output, it is possible to discern a relationship between output and employment.

With the exception of motor vehicles, the classification shows that both the growth record and employment record of all high research intensity sectors in the decade up to 1985 was above the average for manufacturing as a whole. Particularly successful were the office machinery and data-processing equipment industries and some sub-sectors of the electrical engineering industry, where advances in micro-electronics technology paved the way towards the production of more sophisticated products at lower prices and stimulated the development of new markets (the 'microchip' hypothesis explaining productivity growth in the 1980s). However, there is now evidence that the markets for some high-technology products are reaching

Table 2.8 Output trends of manufacturing industries, 1975–85 (in percentages)

SIC 1980		Annual average change		Share of GDP*	
		1975–85	1980–5	1975	1985
	High research intensity				
25	Chemicals and allied products	2.8	3.7	2.3	2.6
33	Office and data-processing machinery	16.4	21.5	0.2	0.9
34	Electronic and electrical engineering	1.4	2.9	2.9	2.8
35	Motor vehicles	−2.9	−3.0	1.9	1.2
37	Instrument engineering	1.9	3.4	0.4	0.4
	Total†	1.8	3.0	8.5	8.6
	Medium research intensity				
21–22	Basic metal industries	−0.8	2.5	1.2	0.9
23–24	Non-metallic minerals and products	−1.5	−1.2	1.8	1.3
31	Finished metal products	−2.2	−0.2	2.2	1.5
32	Mechanical engineering	−2.6	−1.5	5.0	3.2
361	Shipbuilding and marine engineering	−3.9	−2.8	0.5	0.3
48	Rubber and plastic products	1.5	1.5	1.0	1.0
	Total§	−1.8	−0.7	12.2	8.5
	Low research intensity				
411–423	Food	1.2	0.9	2.5	2.3
424–429	Drink and tobacco	0.4	−1.1	1.2	1.0
43, 26	Textiles and synthetic fibres	−2.7	−0.7	1.3	0.8
44–45	Clothing, footwear, and leather goods	−0.3	1.0	1.2	1.0
46	Timber products	−2.1	−1.3	1.0	0.7
47	Paper goods, printing, and publishing	0.4	−0.3	2.5	2.2
	Total	−0.1	0	9.7	8.0
2–4	Total manufacturing	−0.1	0.8	30.4	25.1

*At 1980 constant prices, with adjustments to CSO base weights for 1980 to take account of relative changes in production
†Includes estimate for aerospace equipment (SIC 364)
§Includes railway equipment (SIC 362) and miscellaneous manufactures (SIC 49)

Source: CSO data, Group Economics Department estimates, see Smith (1986)

25

Table 2.9 Trade performance of UK manufacturing industries, 1975–85

SIC 1980*		Trade balance 1985 £ billion	Exports/imports		Imports/home-demand		Exports/sales	
			1975 %	1985 %	1975 %	1985 %	1975 %	1985 %
	High research intensity							
25	Chemicals and allied products	2,366	150	134	23	39	32	46
33	Office and data-processing machinery	−670	107	84	73	102	71	102
34	Electronic and electrical engineering	−1,261	128	84	23	46	30	41
35	Motor vehicles	−2,978	199	58	24	52	39	38
364	Aerospace equipment	1,016	176	136	28	64	42	72
37	Instrument engineering	−290	111	85	51	62	54	57
	Total	−1,787	150	94	29	54	37	52
	Medium research intensity							
21–22	Basic metal industries	−1,113	60	78	29	40	19	35
23–24	Non-metallic minerals and products	−8	192	99	7	16	13	15
31	Finished metal goods	−162	158	88	9	15	14	14
32	Mechanical engineering	2,136	221	135	26	37	44	43
362	Railway equipment	52	274	389	7	11	16	32
48	Rubber and plastic products	−363	155	81	13	26	17	22
49	Miscellaneous manufactures	−212	125	81	24	41	27	30
	Total	330	140	103	19	28	26	30
	Low research intensity							
411–423	Food	−3,748	28	38	25	19	6	7
424–429	Drink and tobacco	594	206	149	4	18	9	25
43, 26	Textile and synthetic fibres	−1,282	100	64	24	45	25	33
44–45	Clothing, footwear, and leather goods	−1,474	58	49	22	38	14	21
46	Timber products	−1,727	16	19	22	32	5	21
47	Paper goods, printing, and publishing	−9,556	51	51	21	26	11	15
2–4	Total manufacturing	−10,938	108	84	22	35	23	30

*The revision of the SIC in 1980 means that the definitions of product groups may not be precisely the same in 1985 as in 1975

Source: Business Monitors MQ10 and MQ12, HMSO, see Smith (1986)

maturity. Smith (1986) argues that as output growth is likely to slow considerably for these products' design, marketing and economies of scale will become increasingly important for the manufacturers. Already, the high research intensity segment has suffered from a considerable erosion of international competitiveness. This is reflected over the past decade by a near doubling of import penetration, a movement into trade deficit (from a £2.4 billion surplus in 1975 to a deficit of £1.8 billion in 1985), and a loss of market share in OECD countries.

Products of high research intensity industries account for half of the UK's manufactured exports and 45 per cent of imports. The success of this segment in the UK is therefore likely to be a critical factor affecting future economic performance. While import penetration tends to be higher so does export opportunity, because it is in these industries that demand is likely to grow more rapidly and where specialized and technologically advanced products permit a high value added per head to be achieved.

Much of the blame for Britain's declining manufacturing trade balance in the past has been associated with differences in inter-country export and import propensities (see, for example, Thirlwall, 1982). It is not so much the UK's relatively high import propensity but a very low income elasticity of demand for UK goods in world markets – due mainly to the supply characteristics of UK goods, such as their design, reliability, delivery, marketing, servicing, and quality in the widest sense. It is exactly these supply characteristics that are becoming more important for the products of the high research intensity industries. Certainly, until the type of goods the UK produces appeal to high-income earners seeking high quality and novelty, it is unlikely that the UK can gain the full benefit from the general increase in real incomes without inducing a deficit on her foreign trade account.

The cost of product development in these areas, however, has restricted the number of entrants and accounts for the important role played by multinational companies. The motor vehicle, aerospace, and computer industries are dominated at the world-wide level by just a handful of manufacturers. Clearly, the marketing and production strategies adopted by multinationals will have an increasingly important impact on the trading structure and position of the UK. The worsening of the UK's motor vehicle trade performance between 1975 and 1985 was partly a consequence of decisions taken by Ford and General Motors to supply a greater proportion of the market from production plants in Belgium, West Germany, and Spain. Creating the right environment to attract investment by multinationals in the UK is, therefore, likely to play a crucial part in shaping future industrial policy.

Turning now to the medium research intensity segment, it is to be noted that industries here have had a particularly poor output and employment record over the past decade. This segment mainly contains the traditional engineering industries. The rapid fall in employment in these industries combined with their relatively poor output performance is perhaps the most striking example of how quickly changes in international comparative advantage can change the structure of output and employment within an economy. Sluggish demand for industrial products left these industries particularly vulnerable, since a large part of the products of the mechanical engineering and basic metal industries consist of intermediate goods. The problems of this segment were compounded by an accelerating loss of international competitiveness for its products, demonstrated by a sharp deterioration of the segment's trade performance. The substantial surplus of £1.5 billion earned in 1975 had all but disappeared by 1985. In 1975, apart from basic metals, all medium research intensity product groups were traded at a surplus. Since 1980, although the position in basic metals has improved, three more sectors have moved into deficit, so that the segment's overall surplus is now almost entirely attributable to the mechanical engineering sector. Even here the position has deteriorated considerably in the last few years. While imports from Japan and other Far Eastern countries have grown relatively quickly in this important sector, their contribution to total UK overseas purchases is still small. In 1985, three-quarters of imports of mechanical engineering equipment originated in the EEC and USA, a proportion which has hardly changed since 1980.[10]

Finally, turning to the low research intensity industries, one finds demand for their products relatively insulated from the effects of recession. This is not surprising since most of the goods produced are demanded by individuals rather than by other industrial sectors, and include products such as food and clothing which are essential items of consumption. Excluding textiles, the losses in employment over the ten-year period to 1985 compare relatively favourably against the manufacturing sector average.

However, in 1985, the level of output in most low research intensity sectors was little different from ten years earlier, reflecting the fairly inelastic domestic demand for this segment's products and little change in its trade position. It was only in the textile industry, which faced intense competition from low-cost producers in Southern Europe and the Far East, that production capacity was severely reduced, particularly during the late 1970s. The modest fall in output of the drink and tobacco industries since 1980 has been the result of changes in consumers' taste in favour of foreign wines at the expense of home-produced beers and spirits; while frequent increases in tobacco excise tax, coupled with the growing awareness of the health dangers of smoking, have contributed to a fall in the demand for tobacco.

The UK trades at a deficit in all but one of the low research intensity product groups. However, the extent of this imbalance – as seen by the ratio of exports to imports – was little different in 1985 from a decade earlier. The UK's imports of manufactured food products exceeds the value of exports by at least a factor of two, because many raw materials cannot be grown in this country, while suppliers of foodstuffs are endeavouring to add value to their produce prior to export. Trends in trade performance in this sector are difficult to assess, since changes in value are just as likely to reflect movements in commodity prices as volume changes. The only low research intensity group to be traded at a surplus is drink and tobacco. The UK has traditionally found large overseas markets for whisky, although wine imports have eroded the surplus considerably during the last few years. The trading position of the textiles and clothing and footwear industries has remained static since 1980, following a marked deterioration in the late 1970s.[11]

Conclusions

Viewed in a long-term context, UK manufacturing performance paints a particularly gloomy picture. Nevertheless, UK manufacturing output has recovered significantly since its nadir in 1981 and is now only marginally below its last cyclical peak in 1979. The recession of 1980–1 has clearly led to a number of changes, the full effects of which may not become clear for some time. More flexible working practices, lower wage inflation, improved productivity and profitability, and stronger company balance sheets have certainly created a more favourable environment for expansion than has existed for some time. The social cost in terms of unemployment and its regional repercussions has nevertheless been high.

The question that clearly remains is whether these changes will be enough to enable manufacturing industry to prosper sufficiently to offset the continuing decline in the non-oil trade balance and create new employment. While the UK undoubtedly has an international comparative advantage in many service sectors (such as financial services, retailing, education, and television), both the employment opportunities and the extent to which services can replace manufacturing as a source of international earnings is still limited.

An examination of the employment, output, and trade performance of particular sectors reveals the importance that must be placed on the development of the high research intensity industries. While these industries have suffered from increasing import penetration over the past decade, the export opportunities and employment prospects are greater. The products themselves, many reaching maturity, are likely to become more highly differentiated in terms of supply characteristics, enabling a higher value added per head to be achieved. If the UK's visible trade position is to improve, it is more likely to be through enhancing export profitability. This can only be achieved by increasing the appeal of UK goods with a high level of value added in world markets. It implies that UK manufacturers must focus on satisfying the needs of new markets, embodying new technologies, and offering new and improved designs. The costs of development of new products is certainly restrictive in the high research intensity industries. This highlights the importance that multinational companies will continue to play in shaping Britain's manufacturing prospects. Nevertheless, the scope for new development does exist throughout the spectrum of manufacturing industries.

With the outlook for UK manufacturing industry brighter than it has been for many years, concentration on the development of high value-added products, with improved design, quality, and marketing characteristics, is now essential. Continued improvements in industrial relations, productivity, and political and economic stability will be essential ingredients to unleash a renewed phase of capital investment and attract multinationals to base more of their production in the UK.

Notes

1. Thirlwall (1982) argues that the absolute loss of jobs in industrial activities, and particularly in manufacturing industry, provides a suitable cause-free definition of de-industrialization. Other 'definitions' of de-industrialization really prejudge the cause of the phenomenon: for example, the thesis of Bacon and Eltis (1976) that Government spending pulls resources out of the industrial sector, and the so-called Cambridge definition of de-industrialization, attributable to Singh (1977), which describe the term as a progressive failure of industry to sell enough exports to pay for the full employment level of imports.
2. See Thirlwall (1982) pp. 28-9.

3. Robinson and McCullough (1986) argue that although manufacturing
   investment has remained relatively low in the UK since 1980, it
   should be borne in mind that, for tax reasons, much plant and
   machinery is now leased (and is therefore recorded in the national
   accounts as investment by financial companies, not manufacturing
   industry).
4. See Coates (1985) p. 86.
5. Meullbauer (1986) p. iv.
6. House of Lords (1985) p. 28.
7. Coates (1985) p. 87.
8. Tables 2.8 and 2.9 are reproduced from the work of Smith (1986).
9. Dunning and Pearce (1985) divide manufacturing industries into three
   segments using the following criteria:
   a) High Research Intensity (HRI): industries where expenditure on
      research and development exceeds 2.8 per cent of sales;
   b) Medium Research Intensity (MRI): industries where expenditure
      on research and development is between 2.8 per cent and 1.1 per
      cent of sales;
   c) Low Research Intensity (LRI): industries where expenditure on
      research and development is less than 1.1 per cent of sales.
10. M. Smith (1986) p. 12.
11. ibid., p. 13.

References

Aritis, M. J., Bladen-Hovell, R., Karatitsos, E., and Divolatzky, B. (1984)
  'The effects of economic policy 1979–82', *National Institute Economic
  Review*, May.
Bacon, R. and Ellis, W. (1976) *Britain's Economic Problem: Too Few
  Producers*, London: Macmillan.
Cherney, H. (1981) *Structural Change and Development Policy*, Oxford:
  Oxford University Press.
Coates, J. H. (1985) 'UK manufacturing industry, recession, depression
  and prospects for the future', in F.V. Mayer (ed.), *Prospects for
  Recovery in the British Economy*, Beckenham: Croom Helm.
Cockerill, A. (1985) 'The British economy: performance, prospects and
  policies', in F. V. Mayer (ed.), *Prospects for Recovery in the British
  Economy*.
Dunning, J. H. and Pearce, R. D. (1985) *The World's Largest Industrial
  Enterprise, 1962–1983*, Gower.
Financial Times (1983) 'The yawning productivity gap', 28 February.
———(1987) 'Time to build on the shake-out', 5 January.
———(1987) 'Computers in manufacturing', 2 June.
———(1988) 'UK industrial prospects', 4 January.
Goodhart, C. and Templeton, P. (1983) *UK Exchange Rate 1979–1981,
  Text of the Overshooting Hypothesis*, Bank of England.
House of Lords *Report From the Select Committee on Overseas Trade*,
  London: HMSO, 30 July.

Jones, D. T. (1976) 'Output, employment at labour productivity in Europe since 1955', *National Institute Economic Review*, August.

Maddison, A. (1979) 'Long-run dynamics of productivity growth', *Banca Nazionale del Lavoro Quarterly Review*, March.

Mayer, F. V. (ed.) (1985) *Prospects for Recovery in the British Economy*, Beckenham: Croom Helm.

Mendis and Muellbauer, J. (1984) *British Manufacturing Productivity 1955–1983: Measurement Problems, Oil Shocks and the Thatcher Effect*, Centre for Economic Policy Research Discussion Paper No. 34.

Morris, R. 'Does Britain really have a wages problem?', *Lloyds Bank Review*, April.

Muellbauer, J. (1986) 'Productivity and competitiveness in British manufacturing', *Oxford Review of Economic Policy* 2 (3), Oxford: Oxford University Press.

Neary, J. P. and Corden, M. (1982), 'Booming sector and de-industrialisation in a small open economy', *Economic Journal*, 92:

Pratten, C. F. (1975) 'Labour productivity differences within international companies', Cambridge, D. A. E. Paper no. 50; Central Policy Review Staff, *Report on the Motor Industry*, HMSO.

Ray, G. F. (1986) 'The changing structure of the UK economy', *National Institute Economic Review*, November.
(1987) 'Labour costs in manufacturing', *National Institute Economic Review*, May.

Robinson B., and McCullough, A. (1986) 'Manufacturing prospects after OPEC III', *Economic Outlook*, London Business School, February.

Singh, A. (1977) *UK Industry and the World Economy: a Case of De-industrialization*, Cambridge Journal of Economics, June.

Smith, M. (1986) 'UK manufacturing output and trade performance', *Midland Bank Review*, Autumn.

Thirlwall, A. P. (1982) 'Deindustrialisation in the United Kingdom', *Lloyds Bank Review*, April.

Chapter Three

Historical perspectives on structural change and economic decline

Stephen Nicholas

Change over time is a central issue in economic history, making the study of structural change a major research topic for economic historians. Structural change is particularly prominent in discussions of economic growth, and the economic histories of Britain, America, Europe, and Japan have been written as success stories within the context of industrialization. The growth and industrialization stories, and their more formal models, were simple: structural adjustment allowed agriculture to yield abundant labour and natural resources for employment and production in the growing industrial sector. Implicit in this emphasis on growth was the idea of sectoral decline, most obviously the shrinking contribution of agriculture to GDP and employment in an industrialized economy.

More important than sectoral decline as a by-product of growth was the economic historian's concern with economic decline, measured by a change in an economy's relative position compared to that of its major trading competitors. While the relative economic decline of Britain since 1870 has dominated Anglo-American economic history research, the rise and decline of Ancient Egypt and Rome, early modern Spain and the war and post-war experience of Japan and Germany have also attracted the historian's attention. Only recently have economists shown a similar concern for economic decline. For example, Angus Maddison, employing the Kendrick-Denison productivity growth approach, has charted the rapid growth in the 1950s and 1960s and the slowdown after 1973 in advanced capitalist economies, particularly the United States (Maddison 1987:649–98). Long-term and systematic factors, including technological catch-up and foreign trade effects, as well as cyclical and *ad hoc* elements, such as the energy price shock, have been utilized to explain the slow growth since the mid-1970s. This chapter argues that many of the causes of post-1973 economic decline find an echo in the past experience of today's capitalist economies. Rather than being a new phenomenon, the economic consequences of structural change are a continuing feature of adjustment in a world of economic progress. A study of structural change in the past provides an analytical context for evaluating economic growth and decline in contemporary western economies.

Economic historians have analyzed structural change as an adjustment mechanism responding to changes in demand, technology, trade, and government policy. Changes in any of these factors can lead to economic growth or economic decline, depending on the particular form of structural adjustment. In the general growth models of W. W. Rostow and Alexander Gerschenkron, the structural adjustments further economic growth. Similarly, at the level of individual national economies, changes in demand, technology, and trade have been viewed by economic historians as inducing industrialization. Using specific examples from the perspective of British, American, and Canadian growth, I survey the role of trade in forcing structural adjustment. First, the positive role of trade in industrialization is discussed before trade-induced structural change resulting in economic decline is analyzed for sixteenth-century Spain and post-1870 Britain. Both these countries experienced deindustrialization due to the impact of natural resource windfalls, offering a direct historical comparison with Britain's current problems arising from the oil discoveries of the 1970s.

The survey is selective both in historical examples and the methodology. It focuses largely on 'representative' examples of structural change through the world economy. Mainly the work of new economic historians who use explicit economic theory and statistical testing is examined. Of course, traditional economic historians have also been concerned with structural changes leading to growth and decline, but their arguments are largely descriptive and their implicit models often unclear and contradictory.

Economic historians have been innovators in formulating general growth models. Both Rostow and Gerschenkron derived models of economic development and growth from their study of history. Generalizing from his work on fluctuations in the pre-1939 British economy, Rostow proposed a stage model of growth which included the traditional society, the preconditions for take-off, the take-off, the drive to maturity, and the age of high mass-consumption (Fishlow 1965). The idea of the take-off is a sectoral, non-linear threshold notion (Rostow 1959; 1960; 1963). The take-off relies on structural change in the form of one or more substantial or leading manufacturing sectors, such as coal, iron, textiles, and engineering with strong multiple linkages with the rest of the economy. The growth process is viewed as a struggle between various industries, where one or two industries accelerate then decline as they are replaced by other leading sectors. In the British case, Rostow argued that the leading sectors, especially cotton textiles, depended on foreign trade. British growth was seen as export-led, with the leading sectors dependent on a growing international economy.

The take-off stage has not fared well at the aggregate level when confronted by the divergent growth patterns of a range of countries. However, the backward and forward linkages forged by the leading sector(s), and their subsequent replacement by new growth industries, provide useful insights into structural change during the industrialization process and have been incorporated within most descriptions of British economic growth.

Rather than the Rostovian process, where industrialization repeats itself from country to country, Alexander Gerschenkron (1962) identified different points (or planes) of departure for industrialization, depending on a country's degree of economic backwardness. Gerschenkron argued that the more backward a country's economy, the more likely was its industrialization to start discontinuously as a sudden 'great spurt'. Describing the spurt, Gerschenkron emphasized the relative dependence on producer-goods as against consumer-goods industries as leading sectors of the more backward economy. Both these general frameworks of growth and development emphasize structural change, but neither 'model' structural change in a rigorous or formal sense.

Rather than the models of Rostow or Gerschenkron, British economic historians look to the empirical work by Phyllis Deane and W. A. Cole (1964) which identified changes in economic structure as being at the centre of the British industrialization process. In *British Economic Growth 1688–1959*, Deane and Cole analyzed, in three successive chapters, the changes in the industrial distribution of the labour force, the changing structure of national product, and the growth of the nineteenth-century staple industries. While they provided detailed measures of structural change, the process was only implicitly modelled. Clearly they had in mind technical improvements at home as the predominant factor in the shift of resources, principally labour, from agricultural to industry. While trade was rejected as the engine of growth, certain export industries were important in furthering the structural transformation of an agricultural economy. Recently, British economic historians have attempted to assess the importance of trade in British industrialization and structural change in the eighteenth and nineteenth centuries.

Analyzing trade as an engine of growth, Donald McCloskey (1981) found that British commodity exports per head grew by 4.4 per cent per year from 1821 to 1873 (almost three times faster than the rate of growth in income per head of 1.57 per cent year over the same period) and 0.93 per cent per year from 1873 to 1913 (12 per cent slower than the rate of growth in income per head of 1.06 per cent for the same years). These data suggest why foreign trade has been cast in the role of a 'leading sector' in British industrialization; as exports accelerated or decelerated, so also did income.

Trade allows domestic production and consumption to differ. Nineteenth-century Britain produced far more manufactured goods than she consumed, and consumed much more food than she produced. This specialization in manufactured commodites meant a much higher commitment to industry in the economy than would have been the case in the absence of trade or at a lower level of trade. In order to measure structural changes induced by Britain's late-nineteenth-century dependence on trade, McCloskey constructed a counterfactual model of the British economy in 1913, specifying the ratio of net imports of commodities to national income of 0.12 (its average 1830s' ratio) in place of the actual ratio of 0.26. A fall in the ratio implies a much lower level of exports, and such a contraction would have fallen largely on manufactures which made up 78 per cent of total exports. To assess the structural change involved in Britain's reliance on exports, McCloskey compared the 1913 counterfactual estimates with the actual 1913 consumption and production levels, distinguishing manufactures, food and other (mainly non-traded) goods and services. McCloskey assumed that all the adjustment fell on production, although changes in relative prices would have meant the consumption side taking some of the burden in practice. If trade in 1913 had been reduced to the ratio 0.12, the share of manufacturing would have fallen to 0.31 from 0.38, the share of food would have risen to 0.22 from 0.16, and the share of non-traded goods and services would have declined to 0.51 from 0.54. While not drastic, such structural adjustments would have been substantial.

Following McCloskey, Crafts (1985) performed the same exercise for the Industrial Revolution economy, choosing France's 1840 ratio of exports to GNP as the comparative standard. Compared with the 'European norm' he found that Britian's specialization on manufacturing for export explained a large measure of the economy's unusually high share of industry in production, making trade an important factor in the structural changes underlying industrialization.

However, Crafts showed that trade did not account for British industrialization, nor was trade the engine of growth in the eighteenth-century economy. During the Industrial Revolution, trade impacted on particular industries, principally cotton textiles and the modernized 'factory' industries. There was, according to Crafts, a broadly based comparative advantage in manufacturing generally, with the traditional industries hardly represented in the trade statistics. Finally, Crafts warned that an agricultural sector which released sufficient resources to permit industrialization due to productivity advance would inhibit structural changes through trade. The more efficient was British food production, the greater the gains from specialization in food and the smaller the gains from specializing in manufactured goods. Of course, the efficiency of food production in Britain did not eliminate the advantage of trade, but the gains from trade and the specialization of industry in the export sector would have been greater in the absence of rapid productivity by growth in agriculture.

Both McCloskey and Crafts provide a measure of structural changes induced by Britain's trade dependence. While British growth was not export driven, the high level of British exports did lead to a higher specialization in tradeable manufactures than would have occurred in the absence of trade. Britain's position as 'workshop of the world' was an important element in shaping the structure of industry at home. It also had important implications for other trading countries.

Britain's early nineteenth-century dominance in world trade, particularly textile production, impacted directly on the structure of Britain's major trading partners. The stylized facts of continental industrialization are that tariffs provided import-industry protection, but, in the later stages of development, reductions of tariffs brought gain from trade. The tariff was a significant factor in shaping industrial structure in a trading world. While the European case is largely descriptive and anecdotal, recent quantitative work on US textile tariffs before the Civil War provides a test of the efficacy of tariffs as a device for structural change.

After the period of major technical and organizational improvements in cotton textiles, Paul David (1975) measured endogenous, experienced-linked improvements in efficiency. Estimating an augmented Cobb-Douglas production function, he found that learning-by-doing (the effects of the accumulation of experience) a powerful factor increasing best-practice productivity. During the period 1833–9, learning-by-doing accounted for about 80 per cent of the average annual growth rate of the total productivity in cotton textiles, falling sharply in the period after 1839 to only a quarter of the 1833–9 level by 1860.

Since all US cotton textile production received blanket protection from 1824 onward, what were the economic implications of the tariff? Protection from British competition meant the establishment of an infant industry which would not otherwise have occurred. The efficiency argument depends on the opportunity for pilot firms to 'learn' to produce efficiently behind a tariff wall. According to David, significant learning-by-doing before the mid-1830s probably out-weighed the welfare burden imposed on American consumers by tariffs. However, David concluded that the rapid fall, after 1839, in annual efficiency improved due to learning, suggested that US tariff policy towards the industry became simply a means of re-distributing income in favour of the cotton textile producers.

The tariff policy employed in pre-Civil War America has direct comparisons with the trade barriers in the international economy today. The various import constraints reflect an attempt to protect employment, diverting trade without, one suspects, any of the learning advantages evident in the pre-1839 American cotton textile case. To attenuate the structural adjustment to a country's industrial structure through the use of tariffs has a long pedigree in the functioning of the world economy.

Besides the industrialization models which adjust through inter-national trade, economic historians have derived so-called 'vent-for-surplus' trade models which describe the impact on the structure and growth of an economy of trade in resources which have no other economic use (see Caves 1965). The existence of 'surplus' resources distinguishes these models from the traditional trade-theory appro-ach involving the reallocation of resources. The original vent-for-surplus model was the 'staple' version derived by Canadian economic historians to explain Canadian development. That approach has been widely applied to similar resource-rich lands of recent European settlement, including Australia, South Africa, and the United States (see Innis 1954, 1929; Watkins 1963; North 1961; McCarty 1964; Sinclair 1976).

The staple vent-for-surplus model posited a succession of natural resources, such as fish, furs, wool, gold, and wheat, which were surplus in the sense of having no use in the recent settlement economy except for export to a developed region. The basic model emphasized the structural impact on the resource-rich economy of exogeneous demand for the staple (see Baldwin 1956; Nicholas 1976). The technology of the exogeneously demanded staple played the key role in the recent settlement area's development. Given the unique technical nature of a country's agricultural production, the produc-tion technology determined the path of economic development through backward and forward linkages, the distribution of income, and the demand for consumer products. In the original formulation, two hypothetical regional economies, a wheat and cotton plantation economy, thinly disguised as the American West and South, were given to provide historical validity to the theoretical aspects of the model.

The salient points of the model may be briefly summarized as follows. The factor inputs, labour and capital, in the two recent settlement areas are drawn from the same 'mother' region. The plantation economy imports unskilled labour while the owner-occupier wheat region's production function requires skilled-labour inputs. Since there is no substitution of labour between the two hypothetical economies and the recent settlement areas are unable to influence factor costs, the factor markets are perfectly competitive. The small-country assumption applies to the product market.

Given the above assumptions, the subsequent development of the two regional economies depends on the production functions which determine the nature of capital and labour imports, the linkages and the distribution of each economy's national income. For the cotton-plantation economy, where a large part of the population is in the very low-income brackets, effective demand consists of a few basic foods, simple clothing and minimum shelter. The plantation crop does not generate linkages into the growing or processing of the staple. In contrast to the plantation economy, the more equitable distribution of income, which arises as the wheat economy develops its export production, leads to the development of domestic industry. The more favourable distribution of income, and thus the relatively large demand for consumer durables, stimulates domestic manufacturing. The wheat production function creates strong linkages, such as farm machinery, railroads, and staple processing. Thus, the wheat economy industrializes while the plantation economy remains backward.

The model implies not only a different industrial structure between the two regions, but also a different structure of social relations. The cotton staple created a plantation economy of the American South which depended on slave labour, while the wheat staple of the American West rested on owner-occupied family farms. Besides this social aspect, the model also claimed direct relevance for development theory. Staple growth through multipliers, linkages, and demonstration effects suggests the positive effects of primary product growth, while the absence of such linkages and fluctuations in export demand and export prices confirm the distrust which less developed economies hold for specialization in primary production.

Recently, Canadian economic historians have more closely specified the staple version of the vent-for-surplus model in order to evaluate the impact of the 1901–11 wheat boom on Canadian per capita income growth (see Chambers and Gordon 1966). The model also has direct implications for the structure of the economy, although these have been understated in the literature. Using a crude general equilibrium model, Edward Chambers and Donald Gordon

(1966) represented the Canadian economy by two competitive industries: the staple 'wheat' export industry and a domestic manufacturing industry producing gadgets, both of which compete internationally. In the simple version of the model, the wheat and gadget constant return production function depend only on labour inputs. Invoking the small-country trading assumption, the prices of both products are exogenously determined. Labour is paid its marginal value product.

Given these assumptions, and the presumption that the slope of the marginal physical product in wheat is negative, any outward shift in the demand for labour in the wheat industry causes the supply curve for labour in the gadget industry to move up horizontally by an equal amount. The effect is a shrinkage in the manufacturing export sector. So long as labour can be drawn from manufacturing, new settlement occurs and cultivation is extended until rent at the margin is zero. Increases in total income are due to rises in rents in the wheat sector. By measuring the rise in rents, Chambers and Gordon calculated that Canadian per capita income growth attributable to wheat production was only 8.5 per cent of the total increase in 1911 national income, concluding that less-developed countries had little to fear from primary-product production. Because Chambers and Gordon were interested in measuring per capita income and growth, the impact of primary exports on industrial structure was not pursued and the implications for economic decline were largely ignored.

In fact, the stylized Chambers–Gordon model contained the seeds of the more complex and well-known Neary–Corden booming-sector models (Neary and Corden 1982). These models have been particularly popular since the concern with the effects of North Sea oil discoveries on Britain's manufacturing sector. The oil boom is simply one example of a class of models dealing with the adjustment effects of exogeneous shocks. When the structural adjustment following an exogeneous shock takes the form of de-industrialization, then the model provides an understanding of economic decline which has been labelled 'the Dutch disease'. The de-industrialization debate is not new to economic historians. The Spanish economy in the sixteenth-century and the late-nineteenth-century British economy have both been analyzed in terms of the Dutch disease. Rodney Maddock and Ian McLean (1984) have discussed the 1850s Australian gold rush in booming-sector terms, and the staple model, as depicted by Chambers and Gordon, can be easily transformed into a version of the booming-sector model.

The industrial decline of Spain, coinciding with the discovery of vast American treasure, is one of the great paradoxes in European economic history. It also has many of the features of the structural changes now affecting the British economy. The application of booming-sector models, offering an alternative to the traditional explanation of Spanish decline, provides a solution to the 'paradox' and an interesting historical parallel to contemporary adjustment problems (see Forsyth and Nicholas 1983).

The traditional historiography of Spanish decline emphasized the silver-induced price inflation as the cause of de-industrialization. Imports of American gold and silver were equivalent to an expansion of the money supply. While the actual production of goods and services was constant, or only growing slowly, the consequence of the gold inflow was a price rise. Domestic inflation saw Spanish manufactured goods priced out of colonial, international, and, finally, domestic markets by the cheaper goods of Spain's foreign competitors. By the middle of the sixteenth century, the industrial base was so eroded that little remained of the specialized branches of Spanish industry. This monetary explanation of the decline of Spain is made all the more plausible by the identification of silver with money. However, the underlying cause of Spanish de-industralization was not monetary; monetary changes simply acted as part of the adjustment mechanism by which more fundamental structural changes were effected.

De-industrialization in Spain displayed a pattern common to all countries where structural changes in industry accompany the discovery of a valuable natural resource. Changes in both its trading patterns and its structure of production was the way in which Spain achieved a new consumption pattern and converted its newly discovered resource into consumables. Even though some gold and silver was consumed directly, most of the resource windfall was converted into goods and services. Some of the new resources were exported, and the new consumption goods imported; however, it was not possible for Spain to obtain the desired pattern of consumption solely through trade. This is because of the existence of non-tradeables, especially services, in the economy.

The core model in the booming-sector literature has three sectors – the booming sector and the lagging sector (which produce tradeables) and the non-tradeable service sector. The small open-economy assumption means that the tradeable goods face given world prices. It is usually assumed that each sector uses specific factors, but that labour is a mobile factor common to all three sectors. The rise in real income from the booming sector increases the demand for both tradeable and non-tradeable commodities. Since the non-tradeable goods must be domestically produced, home factors must be directed to new production at the expense of the tradeable goods. This is labelled the spending effect. The mechanism for adjustment is a rise in the price of non-tradeables relative to the prices of tradeables. The price rise shifts factors to the non-trade sector from both the booming and the lagging sectors. When labour, the mobile factor, leaves the lagging sector, output falls. The result is de-industrialization when the lagging sector is designated as manufacturing.

The second effect is the resource movement effect. As a result of the boom, the marginal product of labour rises in the booming sector and, at a constant wage in terms of tradeables, so too does the demand for labour. This induces a movement of labour out of the lagging sector into the booming sector. The movement of labour out of the manufacturing sector again lowers output, resulting in direct de-industrialization.

This basic model is consistent with the historical evidence on the sixteenth-century Spanish economy. With the discovery of gold and silver, the real wealth of Spain increased, leading both the state and private individuals to demand more of the same types of goods and services while the productive capacity of existing industry did not increase proportionally. To adjust to a new consumption pattern, at least one industry in the tradeable sector must contract absolutely. In Spain many industries contracted, but particularly manufacturing since manufacturing output was most easily replaced by imports.

The Spanish Crown had an income-elastic demand for war in the sixteenth century. There was rarely a year when Spanish armies were not committed to war – in Algeria (1540), in France (1543–4, 1551–9, 1590–8), in Granada (1569–70), in England (1586–94), with the Turks (1570–7) or, from 1560, to the repression of discontent in The Netherlands. The scale of Crown spending, where perhaps 70 per cent of revenue was spent on war, was illustrated by the four-fold increase in debt under Philip II between 1562 and 1582. A significant proportion of military spending occurred within Spain on both tradeable and non-tradeable goods. War was only one form of increased Crown expenditure. The gold and silver from America also financed the Crown's extravagant building and public works programmes and lavish entertainment. Private treasure was also used to consume more goods and services, much of it 'wasteful', conspicuous, and extravagant consumption.

These new patterns of demand were accomplished through a structural decline in Spanish manufacturing. After 1570 there was an unfavourable balance of trade and the increased dominance of foreign manufactures in the cargoes to the Indies. Spain increasingly acted as a 'funnel' for European goods. Perhaps the most obvious sign of declining industry was the demographic and commercial decline of the urban centres after 1580. Although there was rural and semi-rural industry, the urban centres were the home of the textile, glass, sugar, leather, and copper industries. Urban decline in Spain was a proxy for industrial decline.

The structural changes to Spanish industry that resulted from the discovery of gold and silver were effected through inflation. Changes in relative prices which brought the decline in tradeables and a new trade pattern was the only way in which the resource could be converted into consumption. The inflation did not cause the decline of Spain. Rather, the inflation was merely the mechanism through which the strcutural changes occurred.

Structural adjustment leading to de-industrialization in sixteenth-century Spain has close parallels with the impact of North Sea oil on Britain's manufacturing sector today. But Spain's case was an extreme form of adjustment, since the manufacturing base was largely lost. The effect of North Sea oil on Britain's manufacturing sector is unlikely to be so severe, although the Spanish example does provide some useful lessons on the management of structural adjustment. While not stopping de-industrialization, government policy in Spain could have minimized the structural changes involved in its resource windfall. For example, the income increase could have been spread over a much longer time-span through some optional investment strategy. Minimizing the structural adjustments would have arrested the de-industrialization of the Spanish economy, preserving a manufacturing base.

Although trade theory predicts that manufacturing would revive as the inflows of gold and silver declined, this was not the case for Spain. Spain attests to the hypothesis that it is more difficult to create a manufacturing sector than to eliminate it. The shock of capital goods used for production would have depreciated during the boom, requiring a large investment after the end of the treasure inflow to restore the physical base of manufacturing. Further, human capital in the form of skills would have been dissipated. These skills, learned informally and through apprenticeship could not be easily restored. Even though the conditions for a revival of manufacturing industry may have been present after the boom, the entrepreneurial skills needed to turn it into actuality had been lost. Government policy directed to preserving key areas and skills in the manufacturing sector would have provided the basis of re-industrialization after the flow of treasure had been exhausted.

The de-industrialization effects of a natural resource discovery are not new to the later twentieth-century British economy, nor is Spain's experience of decline the only historical parallel. The closest historical parallel to Britain's problems of structural adjustments through the international economy today is with the British economy between

1870 and 1913. In the half-century before the First World War, the British economy declined relatively. Generally, the decline has been seen in terms of foreign industrialization, which reduced the demand for British exports. This story is consistent with the historical evidence which traces the relative decline to the manufacturing sector. Recently, economic historians have suggested that part of Britain's de-industrialization after 1870 can be analyzed in booming-sector terms (see Mathews *et al.* 1982).

Coal was a booming sector in the pre-1913 British economy. The annual rate of growth of coal exports was 4.6 per cent between 1873 and 1913, accounting for 2.3 per cent of GDP and 10.2 per cent of total exports in 1913. The impact on coal on the pre-1913 economy was not as great as that of oil in the 1970s, which accounted for between 4 per cent and 7 per cent of GDP. However, in both cases, the structural shift worked through the spending effect, since little resource movement was required to expand either coal- or oil-production. The effect of the oil boom is to put the balance of payments into surplus, which is then balanced by a contraction in domestic production of traded goods. Since the income increase would be spent partly on non-traded goods, the change in relative prices is the mechanism enabling the reduction in mainly manu-factured tradeable goods. The effect of coal was similar. The increased export earnings strengthened Britain's balance of payments and a deterioration in the balance of trade would keep the overall balance of payments in equilibrium.

While the booming coal sector was unlikely to cause major structural changes by itself, the period 1870–1913 also saw a rise in the transfer of income from Britain's portfolio investment abroad. The export of capital was a second booming sector. Net property incomes from abroad grew from about 2 per cent of GDP in 1855 to over 8 per cent in 1913. Combined with coal, the capital inflow was probably greater than the upper estimate to today's oil boom.

The adjustment mechanism operated under the constraints of the fixed exchange rates of the classical gold standard. The inflow of income earned on the export of capital operated through the current account to augment the money supply. This increased income was converted into goods and services with the adjustment taking the form of the spending effect. Resources were pulled into the non-traded sector from the manufacturing export sector, which declined. In part, the decline in Britain's manufacturing-export sector after 1870 was the inevitable outcome of its fortunate windfall gains from its return on exported coal and capital. This was not a reflection of failure on the part of the economy; rather, de-industrialization was the inevitable structural adjustment due to a booming sector.

References

Baldwin, R. E. (1956) 'Patterns of development in newly settled regions', *Manchester School of Economics and Social Studies* 24: 161–79.

Caves, R. (1965) '"Vent for surplus" model of trade and growth', in R. Baldwin *et al.* (eds) *Trade, Growth, and Balance of Payments*, Amsterdam: North–Holland, pp. 95–115.

Chambers, E. J. and Gordon, D. F. (1966) 'Primary products and economic growth: an empirical measurement', *Journal of Political Economy* 74: 315–32.

Crafts, N. F. R. (1985) *British Economic Growth During the Industrial Revolution*, Oxford: Clarendon Press, pp. 127–9.

David, P. (1975) *Technical Choice, Innovation and Economic Growth*, Cambridge: Cambridge University Press, pp. 95–168.

Deane, P. and Cole, W. A. (1964) *British Economic Growth 1688–1959*, Cambridge: Cambridge University Press.

Fishlow, A. (1965) 'Empty economic stages?', *Economic Journal* 75: 112–25.

Forsyth, P. J. and Nicholas, S. (1983) 'The decline of Spanish industry and the price revolution: a neoclassical analysis', *Journal of European Economic History* 12: 601–10.

Gerschenkron, A. (1962) *Economic Backwardness in Historical Perspective*, Cambridge, Mass.: Harvard University Press.

Gordon, M. (1985) 'Blooming sector and Dutch disease economics: survey and consolidation', in M. Gordon (ed.) *Protection, Growth and Trade: Essays in International Economics*, Oxford: Basil Blackwell.

Innis, H. A. (1927) *The Fur Trade in Canada: An Introduction to Canadian Economic History*, Toronto: University of Toronto Press.

——(1954) *The Cod Fisheries: The History of an International Economy*, Toronto: University of Toronto Press.

McCarty, J. (1964) 'The staple approach in Australian economic history', *Business Archives and History* IV.

McCloskey, D. (1981) *Enterprise and Trade in Victorian Britain*, London: George Allen & Unwin, pp. 139–54.

Maddison, A. (1987) 'Growth and slowdown in advanced capitalist economies', *Journal of Economic Literature* XXV: 649–98.

Maddock, R. and McLean (1984) 'Supply–scale shocks: the case of Australian gold', *Journal of Economic History* XLIV: 1047–67.

Mathews, R. C. O., Feinstein, C. H., and Odling-Smee, J. C. (1982) *British Economic Growth, 1856–1973*, Oxford: Clarendon Press.

Neary, J. P. (1975) 'Theory and policy of adjustment in an open economy', in D. Greenaway (ed.) *Current Issues in International Trade: Theory and Policy*, London: Macmillan pp. 43–61.

Neary, J. P. and Corden, M. (1982) 'Booming sector and de-industrialization in a small open economy', *Economic Journal* 92.

Nicholas, S. (1976) 'The staple theory of economic development: an economic criticism', University of New South Wales Discussion Paper, pp. 1–25.

North, D. C. (1961) *The Economic Growth of the United States, 1790–1860*, Englewood Cliffs, N. J.: Prentice-Hall.

Rostow, W. W. (1959) 'The stages of economic growth', *Economic History Review*, 11: 1–16.

—— (1960) *The Stages of Economic Growth*, Cambridge: Cambridge University Press.

—— (1963) *The Economics of Take-off into Sustained Growth*, London: Macmillan.

Sinclair, W. A. (1976) *The Process of Economic Development in Australia*, Melbourne: Longman Cheshire.

Watkins, M. (1963) 'A stable theory of economic growth', *Canadian Journal of Economics and Political Science* XXIX: 141–58.

Part Two

Causes of change in the world economy

Chapter Four

Competition, innovation, and industrial performance

Kirsty S. Hughes

Introduction

This chapter analyzes the role of innovation in the changing structure and performance of four of the main advanced industrial economies – the US, UK, Japan, and West Germany.

These leading, advanced industrial countries have experienced, and are likely to continue to experience, major shifts in their relative positions in terms of output, output growth, trade, innovation, and so forth. Within their economies the relative performance of different industries has also been changing, as comparative advantage alters and as demand shifts. One important factor in these changes is the role of innovation. By its very nature, innovation leads to change, but the effects of innovation on countries' relative structures and performance is compounded by their different comparative advantage in innovation and by changes in the process of creation and transfer of technological knowledge itself. Thus, the spread of multinational enterprises, the increasing importance of co-operative R&D, the speed and cost of imitation of innovation, all have potentially profound implications for the role of innovation in the competitive process.

Furthermore, countries' abilities in innovation are not static, not only because their relative inputs into innovation change, but because there are many potential cumulative advantages to success in innovation – the role of learning, clustering, and sequences of innovation, production experience, marketing, and so forth. Such cumulative effects could be destabilizing at a global level if the performance of different economies diverges to a large extent. This may be of particular concern at times of global recession with slow growth in world trade – when firms are fighting for increased market share, in markets that are only expanding slowly. The major advanced industrial economies are also under pressure from other economies – both advanced and newly industrializing – which threaten to break into and expand in markets wherever possible. The 1987 UNCTAD report considers that the world economy is again on the brink of recession. They argue that a technology war may result from the intensified rivalry between Japan, the US, the European Community, and leading developing countries, such as Brazil or South Korea – a war that would be inconsistent with the expansion of world trade. UNCTAD also suggests that, if the industrial economies try to link trade liberalization to increased protection of intellectual property rights, this could create tensions and conflict. Nevertheless, if technological knowledge is at present transferring more quickly and more easily, there are increasing pressures on the advanced economies both to develop innovations faster, and to be competitive in all other aspects of the production process. Innovation remains of central importance to the advanced industrial economies; it is not, however, innovative ability alone that will ensure their success. Not only are there many other important parts of the productive and competitive processes, but there is, at least, a two-way relationship between growth and innovation. Innovative effort and success may be much greater in an economy with sustained and relatively stable growth, so allowing for a cumulative advantage in those economies that are successful in growth and innovation.

In the light of these various dynamics, further change and development in the nature of global competition, and of international market structures, are likely. While many of these developments may be positive, there is no reason to expect even development across or within economies. Equally, faced with such changes, and the changing nature of innovation, it would be difficult to argue that there are any simple policy solutions.

To explore these issues further, the first section of this chapter looks at the relative positions of the US, UK, Japan, and Germany, in terms of innovative effort and economic performance, and at the changes in these indicators over time. The second section considers in more detail some of the recent trends raised in this introduction. The third section suggests some likely future issues and developments.

Innovation and performance

The relative performance of the US, UK, Japanese, and German economies over the last thirty years is well known – the spectacularly fast growth of Japan, the relatively fast growth of Germany, and the relatively slow growth of the US and UK. Japan was, however, starting from much lower levels of output per head and productivity, so that it was not until 1980 that Japan's GDP per head exceeded that of the UK. This is illustrated in Table 4.1. Despite Japan's high rate of

Table 4.1 GDP per head of population (in 1975 $US)[a]

	1953	1963	1973	1983	Percentage growth per annum 1953–83
US	4,946	5,503	7,371	8,037	1.6
UK	3,125	3,855	5,097	5,506	1.9
Japan	1,054	2,245	4,974	6,010	5.8
Germany	2,319	3,866	5,628	6,291	3.3

[a]Exchange rates based on purchasing-power parity

Source: Rowthorn (1986)

growth, by 1983 her GDP per head was still below that of the US and Germany. Similarly, although the German economy was growing on average twice as fast as the US economy, her GDP per head in 1983 was three-quarters of that in the US. Germany and the US also remain the largest participants in world trade.

A similar picture obtains if we look at manufacturing industry. Table 4.2 presents data on labour costs, productivity, and unit labour costs. Japan's average productivity is lower than that of the US and Germany, though she is competitive in terms of unit labour costs. The UK's low labour costs fail to translate into a competitive advantage in unit labour costs due to her low labour productivity.

Table 4.3 presents rates of growth of manufacturing industry 1972–81, where again the superior productivity growth of Japan and then Germany is clear. The US was the only one of the four to show an increase in workers employed over the period, while the UK had the largest negative growth rate of employment. The UK was the only one of the four to show a negative growth rate in numbers of researchers employed.

As was stressed in the introduction, high levels and rates of growth

Table 4.2 Productivity and unit labour costs in manufacturing industry (UK = 100)

	Total hourly labour costs		Output per person hour		Unit labour costs	
	1980	1984	1980	1984	1980	1984
US	126	194	273	267	46	74
Japan	80	109	196	176	41	62
Germany	165	153	255	232	65	66
UK	100	100	100	100	100	100

Source: Ray (1987)

Causes of change in the world economy

Table 4.3   Annual average growth of manufacturing industry, 1972–81

	Output	Apparent labour productivity	No. of workers employed	No. of researchers
US	2.6	1.3	0.6	4.7
Japan	4.1	6.9	−0.4	5.1
Germany	1.2	3.0	−0.9	3.4
UK	−1.3	1.6	−1.9	−0.2

Source: OECD (1986)

of output, exports or productivity cannot be linked to innovative efforts alone. Nevertheless, many recent studies have demonstrated links between R&D and productivity growth (see Griliches 1984 for recent evidence) and R&D and trade performance (see Hughes 1986 for a survey). (R&D expenditures are, of course, not a comprehensive measure of innovative activity, or innovative success. They are used here as the best available measure for cross-country, cross-industry, and over-time comparison.) The OECD (1986) picks out two extreme cases of R&D and growth – Japan with the highest growth rates in both output and R&D, 1972–81, and the UK 'where low R&D growth is accompanied by a decline in industrial output'. In the US, output and R&D grew at roughly the same rate; in Germany, R&D grew at a faster rate than output. High R&D intensity industries tend to be the high growth industries – average annual growth of over 4 per cent 1970–80 (OECD 1986) – although some medium R&D intensity industries also fall in this category. However, absolute levels of labour productivity 'seem to be higher in the mature industries than in the high R&D intensity ones' (OECD 1986).[1]

Table 4.4   Importance of high R&D industries in total manufacturing output and exports (proportion of total)

	Output		Exports	
	1970	1982	1970	1982
US	14.6	10.8	25.8	31.1
Japan	14.1	13.4	20.2	26.9
Germany	11.9	12.0	15.5	17.7
UK	12.2	12.5	16.8	24.8

Source: OECD (1986)

High R&D intensity industries account for a relatively small proportion of output in all four countries, but for a higher, and increasing, share of exports – as shown in Table 4.4. In terms of trade performance, as shown in Table 4.5, positive net trade balances tend to be found in the high and medium R&D intensity industries, although Japan also has a positive balance in low R&D intensity, while the UK shows a recent negative balance in the high R&D intensity group.

Tables 4.6 and 4.7 demonstrate the trends in export market share

Table 4.5   Trade balance of manufacturing by technology group, 1970–84

	High R&D	Medium R&D	Low R&D
US	Positive[a]	Positive[b]	Negative
Japan	Positive	Positive	Positive
Germany	Positive	Positive	Negative
UK	Positive[c]	Positive[c]	Negative

[a] Negative in 1984
[b] Negative from 1982
[c] Negative in 1983 and 1984

Source: OECD (1986)

Table 4.6   Export market shares of manufacturing by technology group

	High R&D		Medium R&D		Low R&D	
	1970	1980	1970	1980	1970	1980
US	28.3	25.6	19.5	15.8	11.3	9.9
Japan	12.0	24.5	7.6	16.5	11.1	10.7
Germany	16.0	12.9	20.7	18.5	12.6	12.8
UK	9.5	8.3	10.7	6.7	7.6	5.9

Source: OECD (1986)

Table 4.7   Import penetration of manufacturing industry by technology group

	High R&D		Medium R&D		Low R&D	
	1970	1980	1970	1980	1970	1980
US	4.8	14.3	7.0	11.2	4.8	6.1
Japan	6.6	7.9	5.5	6.9	3.5	5.4
Germany	21.6	42.5	22.8	33.4	16.8	27.4
UK	18.6	44.2	22.0	43.1	13.4	18.4

Source: OECD (1976)

and import penetration by technology groups, 1970–80. In both the high and medium R&D groups, Japan was the only country to increase her export market share. The UK in particular lost a large part of her market share in the medium R&D group. The US retained the highest market share in high R&D products, though closely followed by Japan. Germany had the highest market share in the medium group, and was the only one to have a higher share in this group than in the high R&D group. The UK's share was the lowest in all groups, and was particularly low in the high and medium groups.

The import penetration figures show a somewhat different picture. The UK and Germany are quite similar in this regard – both having high levels of penetration in 1970 and showing sharp increases by 1980, particularly in high-technology products. The US also has a large increase in import penetration in high technology products, but still at a relatively low level. By 1980 Japan has the lowest levels of import penetration in all three groups. The asymmetry between Japan on the one hand and the UK and Germany on the other is particularly striking.

Tables 4.8 and 4.9 give a more detailed account of changing trade performance by looking at the changes in the export/import ratio for each industry in the high- and medium-technology groups. Table 4.8 shows again a relative deterioration in virtually all high-technology

Table 4.8   Export/import ratios of the high-technology groups

	Aircraft		Office machines and computers		Communications equipment and electronic components	
	1969	1984	1969	1984	1969	1984
US	8.8	2.7	2.8	1.4	2.2	0.6
UK	1.1	1.4	0.7	0.7	1.5	0.8
Japan	0.3	0.1	0.9	5.6	3.3	7.2
Germany	0.6	1.1	1.3	0.8	1.8	1.1

	Electrical transmission equipment		Scientific instruments		Drugs	
	1969	1984	1969	1984	1969	1984
US	2.8	1.3	1.9	0.7	4.3	1.7
UK	1.5	1.1	1.6	0.9	4.4	2.2
Japan	2.3	4.1	3.6	5.8	0.3	0.3
Germany	2.6	1.9	2.4	1.5	3.1	1.8

Source: OECD/STIIU databank

Table 4.9 Export/import ratios of the medium-technology groups

	Motor vehicles		Chemicals		Other manufacturing	
	1970	1982	1970	1982	1970	1982
US	0.5	0.6	2.0	1.8	0.4	0.4
UK	1.9	0.7	1.3	1.3	1.0	0.7
Japan	25.1	48.2	2.2	1.3	1.1	3.2
Germany	3.4	4.4	2.0	1.7	1.1	1.1
	Non-electrical machinery		Rubber and plastics		Non-ferrous metals	
	1970	1982	1970	1982	1970	1982
US	2.5	2.4	0.4	0.2	0.3	0.4
UK	2.1	1.6	1.3	0.5	0.7	0.8
Japan	2.8	7.4	10.0	4.0	0.2	0.3
Germany	3.8	3.8	1.2	0.6	0.5	0.8

Source: OECD (1984)

industry groups for the US, UK, and Germany, and a sharp improvement in most for Japan. The UK in 1984 has a trade balance of less than one in three industries out of six; the US, Japan and Germany in only one or two industries. The picture in the medium-technology industries (Table 4.9) is more varied. The US and Germany show relatively little variation at the level of these broad industry groups. Japan shows an improvement in four out of six industry groups, most notably in motor vehicles and non-electrical machinery. The UK shows a deterioration in four industry groups, particularly in motor vehicles.

To summarize briefly, the data presented above indicated that Japan continues to increase her market share, and to improve her overall performance, while the UK, in particular, has a relatively poor performance and low market share. Relative performance varies across industry groups, and although Japan outperforms the US and Germany in many industries in terms of trade performance, she still has not completely closed the gap at an aggregate level.

A comparison of R&D activities gives a similar though not identical picture. Japan is the second largest R&D spender – after the US, as shown in Table 4.10. Both Japan and Germany overtook the UK by 1970 in terms of absolute R&D spending, and France had overtaken the UK by 1983. Thus, in less than twenty years, the UK has moved from being the second largest to the fifth largest OECD R&D spender. The US remains the largest, though her share has fallen, as indicated by Table 4.11. The fall in the US share can be seen to be matched by the increase in Japan's share – which almost doubled between 1969 and 1983. In terms of basic research, Japan is performaing a smaller proportion than her overall R&D share, though Japan is now aiming to concentrate more on basic research.

Table 4.12 presents R&D as a percentage of GDP, thus adjusting for size – although, given the existence of an R&D/GDP growth relation, such ratios taken alone can be misleading. In terms of this ratio, the UK position appears to be better, with little change for 1969–1981; Japan and Germany both show large increases. Given the UK's poor growth record the constancy of this ratio cannot be interpreted as a very positive indicator – as underlined by the absolute figures in Table 4.10.

The government's role in R&D varies considerably between these countries, not simply in terms of absolute expenditures, but also in terms of the direction of those funds and in terms of the institutional structures supporting government involvement in R&D. Table 4.13 shows the proportion of total R&D funded by governments in 1969

Table 4.10   Gross expenditure on R&D (GERD): constant 1975 prices (in $US million)[a]

	1969	1975	1981 % of OECD total	Total 1981	Compound real growth rates 1969–81
US	37,735.1[b]	36,723.7	47,122.8	46.3	1.8
UK	5,656.8	6,122.7	8,203.3	7.2	2.2
Japan	6,790.2	10,976.3	17,341.0	16.1	8.1
Germany	5,348.3	7,656.0	9,934.8	9.9	5.4

[a] Purchasing power parities.
[b] 1970

Source: OECD/STIIU databank; OECD (1986)

Table 4.11   R&D in the OECD area

	Total R&D expenditure				Basic research
	1969	1975	1981	1983	1981
US	55.1	47.5	46.3	46.0	44.0
Japan	9.3	13.5	16.1	17.4	10.0
EEC	28.0	30.8	29.6	28.7	36.0
Other	7.5	8.2	7.9	7.8	10.0
Total OECD	100.0	100.0	100.0	100.0	100.0

Source: OECD (1986)

and 1984, and the proportion of industry R&D financed by industry. Public funding has fallen in all four economies. Japan funds about a quarter of R&D relative to one half in the US and UK. Similarly, in the business enterprise sector, Japan and Germany have a much higher proportion of R&D financed by industry itself. However, once account is taken of defence R&D, Japan's public funding can be seen to be similar to the other countries. Equally, the proportion of non-defence industrial R&D financed by industry in the US and UK would be much closer to that of Germany and Japan.

Table 4.14 presents further evidence on the level and composition of government R&D funding to support this explanation. Government civil R&D funding as a percentage of GDP is highest in Germany, and similar to each other in the US, UK, and Japan. The

Table 4.12 Gross expenditure on R&D as a percentage of GDP

	1969	*1975*	*1981*	*1984*
US	2.8[a]	2.4	2.5	2.7
UK	2.3	2.2	2.4	2.3[b]
Japan	1.7	2.0	2.3	2.6
Germany	1.8	2.2	2.5	2.6

[a]1970
[b]1983

Source: OECD/STIIU databank

Table 4.13 Funding of R&D

	% of total R&D financed by public sources		*% of BERD[a] financed by industry*	
	1969	*1984*	*1969*	*1984*
US	59.8[b]	49.1	53.8	67.6
UK	51.3	50.2[d]	63.4	63.0[d]
Japan	28.9[c]	22.5	98.7[b]	98.0
Germany	41.8	38.7	86.4	82.7

[a]R&D in the business enterprise sector
[b]1970
[c]1971
[d]1983

Source: OECD/STIIU databank

Causes of change in the world economy

Table 4.14   Government R&D funding

	Government R&D funding as % of GDP		Government civil R&D funding as % of GDP		Defence R&D as % of Government R&D		
	1975	1984	1975	1984	1975	1980	1984
US	1.2	1.2	0.6	0.4	50.8	50.2	66.2
UK	1.4	1.3	0.8	0.7	45.2	51.8	50.9
Japan	0.6	0.6[a]	0.6	0.6[a]	1.9	2.0	2.4[a]
Germany	1.2	1.1	1.0	1.0	11.1	10.2	10.0

[a]1983

Source: OECD/STIIU databank

US shows a sharp drop by 1984, which is a result of the increase in defence R&D, attributable mainly to the Star Wars programme.

Focusing on business enterprise R&D (though still including defence spending), Japan spends about one-third of the US total, Germany one-fifth, and the UK about one-tenth. This is shown in Table 4.15. Growth rates of business enterprise R&D vary both across countries and over time, with Japan and Germany both averaging high rates of growth, and the US and UK experiencing negative growth in some sub-periods, although most recent figures for the UK do show a renewed spurt of growth in 1983–5.

A picture of R&D strengths in different industries is given in Table 4.16, which gives the proportion of OECD R&D each country carries out in each industry group. Aerospace is dominated by the US, and then the UK, reflecting the defence picture. Japan has a relatively strong presence in basic metals, reflecting her tendency to spread its R&D more widely across industries rather than just focusing on high-technology industries. This is also shown in Table 4.17 which presents the percentage distribution of R&D within countries. Japan and Germany again have low, or zero aerospace proportions, and Japan

Table 4.15   Business enterprise R&D – rate of growth

	Million US $ 1983	Compound real growth rates (%)			
		1969–81	1969–75	1975–81	1981–83
US	62,816.0	1.9	−1.6	5.4	4.4
Japan	21,270.0	8.4	7.6	9.2	10.7
Germany	12,649.0	5.9	5.6	6.2	2.9
UK	7,662.9	2.0	−0.1	4.1	−1.3

Source: OECD (1986)

has more R&D concentrated in industries such as non-ferrous metals, food, drink and tobacco, rubber and plastics, and stone, clay and glass This more diversified, flexible nature of Japanese R&D may be an important source of strength. The US and UK both have very high proportions in aerospace. The relatively low UK proportion in motor vehicles is also notable.

In summary, Japan has a very strong position in R&D, both in absolute levels and rates of growth, though the US remains absolutely larger, by a factor of two in civil R&D. Germany has also shown strong rates of growth, while the UK's relative – and at some points absolute – position has deteriorated. Countries' strengths and weaknesses vary across industries, although overall patterns of R&D (excluding defence) expenditure are fairly similar.

In terms of both trade performance and R&D we have a picture of Japan continuing to improve her performance strongly over time. The US shows much lower rates of growth or deterioration in relative performance on a number of indicators, but remains ahead of the other countries in terms of levels of R&D, levels of overall productivity, and GDP per head. Germany has been increasing her R&D effort at a· fairly high pace, remains ahead of Japan in overall productivity and GDP per head, but has experienced some deterioration in trade performance, although remaining the largest world exporter. The UK has witnessed a dramatic decline in her R&D position – from second to fifth place – even without excluding defence R&D. Her trade performance has also deteriorated – she

Table 4.16 Proportions of industries' R&D 1981 (OECD = 100)

	Electrical	Chemical	Aerospace	Other transport	Basic metals
US	46.1	40.9	75.3	47.2	35.7
Japan	16.9	16.0	0.0	22.7	30.3
Germany	11.3	14.0	4.3	12.7	11.4
UK	9.7	6.5	9.2	3.0	4.0

	Machinery	Chemical linked	Other manufacturing	Services
US	62.0	37.1	49.6	38.8
Japan	12.3	25.9	19.8	18.5
Germany	10.2	7.9	6.3	4.6
UK	5.0	7.7	4.5	6.1

Source: OECD (1986)

Table 4.17 Distribution of manufacturing R&D within countries, 1983

	US[a]	Japan	Germany	UK
Electrical machinery	7.1	8.5 ⎫		3.0
Electronic equipment and components	14.4	20.3 ⎭	25.4	31.2
Chemicals	6.7	11.4 ⎱	23.2	9.2
Drugs	4.2	6.8 ⎰		9.7
Petroleum refineries	3.6	1.2	0.8	0.8
Aerospace	21.6	0.0	5.6	18.5
Motor vehicles	11.6	14.2	16.0	6.2
Ships	0.4	2.3	0.2	0.2
Ferrous metals	1.0	4.4	2.0	0.7
Non-ferrous metals	0.6	1.7	0.7	0.6
Fabricated metal products	1.3	1.9	2.8	1.1
Instruments	7.1	3.7	1.8	1.3
Office machinery and computers	9.3	4.4 ⎱	15.2	6.6
Machinery n.e.c.	4.6	7.3 ⎰		5.9
Food, drink, and tobacco	1.5	2.8	1.2	2.1
Textiles and clothing	0.3	1.2	0.5	0.4
Rubber and plastics	1.6	2.6	1.8	0.6
Stone, clay, and glass	1.0	2.7	1.2	0.9
Paper and printing	1.1	0.9	0.4	0.5
Wood, cork, and furniture	0.3	0.5	0.5	0.1
Other manufacturing	0.8	1.1	0.3	0.5

[a] 1980

Source: OECD/STIIU data bank

has much lower export market shares than the other countries and her net trade balances have declined across many industries.

Innovation differences across countries

The causes of the differences in innovative and economic performance set out in the previous section are both varied and complex. There have been many analyses and explanations of Japan's exceptional performance and of the UK's poor performance. More recently, some writers have suggested that the US is also suffering from some of the same de-industrialization problems as the UK (see, for example, Thompson 1987). While different arguments abound, there is widespread agreement that innovative ability is an important ingredient in a country's economic performance – taking innovation to mean the whole process from R&D through to marketing. It is of interest, therefore, to consider the causes of differences in innovative efforts and innovative success. It should be recognized, though, that to stress the importance of innovation is not necessarily to imply that success in the high-technology industries is crucial to a country's growth and general economic performance. Thus, Nelson (1984) distinguishes carefully between the notion 'that high-technology industries often are "leading" in that they tend to drive and mould economic progress across a broad front' and the argument 'that national economic progress and competitiveness are dependent upon national strength in these industries, and governmental help is warranted to ensure this strength'. Furthermore, as firms and technological knowledge become increasingly internationalized, serious questions arise about the relation between the performance of firms of a particular nationality and that nation's economic performance. This is discussed further in the final section of this chapter.

Here, we briefly focus on some of the main arguments that have been put forward to explain differences in innovative performance. First, as stressed in the introduction, the impact of current macro-performance should not be underestimated. Nelson (1984) concludes that general economic strength is a necessary condition for success in leading industries. Patel and Pavitt (1986) report management studies that find low-demand growth is a particular hindrance to innovation in the UK. Similarly, Ergas (1986) states, with respect to the strength of Japanese industry, that 'the first, most obvious and in some respects most pervasive factor is the very favourable macro-economic context'. Thus, where countries, for whatever reasons, have successful macro-economic performances, this is likely to be an important stimulant to innovation through fostering confidence in growing demand, access to finance, investment and so forth, and so generally improving expectations and attitudes to risk and uncertainty. Such circumstances may well, of course, result in 'virtuous circles' or cumulative causation, with growth leading to investment and innovation, resulting in further growth. The impact of a poor macro-economic performance or of recession on innovation may then be very serious. The OECD (1980) refers to tendencies in the UK and US for innovation to be directed at short-run and safe projects under such circumstances. Further, to the extent that spillover, and interaction between industrial sectors is important in spreading innovations, technological knowledge, and – more broadly – demand and positive expectations, then it will become increasingly difficult for the slower-growth, less innovative economies to compete in any one specific sector. Taken further, such an argument would imply that an economy like Japan's depends on its competitive advantage and growth, on success and interaction across a broad front – thus, its development requires a broad asymmetry between it and its competitors.

Many writers have suggested that the distribution of R&D may be a crucial factor in addition to its absolute level (see, for example,

Freeman 1978, Ergas 1986). Thus, it is argued that the heavy emphasis on defence R&D in the US, UK, and France has, in effect, crowded out civil R&D, while Germany and Japan have both benefited from low or zero levels of government defence R&D. Ergas (1986) referring to the UK, states:

> The indirect spin-offs have been low, creating a 'sheltered workshop' type of economy, a small number of more or less directly subsidized high-technology firms, heavily dependent on and oriented to public procurement, and a traditional sector which draws little benefit from the high overall level of expenditure on R&D.

However, while there is no doubt that defence spending has distortionary effects on the industrial structure generally, as well as on innovation, a straightforward crowding-out hypothesis is too simplistic. As shown in the previous section, the UK has been falling behind in terms of absolute spending (including defence) on R&D since 1970, so there would appear to be a problem of absolute levels, not simply distribution, of R&D. Freeman (1978) argues that, for the UK, the problem is one of the distribution, since in the early and mid-1960s she had high absolute levels of R&D but poor performance. However, the question arises as to why firms working in non-defence areas did not – and do not – spend more on R&D. If defence R&D directly crowded out civil R&D, through absorbing scientific and technical personnel, this should show up in an increase in R&D labour costs in the civil sector, as firms bid up wages in an attempt to increase their R&D personnel. It is not clear that this happened – certainly in the early to mid-1970s UK R&D labour costs were well below those of the US. If it is firms' profits, expectations, time horizons, management ability, and so forth that affect R&D, then a reduction in defence R&D *per se* may not solve the problems of low civil R&D. It would certainly release some scientific personnel, it would also release government funds – but there is no guarantee that these funds would then be directed at civil R&D, or that they would be competently used. Thus, Patel and Pavitt (1986) comment:

> There is widespread concern in W. Europe and the USA about the harmful effects on innovative activities of top management's reliance on short-term planning and profit horizons, and of its lack of competence and commitment in technology.

Patel and Pavitt also stress the difficulties of obtaining development finance in the US and UK. While, then, the commitment to defence R&D is an important distinction between the UK and US on the one hand, and Germany and Japan on the other, it should not be seen as a

62

comprehensive explanation of innovation differences, or as providing simple policy guidelines.

A further area that receives much attention is that of government policies with respect to R&D, apart from defence R&D policies. Here attention tends to focus most strongly on Japan. The role of MITI – the Ministry of International Trade and Industry – is seen as particularly important. MITI has played a wide-ranging role in the Japanese economy, from targeting sectors and industries where the economy should be developing, to funding and encouraging specific research projects, diffusion of information, and so forth. Nelson (1984) comments:

> What seems special about Japanese policies towards high technology industries is that MITI has played an active role in funding and orchestrating various large-scale co-operative research efforts aimed at helping the Japanese firms reach and then surpass foreign technological capabilities.

Such policies cannot be seen in isolation from other aspects of Japan's industrial structure, such as the large industrial groups, including banking and financial institutions, which provide the institutional structure within which these policies take effect. Interdependence and close communication appear to be important aspects of Japan's success. Thus, a 1987 seminar of the Japan Technology Transfer Association (reported in the *Financial Times*, 12 March 1987) stressed that:

> The Japanese have two powerful weapons: a cohesive national policy on technological development, funded by the government, and a scientific old-boy network that extends to every board room and laboratory in the country.

MITI's most recent industrial strategy – the Technopolis programme – now aims to build a national network of research cities, with the emphasis on small firm science centres.

Contrasts are also frequently drawn between the technology policies of Germany and of the US and UK (see, for example, Nelson 1984, Ergas, 1986), partly in terms of defence, partly in terms of US and UK reluctance to be very directly involved in civil industrial activity (Nelson 1984). Ergas suggests that Germany is more 'diffusion orientated' in that she is 'largely concerned with upgrading the capacity of firms to respond to new technologies'. A recent white paper on UK R&D (July 1987) recognizes some of the problems of UK R&D effort and calls for more co-ordination and a greater focus on commercially exploitable areas of science. The white paper proposes to establish a new committee, chaired by the Prime

Minister, and advised by the Advisory Council on Science and Technology (ACOST). The effectiveness of such institutional changes remains to be seen; unless more innovative effort is forthcoming, however, their success is in doubt.

More generally, the effectiveness of any technology policies cannot be seen in isolation from the rest of the economy or the role and actions of government in the rest of the economy. Furthermore, as Nelson (1984) points out, the purpose of national technology policies in an increasingly interconnected world economy may need rethinking. In addition, given the disequilibrium and uneven nature of growth, it is not to be expected that all economies can perform equally successfully, or that there will be five, or fifty, Japans. As Nelson (1984) put it:

> Five countries cannot all be first in the product cycle race, and the competition appears to have reduced the size of the prize and increased the costs of entry.

Future developments

This final section briefly considers some recent developments in the process of creating and transferring technological knowledge and discusses some of the issues and problems they potentially raise. Two developments are focused on, in particular, the increase in co-operative R&D, and the increasing importance of multinational enterprises (MNEs).

As discussed above, Japan's R&D efforts have been based in part on both formal and informal co-operative efforts, in particular in the earlier or more basic stages of research. Various types of co-operative R&D ventures are now also seen in the US and Western Europe. These take various forms, such as firm–university co-operation, inter-firm joint ventures (including firms of different nationalities), government-sponsored or -organized co-operation, and inter-governmental-sponsored or -organized co-operation, such as the many initiatives established by the European Economic Community. Such co-operation may be seen as a positive development, as it avoids duplication of research and encourages faster and more widespread diffusion of knowledge and information. At the European level it may be argued that such initiatives are also necessary to provide effective competition against Japan and the US.

However, there are various potential difficulties and contradictions here. First, although duplication is wasteful, it may nevertheless be necessary. Since research is by nature uncertain, it is desirable that there should be a diversity of approaches to a particular area or problem – the cost of this is some duplication, the cost of not doing it is a narrowing of research and a limiting of technological change. Second, the issue of co-operation raises the old question of the public and private nature of knowledge – i.e. that, without some degree of appropriability, firms will not attempt to innovate. As co-operation increases, as speed of imitation of innovation increases, the degree of appropriability falls. Is it then to be expected that in future there will only be free technological competition between the three blocs – US, Japan, and Europe, and not within them, or might there be US/European co-operation but new competitors emerging on the Pacific Rim? Alternatively, if appropriability falls dramatically, the competition may come to be based on more traditional aspects of comparative costs.

Such developments are complicated further by the spread of multinational enterprises. As MNEs of many nationalities increasingly expand across Europe, the US and, to a lesser extent, Japan, the whole concept of technological advantage of a particular economy becomes more tenuous. This raises the issue of the extent to which technological advantage is firm-specific or country-specific. As Nelson (1984) states: 'Increasingly, technological knowledge and capability are international rather than national'. The question then arises, if the European Community is organizing collaboration and co-operation between firms on specific areas can it – and should it – exclude foreign MNEs based in the EEC? If these MNEs are included, then this may tend to undermine further the basis of US/Japan/European competition. Furthermore, to the extent that firms do still derive particular strengths and weaknesses from their parent country, they are, nevertheless, highly mobile internationally. If technological leadership cannot be guaranteed except for short periods, then these firms may be moving increasingly, and more quickly, to sources of low-cost supply. Thus, the advantages or competitiveness of firms of a particular country may have a smaller and smaller impact on the performance of that country.

The evidence presented in the first section of this chapter stressed the differences in innovation and economic performance between countries. Here, it is suggested that this may be a less appropriate level of analysis in the light of future trends, unless supplemented by more detailed information on MNEs and the transfer and creation of technological knowledge. Thus, the increasingly global nature of firms, and the increasingly global and social nature of technology raises a number of important questions and problems – a few of which have been briefly discussed here. The internationalization of firms and of technology is an important development – its implications and likely future trends need consideration by policy analysts and economists alike.

65

References

Ergas, H. (1986) 'Does technology policy matter?', Paris: OECD, mimeograph.

Freeman, C. (1978) 'Technical innovation and British trade performance', in F. Blackaby (ed.) *De-industrialisation*, London: Heinemann.

Griliches, Z. (ed.) (1984) *R&D Patents and Productivity*, Chicago: NBER, University of Chicago.

Hughes, K. (1986) *Exports and Technology*, Cambridge: Cambridge University Press.

Nelson, R. (1984) *High Technology Policies – Five Nation Comparison*, Washington: American Enterprise Institute.

OECD (1980) *Technical Change and Economic Policy*, Paris: OECD.

—— (1984) 'Specialisation and competitiveness in manufacturing industries of high, medium and low R&D intensity', DSTI/SPR/84.49, mimeograph.

—— (1986) *Science and Technology Indicators*, No. 2 – *R&D, Invention and Competitiveness*, Paris: OECD.

Patel, P. and Pavitt, K. (1986) 'Is western Europe losing the technological race?', mimeograph.

Ray, G. F. (1987) 'Labour costs in manufacturing, *National Institute Economic Review*, May, pp. 71–4.

Rowthorn, B. (1986) 'Deindustrialisation in Britain', in R. Martin and B. Rowthorn, *The Geography of Deindustralisation*, Basingstoke: Macmillan.

Thompson, G. 'The American industrial policy debate: any lessons for the U.K.?', *Economy and Society* 16 (1): 1–74.

Chapter Five

The role of services in global structural change

H. Peter Gray

Introduction

One of the most striking features of the economic development of the industrialized world over the last twenty-five years has been the steady and general growth of the ratio of value-added in services to GNP in virtually all countries. This trend has been experienced in virtually all industrialized countries. The growth of the importance of international trade in services (relative to tangible goods) has also been substantial.

This chapter examines the implications of the increasing importance of services for the evolving structure of the global economy. The main focus is necessarily the effects of the growth in the international exchange of services (the direct effects); to a lesser degree, the chapter explores the indirect effects of the growth of domestic value-added.

Over recent years, the service sector has contributed disproportionately to employment in industrialized countries. This change, well illustrated for the United States by McCulloch (1988: 380–8), is attributable not only to the growth of value-added in services but also to the lower productivity of many service jobs. While the service sector has contributed to total employment in this way, the main growth in jobs has been in the traditional services, particularly wholesale and retail trade. In addition, the main growth sectors have been financial services, 'business repair', and health services (McCulloch, 1988: 384). One of the side effects of this phenomenon has been to generate a much less equal distribution of income as high-productivity, high-wage jobs in manufacturing have been eliminated by technological innovations. There is concern in the United States for the 'disappearing middle class', as those high-paying jobs which are created in the service industries tend to be professional jobs and are very well paid. Of particular importance are the effects of the service-oriented technological innovations for the international division of labour. These innovations, particularly those in communications and knowledge-intensive industries, have already had major effects on the structure of the global economy since they are catalysts to the global integration of financial markets and the centralization of production decisions in headquarters of multinational corporations. The potential for further international growth of the industries which use them, has also led to the inclusion of international trade in services in the Uruguay Round of multilateral trade negotiations[1] and to the possibility of a significant broadening of the scope of the General Agreement on Tariffs and Trade (GATT) (see Giersch, 1989). It is possible that the growing contribution of information technology to management will constitute an additional reason to the four cited by Cantwell in Chapter 6 of this book for the growing internationalization of industry.

This chapter seeks to identify those features of the range of service industries which are likely to affect global economic structure and the international division of labour. To a very important degree, these effects will depend upon the way in which countries with comparative disadvantages in particular services do not deliberately impede or blockade imports: that is, the degree of success and the breadth of inclusion of countries in negotiations on services in the Uruguay Round are important in any attempt to gauge the effect of services on global economic structure.

The following section identifies and categorizes the many types of service that exist and provides some basic data. The next section examines the growth of trade in services among the industrialized nations as a source of structural change in the international economy, and the penultimate section is concerned with the implications of the growth of value-added and international trade in services for the pattern of global production, the division of labour, and the stability of the economic system. In conclusion, the final section offers *the intrusion hypothesis* which states that: because growth in international trade in service activities (particularly financial services and data-processing services) is capable of penetrating more closely to the heart of a nation's individual concept of economic independence than will an equal volume of trade in tangible goods, the implications for nations of growth in trade in services will be more fundamental and far-reaching. Encouragement of open (free) trade in services is therefore likely to warrant and receive far more careful consideration than open trade in goods: nations are unlikely to renounce controls over the foreign supply of services merely to gratify a time-honoured but abstract argument for free trade and one which does not acknowledge any value for individual national identity. These reservations may be expected to apply more severely to Third World nations where an efficient indigenous service sector is lacking but will also apply to those industrialized nations that place a high value on their own economic identity.

The growth of service activities

Services are intangible and, as such, have quite different economic characteristics than do goods. A pure service requires virtually simultaneous presence between the producer and user: it is only the recent rash of advancements in communications technology that has allowed services to be traded internationally without some international movement of the product and consumer. Any analysis of the role of services in the world economy must delineate quite carefully what range of service activities is to be included. Services are as heterogeneous as goods but there is one distinction which is particularly important in any consideration of their role in the international economy. 'Services' can comprise inputs by primary factors of production as well as 'produced services', so that it is possible to distinguish between, say, the services provided by a commercial bank (produced or non-factor services) and the services provided to the bank by people employed there (primary or factor services). Most analyses of the role of services in a national economy are concerned with the effects of produced or non-factor services. Non-factor services can be either final products or intermediate products. As noted above, much of the growth in employment in service industries has been generated in the distributive industries and would be categorized as goods-related trade. The distinction between factor and non-factor services becomes even more important in an international context given that multinational corporations are transferers of capital among nations and the return on that capital (repatriated profits) is essentially a payment for a primary or a factor service to a foreign resident.[2]

A strict definition of a service requires that it be non-storable, so that immediate contact between supplier and user must exist at the moment of the production of the service (Hill 1977). This may once have been a valid requirement of the definition of a service but it is not an operational one – consider the list of internationally traded activities included in the definition of services in Table 5.3 on p. 74. It is now possible for many (but not all) services to be provided at a distance either by electronic communication devices (including fax machines) or by their embodiment in a tangible object for delivery purposes (e.g. blueprints serve to make engineering services available through time and space but this practice does not make engineers producers of a commodity). This distinction leads to non-factor services being referred to as either 'factor-embodied', in which the factor of production or consumption moves to the location of consumption or production, or as 'other services' (a residual category), which achieve delivery by some other (possibly electronic) medium than the movement of a primary factor. Transportation of passengers and goods, foreign travel (including tourism and non-pleasure travel), and the acquisition of education and health services are all time-honoured categories of internationally exchanged services which are factor-embodied. While these categories are quantitatively important and are likely to remain so, they are not, with the exception of air freight and container ships (see below), the categories of service which feature rapid technological innovation likely to bring about structural change of major proportions. In the third and fourth sections of this chapter, the emphasis will be on those services in which rapid technological development has recently occurred and/or is still occurring.

A final word of caution is in order before considering the magnitude of value-added and trade in services. The reliability of data on international trade in services is probably much lower than that which applies to tangible goods if only because it is much more difficult to obtain accurate reports on the amount traded from the basic sources. The US Office of Technology Assessment (1986, Ch. 4) undertook a detailed assessment of US international trade in services and found the newer services to be the more seriously *under*estimated. Published data on trade in services are subject to even greater errors than most economic data and should be used with more care than is usually applied in empirical work.[3]

Table 5.1 provides a breakdown of the change in the division of sectoral (value-added) contributions to gross domestic product (GDP) for five industrialized countries from 1960 to 1984. In all countries the proportion of GDP attributable to services has increased steadily.[4] This fact can be attributed to five separate developments.

First, consider what may be described as 'goods-related' services, such as transportation. These services have grown with the volume of international trade. Second, consider the other factor-embodied services which have also grown substantially over recent years. Tourism, health services, and education are all income-elastic and have registered impressive growth during the last quarter of a century. Causes of rapid growth of international trade and production of 'other services' derives first from structural changes in national economies themselves; second, as a result of 'splintering'; and third, from the huge technological advances in knowledge-intensive services. One example of the common structural developments in

Table 5.1 Sectoral shares of GDP for five developed nations, 1960–84 (in percent – in current prices)[a]

Country	Agriculture				Manufacturing				Other industry[b]				Services			
	1960	1970	1980	1984	1960	1970	1980	1984	1960	1970	1980	1984	1960	1970	1980	1984
Canada	6.7	4.3	4.4	3.7	27.5	24.5	21.1	18.7	13.0	13.2	16.3	15.5	52.8	58.5	58.2	62.1
Germany (Fed. Republic)	5.8	3.4	2.2	2.0	42.9	40.8	34.6	32.9	12.5	11.7	10.7	10.0	38.7	44.1	52.5	55.0
Japan	—	6.0	3.6	3.2	—	35.2	28.7	29.3	—	10.4	12.4	10.9	—	48.4	55.3	56.6
United Kingdom	4.0	2.8	2.1	2.0	36.4	33.1	26.4	24.0	11.8	13.8	15.1	15.8	47.7	53.6	56.5	58.2
United States[c]	4.0	2.7	2.7	2.0	28.3	25.1	22.0	20.7	9.4	3.9	10.7	10.3	58.3	63.2	64.6	67.0

[a]Details may not add to totals because of statistical discrepancies
[b]Mining, quarry, electricity, gas, water, and construction (includes petroleum)
[c]1983 data are latest available

Sources: UN Yearbook of National Accounts Statistics, 1970 (New York: United Nations, 1972) and National Accounts Statistics: Main Aggregates and Detailed Tables, 1984 (New York: United Nations, 1986)

modern industrialized economies has been the ever-increasing proportion of women employed in the official (directly remunerated)
labour force. This development has liberated many women from their
traditional home-oriented role, so much so that Grubel (1989) found
the rate of female participation in the labour force was a statistically
significant and important explanatory variable of the growth in
restaurant services in Canada. 'Splintering' is a phenomenon identified by Bhagwati (1984) and describes the spinning off into separate
corporations of certain activities which previously had been performed within a large goods-producing corporation. Service activities
have been spun off in this way to an important degree. Since value-
added in services is determined by reports filed from firms which
produce services, as distinct from those whose end-product is goods,
then the separation of a service activity from a goods-producing
entity will enhance the reported value of services performed in an
economy. Splintering, therefore, gives rise to a spurious reported
increase in service production proper, since the volume of services
performed in the economy has not increased in any real sense. Third,
the growth of data-processing activities and the transmission of
knowledge by electronic communications devices have increased
severalfold in recent years, at the same time as the means of
transmission has shifted from being hardware-intensive to software-
intensive.

The importance of the growth of the information-intensive services
can be inferred from Table 5.2 which provides (constant-price) 1970
and 1983 data for some selected services for the Federal Republic of
Germany and the United States. In addition to significant rates of
increase in the provision of health-related services, the two spectacular gainers in both countries are 'communications' and 'financial
institutions'. This reinforces the point made above that the major
effect of the services sector on global structural change can be found
mainly with those services which have enjoyed such striking
technological advances in recent years (freight transportation and
communications/data processing services).

Table 5.3 provides a detailed breakdown of US international trade
in non-factor services.[5] The tabulation indicates the large number of
individual services which are traded annually among residents of
different nations. Of these, the following are 'factor-embodied':
construction; education; health; leasing; management/consulting;[6]
transportation; and travel.

Clearly, the two major activities are transportation and travel,
which account for more than 50 per cent of both exports and imports.
Next in quantitative importance are 'financial services' (comprising
both insurance and investment banking/brokerage), which are es-

Table 5.2   Selected components of service activities, 1970 and 1983

	Germany (millions of 1980 DM)		United States (millions of 1975 US$)	
	1970	1983	1970	1983
Wholesale and retail trade	109,280	141,200	222,301	336,497
Restaurants,	16,450	18,150		
Hotels and lodging			8,539	11,182
Transport and storage	41,770	52,070	51,696	57,348
Communications	17,210	37,720	28,903	65,240
Financial institutions	29,300	54,660	31,494	49,256
Insurance	10,360	16,440	19,397	26,871
Health	20,100	32,160	42,479	79,157
Community, social, and personal services (excluding health)	82,300	142,490	62,044	76,889

Source: *National Accounts Statistics. Main Aggregates and Detailed Tables, 1984* (New York: United Nations, 1986)

timated to generate international revenues in 1984 of $14 billions and expenditures of $13.5 billions. These services almost inevitably involve significant offsets: for example, premium income earned by insurance companies almost has to involve some pay-out in the form of claims. The data in Table 5.3 do *not* include estimates of receipts from commercial banking. For this industry, the question of what is and what is not a balance-of-payments transaction is extremely difficult to define and reliable data are extremely difficult to obtain. The Office of Technology Assessment (1986) report provides an estimate for total international revenues and expenditures by the United States but does not distinguish these revenues between 'direct exports' and 'foreign-affiliate sales'. An approximate estimate of direct US exports (imports) by the three financial services combined in 1984 would be $20 (25) billions.

International trade in services comprises a wide variety of types of transactions and it would be extremely difficult to attribute this array of activities to a single root cause which leads to international trade. Moreover, as noted above for insurance, international trade in services inevitably involves a great deal of cross-hauling. Ships and aircraft do not travel full in one direction and empty in the other; travel involves both incoming and outgoing travellers as home and foreign business people visit export markets and foreign subsidiaries, and as tourists seek to familiarize themselves with foreign countries for the sake of going abroad. To the extent that international trade in services is intra-firm trade conducted under the auspices of MNCs,

Table 5.3 Estimates of US service balance of payments, 1982–4[a]

	Exports (receipts) (billions of dollars)			Imports (payments) (billions of dollars)			Net exports[b] (billions of dollars)		
	1982	1983	1984	1982	1983	1984	1982	1983	1984
Accounting	0.2–0.5	0.2–0.5	0.2–0.5	—[c]	—[c]	—[c]	0.2–0.5	0.2–0.5	0.2–0.5
Advertising	0.1–0.5	0.1–0.5	0.1–0.5	—[c]	—[c]	—[c]	0.1–0.5	0.1–0.5	0.1–0.5
Construction	5.6	4.8	4.0–6.0	0.0–2.2	0.0–1.7	0.0–2.0	3.4–5.6	3.1–4.8	2.0–6.0
Data processing	0.1–1.2	0.1–1.2	0.1–1.2	0.0–2.0	0.0–2.0	0.0–2.0	(1.9)–1.2	(1.9)–1.2	(1.9)–1.2
Education	1.5–2.2	1.6–2.3	1.8–2.5	0.1–0.3	0.0–2.0	0.1–0.3	1.2–2.1	1.3–2.2	1.5–2.4
Engineering	1.2–1.7	1.1–1.6	1.0–1.4	0.1–0.3	0.1–0.3	0.1–0.3	0.9–1.6	0.8–1.5	0.7–1.3
Franchising	0.2–1.0	0.2–1.1	0.2–1.2	—[c]	—[c]	—[c]	0.2–1.0	0.2–1.1	0.2–1.2
Health	1.0–2.5	1.0–2.5	1.0–2.5	—[c]	—[c]	—[c]	1.0–2.5	1.0–2.5	1.0–2.5
Information	0.0–2.6	0.0–2.9	0.0–3.1	0.0–1.0	0.0–1.0	0.0–1.0	(1.0)–2.6	(1.0)–2.9	(1.0)–3.1
Insurance	5.6–7.7	6.1–8.2	6.9–9.1	6.3–8.6	6.7–9.1	7.4–9.8	(1.1)–(0.5)[d]	(1.1)–(0.4)[d]	(0.9)–(0.2)[d]
Investment banking/brokerage	2.1–4.8	3.2–6.4	3.2–8.5	3.6–4.1	4.3–4.8	4.3–5.6	(2.0)–1.2	(1.6)–2.1	(2.4)–4.2
Leasing	0.2–1.2	0.2–1.2	0.0–1.2	0.0–1.0	0.0–1.0	0.0–1.0	0.8–1.2	0.8–1.2	0.8–1.2
Legal	0.0–2.0	0.0–2.0	0.0–2.0	0.0–1.0	0.0–1.0	0.0–1.0	(1.0)–2.0	(1.0)–2.0	(1.0)–2.0
Licensing	5.2	5.2	5.5	0.7	0.8	1.0	4.5	4.4	4.5
Management/consulting	0.5–1.1	0.6–1.4	0.6–1.6	0.6–1.1	0.6–1.1	0.6–1.1	(0.6)–0.5	(0.5)–0.8	(0.5)–1.0
Motion pictures	1.6	1.9	1.9	0.1–1.4	0.1–1.7	0.2–2.7	0.2–1.5	0.2–1.8	(0.8)–1.7
Retailing	—[c]	—[c]	—[c]	—[c]	—[c]	—[c]	—[c]	—[c]	—[c]
Software	1.6–1.7	2.5–2.6	2.8–2.9	0.0–1.7	0.0–2.2	0.0–2.7	(0.1)–1.7	0.3–2.6	0.1–2.9
Telecommunications	1.1	1.3	1.3	1.9	2.0	2.4	(0.8)	(0.7)	(1.1)
Transportation	16.7	17.1	18.5	17.7	19.1	22.8	(1.0)	(2.0)	(4.3)
Travel	15.7	14.1	13.7	13.7	15.8	16.4	2.0	(1.7)	(2.7)
Miscellaneous	4.7	5.3	5.7	1.8	1.9	2.1	2.9	3.4	3.6
OTA total	65–81	67–84	69–91	47–61	52–66	57–74	6.3–32.8[d]	2.7–30.7[d]	(3.5)–31.5[d]
OTA mid-range estimate	73	76	80	54	59	66	20	17	14
BEA total	41.7	41.8	43.8	32.6	35.4	41.5	9.1	6.4	2.3

[a] Commercial banking is excluded from this table, for reasons discussed on p. 76 of the above publication
[b] Parentheses indicates negative balance
[c] Negligible
[d] Range of estimates for net exports, not that implied by ranges for exports and imports, for reasons explained on p. 76 of the above publication

the existence of inward and outward foreign direct investment in the same industry (intra-industry FDI) will also augment intra-industry trade in services.

Direct implications of a larger volume of trade in services

The increase in the relative output of international trade in services and of the technological developments in the service sector affect the international division of value-adding activities in several ways. This section considers first the effect of these developments on the pattern of international trade in goods. The second area of interest is the pattern of growth of international trade in services. The growth of international trade in services has important implications for the existing institutional apparatus of international economic co-operation on trade issues. Finally, it is possible to provide some indications as to how greater international trade in services will affect the international division of labour.

The effect on goods trade

All trade in goods contains some embodied services (and, equally, all trade in services contains some embodied goods)[7]. To the extent that there are differences between countries in the relative costs of intermediate services which are used (embodied) in the production of tradeable goods, the cost-competitiveness of the traded goods will depend directly upon the differences in the costs of service inputs (Grubel 1987). What is probably more important than the actual relative costs of the service inputs is any difference in the technological sophistication of services available in different countries and the contribution of such services to international competitiveness. In context, competitiveness must be defined as having both a design/quality dimension as well as a cost (or financial) dimension. Differences in technological sophistication in two countries can enable a country's economy to allocate resources more efficiently in the traditional static sense or, dynamically, to adapt design and production methods more quickly as local firms are better able to use such new systems as computer-aided design and computer-aided manufacture (CAD/CAM). This advantage is likely to be more important in the dynamic than in the static sense, since it will permit a national industry to maintain its comparative advantage by adopting basic R&D more quickly than its foreign competitors. The advantages that derive from the use of computer-aided production are likely to involve a reduction in the amount of labour needed per unit of output – largely replacing semi-skilled production workers by a much smaller number of highly-trained technical workers. To the extent that this applies, the processes are likely to reduce the major source of comparative cost advantage in the Third World and to weaken the ability of such countries to provide manufactures at a competitive price. A sophisticated financial sector using data-processing and communication techniques intensively, adds to the efficiency of the allocation of new investments and will provide another source of increased efficiency which will be preponderantly available to the developed world.

Some services are best described as 'trade-in-goods-related'– these include freight transportation and the associated financial services. In recent years, freight transportation has experienced a major technological change-containerization. Containerization is a mode of transportation by which general cargoes can achieve some economies of scale in handling that specialized facilities and ship design accord to bulk cargoes – by loading goods into standardized 40 foot containers at the factory and shipping them to receiving depots equipped to handle them. In addition to the savings in commodity costs from easier handling and in vessel costs from quicker turnaround, the shipper also gains from reduced pilferage and reduced breakage (Gray 1982). These savings substantially reduce the costs of freight transportation and, since they apply mainly on routes in which the containers can be shipped full in both directions, the savings are especially relevant to the planned combination of production in different countries according to perceived cost advantages and available capacity. Containerization, by reducing transportation costs, has contributed to the greater integration of national economies through the exchange of goods: containerization has its greatest effect on global structure by virtue of the way in which it facilitates joint production under the auspices of MNCs and will therefore contribute mainly to North–South trade.

The growth of trade in services

The truly revolutionary technologies which have contributed to growth in services are those in data-processing and communications – in international transactions the category of *transborder data flows.*[8] These innovations have led to the creation of new (service) industries as well as exerting profound changes on older (goods and service) industries. The fact that many existing industries grew to incorporate the new technologies and to rely upon the availability of massive amounts of data, is reinforced by the fact that data technology permits interlinkage of different processes so that old lines of endeavour are transformed. Moreover, management of

MNCs became increasingly dependent on the use of international data communications as a means of maintaining competitiveness in world markets during the global economic turbulence triggered by the two oil-price shocks of 1974 and 1979. 'Of particular importance is the rapid internationalization of the service industries – banking, insurance, transport-producer services – whose products typically involve a substantial information component' (Sauvant 1986a: 81). These industries rely upon data availability to achieve the gains which international co-ordination of activities made possible and, as they grow, the demand for such data increases.

In all of these developments, the reliance of *financial* activities of MNCs, commercial banks, insurance companies, and investment banks on transborder data flows has been the most spectacular. It is in this area that the innate resistance to unlimited international trade in services was to find resistance. History has shown that an unregulated financial system is capable of severe instability and most countries choose to regulate financial transactions conducted within their borders. Here is a classic example of discrepancies between the optimum political and optimum economic size of units (Kindleberger 1984). Economies of scope and scale offer great gains in cost efficiency for financial firms allowed to operate across boundaries and without political regulation or restraint. Yet a desire for national identity and concern for the stability of domestic economic and financial systems requires the supervision of the home government.[9] It is not unreasonable to suppose that firms based within a country will be more responsible to financial contracts and more susceptible of regulation than those headquartered elsewhere. Thus, complete freedom of trade in services is unlikely to take place without safeguards imposed in the interest of financial stability in the local region.[10]

Yet another impediment to the free exercise of international trade in data flows is the concern of some countries with the possibility of infringements of personal privacy. Purveyors of data-bases are seen as potential 'Big Brothers'. Currently, several European nations have imposed regulations and/or drafted laws concerning the international transmission of personal data. While progress has been made, no consensus has yet appeared on how to resolve the conflict between the gains from freedom of data transmission and safeguarding personal privacy.

To the extent that a country's international trade is dominated by dometic and foreign MNCs, differences in the efficiency of the domestic service sector will exert only a small influence on the pattern of international trade or its development. MNCs will have access to and will make use of efficient service industries in those countries in which they are available. It is domestic-based firms, possibly pre-dominantly concerned with the production of non-tradeable goods, which will suffer from the disadvantage of an archaic set of knowledge-intensive service industries.

The need for a controlled delivery system in export markets

One of the main differences between international trade in services and goods is the need of exporters of services for related or closely controlled delivery systems in the market country. In principle, a foreign market can be serviced by exports made in the home country, by the establishment of a foreign subsidiary in the foreign market and supplying the market wholly from that source, and from a combination of domestic and local foreign production. This third modality of servicing a foreign market is especially important for information-intensive services. There are three reasons why a service firm might need to establish its own marketing-and-distribution subsidiary (and production unit) in a foreign market. These are, first, to service local after-sales support systems, which are important for industries such as management consulting and software; second, for the adaptation of a standardized service produced in the home country that requires to be made compatible with local traditions and/or regulations; and third, there are likely to be advantages of scale and scope to be gained from centralizing some of the more complex and basic operations in the headquarters of the exporting firm and combining the services produced with local inputs in the country of final sale. The contribution of an 'own' or subsidiary marketing-and-distribution (M&D) outlet is increased if the type of service provided is client-idiosyncratic to the point that knowledge of the client's business increases the likelihood of additional sales.[11]

To the extent that international trade in information-intensive services requires an 'owned' delivery service in the market economy, it is possible to preclude free trade in many services simply by denying foreign firms the ability to create the necessary foreign M&D and production subsidiaries (denying the 'right of establishment') or if foreign firms are allowed to create subsidiaries, by discriminating against these firms by denying them the same treatment as is accorded to indigenous firms (denying so-called 'national treatment'). If freedom to establish local M&D and (production) subsidiaries – either wholly owned joint ventures – is a necessary ingredient in open access of local markets to the foreign supply of services, then the inclusion of trade in services on the agenda for the Uruguay Round has major implications for the structure of the GATT. This organiz-ation has hitherto steadfastly refused to be drawn into the area of agreements over foreign direct investment and must now confront such a possibility because the addition of services to the agenda has made the trade and investment dimensions inseparable. Most complex questions of trade policy that do not involve simple quantitative measures have been resolved by agreeing to 'codes' which set out rules of good behaviour which are obeyed by signatories in so far as the economies of other signatories are affected.

Effects on the international division of labour

The introduction of new technologies in knowledge-intensive industries is likely to have substantial implications for the international allocation of value-adding activities and of labour. The effects can be considered in terms of North–North and North–South trade sequentially. Undoubtedly, it is the industrialized North that enjoys a technological lead (and therefore a comparative advantage) in knowledge-intensive services. Most of these are intermediate services and their effects will be felt unequally across the whole range of goods and services involved in international trade. The surge of technological innovation in telecommunications and data-processing has not yet been exhausted and the gap in technological efficiency between North and South may be expected to widen.

The optimistic scenario is for trade in services among the industrialized countries of the North to be relatively open. The basic reason for such optimism, irrespective of the success in negotiations on services at the Uruguay Round, is that the national inequalities in technology possession are less pronounced among the industrialized countries. Each of them is likely to have one industry or sub-industry in which it is a leader. The gains from greater North–North trade in services will be widely spread among firms, industries, and nations. Much of the technology may be held by individual firms so that the patterns of intra-industry trade in manufactures are likely to be repeated in services. One of the important features of rapid growth in intra-industry trade was that the ratio of social costs of adjustment to gains from increased trade was quite low (Gray 1985; 54–62). The prospects for such optimism are particularly good on a regional basis: the European Community has agreed to dismantle its maze of regulations on nearly all aspects of intra-community transactions by 1992, and Canada and the United States are committed to free trade in services as in goods.[12] The mutual quality of benefits in terms of domestic economic efficiency from the local availability of best practice as well as from international trade *per se* are well enough identified for progress to be made.[13]

The prospects for increases in North–South trade in knowledge-intensive services are less good. In addition to the problems presented by the 'intrusion factor' developed in the concluding section of this chapter, the developing countries are very clearly aware that they are at a strong comparative disadvantage and can expect to see their indigenous service sectors destroyed by competition from technologically advanced northern corporations. The defensive posture of the Prebisch hypothesis must be seen as a probable strategy for developing governments – particularly in countries in which the vulnerable indigenous service industries have political clout.

The implications of increased international trade in services for the division of labour are, then, relatively small. Intra-North trade will probably not bring about substantial changes in the balance of trade on 'other services' even though the volume may increase impressively. The volume of North–South trade is not likely to increase as impressively and the direct effects on the division of labour will be small, but the effects on trade in goods of this scenario may be quite pronounced. To the extent that adoption of the new technologies allow the efficiencies of manufacturing sectors in the North to be increased, the competitive advantage to be derived from cheap labour will be substantially reduced. This propsect of a loss of goods markets should encourage the newly industrializing countries to adopt an open policy so that they may preserve their export markets for manufactures.

Indirect implications of increased trade in services

There exist three major indirect implications for global economic structure as a combined result of the innovations in and increased internationalization of the service industries. These are:

(1) The greater potential for serious financial instability associated with much greater volume of cross-hauling financial investments and the integration of national money, capital, and equity markets in a world of national currencies;

(2) The ever-increasing capacity for centralization of production decisions in the headquarters of multinational corporations;

(3) The likelihood of greater inequality of income distribution within the industrialized nations and between the two blocs of developed and developing countries.

Integration of global financial markets

There exist two majors sources of potential instability in the international financial system and both are attributable to a significant degree to technological innovations in 'other services'. First is the huge debtor/creditor imbalance of the key-currency nation brought about by the profligate deficit spending of the Reagan administration in the United States (Schlesinger 1988). This has led to huge current deficits financed in part by a massive volume of relatively liquid liabilities of the US financial system being owned by non-residents. At the end of 1987 these claims which were either fully liquid or were traded in efficient markets amounted to approximately $1.3 trillion and could be expected to reach $2 trillion even if the US current account deficit were, relatively optimistically, to be reduced to zero by 1995. This huge indebtedness in relatively liquid instruments (see Tables 5.4 and 5.5) has been caused by the relatively high inflation-compensated (real) interest rates which followed from the large net increase in the federal demand for loanable funds. The existence of improved communication and data-processing techniques as well as new financial instruments which offer the promise of risk reduction (in a stable financial environment), made it easier for the United States to use its status as the key-currency nation to finance a large proportion of its federal deficits by attracting foreign saving. The essential problems are the decrease in the international net worth of the United States in recent years (Table 5.4) and the financing of the cumulative current account deficits by attracting foreign saving as *liabilities of private financial institutions* which are, by their very nature, highly leveraged or geared.[14] Self-evidently, large repatriations of assets by non-residents in the face of some adverse shock or disturbance or as a result of a lapse of confidence in the United States' ability or willingness to pay a realistic total rate of return[15] on the invested assets could bring about a financial panic or crisis with devastating repercussions for the solvency of deposit intermediaries.

The increase in the integration of financial markets and the

Table 5.4 The international net worth of the United States[a] ($ billions at end of year)

	1983	1984	1985	1986	1987[P]
INW at end of preceding year	137.0	89.6	3.6	− 111.9	− 269.2
Current account balance	− 67.0	− 112.5	− 122.1	− 141.4	− 160.7
Adjustments[b]	+ 19.6	+ 26.5	+ 6.6	− 15.9	+ 61.7
INW at end of year	+ 89.6	3.6	− 111.9	− 269.2	− 368.2

[a] Includes the official US gold stock valued at $42.22 per troy ounce. This valuation results in an underestimate of US international net worth of roughly $100 billion for all end-of-year data. (Gold holdings are valued officially at $11.2 billion.)
[b] Includes the effect of price changes for assets or liabilities and of exchange rate changes. The 1987 data include the upward revaluation of foreign US assets due to the weakening of the dollar as well as substantial losses in the value of US corporate securities held by non-Americans.
[P] preliminary
Source: Survey of Current Business (June, 1987), pp. 39–40 and 54–5, and (March, 1988), p. 41

Table 5.5 Outstanding financial assets of non-Americans in US financial markets: end-of-year data ($billions of US dollars)

	1982	1983	1984	1985	1986	1987ᴾ
Foreign official assets	189.2	194.5	199.0	202.5	241.7	283.1
Foreign private assets	378.1	456.0	527.8	674.1	1,098.9	1,252.9
US treasury securities	25.8	33.9	56.9	83.6	91.5	78.4
Corporate and other bonds	16.8	17.5	32.3	82.5	142.1	171.0
Corporate stocks	76.8	97.3	95.9	124.1	166.7	173.4
Liabilities of non-bank concerns	27.5	26.8	30.5	29.4	26.7	28.8
Liabilities of banks	231.3	280.6	312.3	354.5	451.6	539.4

ᴾpreliminary
Source: Survey of Current Business (various issues).

innovations which allowed this integration to take place,[16] are quite capable of creating fragility or vulnerability in the global financial system even in the absence of a huge net debtor position by the United States. What the new technologies (including innovations in instruments) have wrought is the creation of what is near to being a single set of financial markets for investors and speculators whose 'home' or functional currency can be quite different from the currency of denomination of a large proportion of the assets in their portfolios. Most vulnerable are deposit intermediaries. Whatever the degree of leverage of the financial institutions involved (The Bank for International Settlements [1987] is developing an international consensus to increase the capital adequacy of the major international banks by establishing a common set of regulations requiring higher ratios of capital to liabilities in the G-10 countries), the possibility of sudden and huge movements of funds out of one currency and into another cannot but constitute an important source of fragility for the international financial system. If violent shifts in exchange rates ensue, then there is a real possibility of the failure (insolvency) of large financial institutions. Similarly, if equities markets move in sympathy with changes in the strength of national currencies, a sudden withdrawal of funds from assets denominated in a particular currency will trigger a severe downward movement in equity prices denominated in that currency and will, in all probability, seriously impair the equity positions of non-deposit financial institutions. The two possibilities will feed on each other and increase the amount of equity capital needed in financial institutions. This possibility suggests that the world's financial system will have a much greater sensitivity to disturbances in major national markets as well as to changes among such markets.

Both possible causes of major global financial instability are reinforced by another development which owes its existence to the increase in breadth of access to large amounts of data by means of trans-border data flows. Increased data availability has allowed large creditworthy borrowers to borrow directly from lenders (securitization) and to bypass commercial banks. This process has brought about an inevitable deterioration in the quality of the loan portfolios of the major commercial banks and rendered them more susceptible to large panics or crises.

International trade in financial services increases the allocative-efficiency of the world economy, as all potential investors confront similar financial conditions (Bryant 1987). These gains have been achieved at significant costs in terms of stability-efficiency (Gray and Gray 1981: 55–61). Moreover, the rapid pace of technological innovation in financial services renders difficult, if not impossible, the task of imposing some regulatory framework which will diminish any tendency toward instability.[17]

Centralization of MNC management

The increase in the ability of units to process information regarding relative international costs of factors of production and marketing conditions in different countries both quickly and cheaply will undoubtedly lead to a greater tendency to concentrate production plans and marketing strategies at the headquarters of multinational corporations. This is probably a structural change in degree rather than in any fundamental sense, since multinationals have always desired to centralize their strategic decision-making at the head office and the easier availability of data now makes this possible. Again, this development is likely to present allocative-efficiency gains (from a global perspective) and stability-efficiency losses (from a national perspective). Vernon (1979) adumbrates the existence of information-rich multinational corporations when he conjures up the notion of a multinational corporation with complete information. This state of affairs allows the corporate planners to locate production in its least-cost locale and to serve markets from the least-cost supplier. But the information also allows the MNC to shift the production of manufactures around much more quickly and the decisions will, in the absence of controls, be constrained only by private costs and benefits. The social costs of the sudden switching of production facilities will not be a variable in the decision process and local economies could be badly damaged by decisions by seemingly unconcerned people thousands of miles away. The history of the behavior of the *maquiladoras* in northern Mexico reinforces this thesis of MNC behaviour. The availability of cheap global information provides a new dimension to the age-old problem of employer–employee relationship and strengthens the hand of the employer. When the employer is an MNC, the matter takes on overtones of international politics and can induce rapid structural change.

The potential benefits from best-practice service technology

Virtually all the theory of commercial policy is set in terms of a 'home' industry seeking to protect itself from foreign competition in a static setting and in the absence of severe externalities (Bhagwati 1988). Thus, the use of commercial policy to keep out foreign-generated goods or services has an obvious cost for the welfare of the average consumer of those goods or services inside the home nation. What is insufficiently recognized is that the home nationa may face much greater externalities (and costs) by keeping out foreign services than in keeping out foreign goods. The crucial distinction is that it is possible for a country to acquire much foreign technology embodied in capital goods, and that a rational tariff structure will allow easy (duty-free) importation of capital goods which contribute appropriately to the country's technological base. There may be some resistance to allowing the acquisition of technology which requires allowing an MNC to establish itself in the country, but such a decision is usually relatively narrow in the sense that goods-producing MNCs will produce externalities only in their own manufacturing sector. Similarly, the effect of foreign direct investment of this kind on the home industry is likely to eliminate only a relatively small and technologically backward group of firms, if any. Permitting the importation of services can have far more widespread effects. It is much more likely that foreign best-practice technology can be acquired in services only through foreign direct investment. The newly established subsidiaries are likely to dominate the 'home' market and preclude the development or survival of indigenous firms as they fail to incorporate equivalent technology. The argument for keeping foreign firms out of the home market for services is a straightforward question of balancing the benefits of having foreign best-practice available in the country for the provision of the service in question against the costs of adjustment and the possibility of ultimate dependence on foreign firms for those services. If the availability of best-practice information-intensive services is necessary as an infrastructural feature of the home economy, then the externality (the more efficient development and growth of other sectors) may be very large and positive. It is quite likely that developing countries may not give sufficient weight to the infrastructural costs of imposing barriers to free trade in services (with attendant rights of establishment and national treatment) irrespective of the clamour for protection from those firms threatened with extinction.[18] The breadth of effect of efficient service industries may be an important argument for allowing inward FDI: the fact that service industries are often central to the sense of national economic identity suggests that nations will and should explore alternatives to allowing unrestrained FDI in services (though not at the expense of allowing the continued quiet existence of domestic oligopolists).

Conclusion: the intrusion hypothesis

Inevitably, the preceding sections have focused on differences of degree between the effects of growth of output and trade in services and in tangible goods for the global economic structure. What shows through clearly is a general tendency for growth of trade in services and technological developments in services to reduce national independence to a greater degree than does an equivalent amount of growth in trade in goods. Services *intrude* (or penetrate) to a greater degree and more irreversibly into the structure of individual domestic economies than do goods. Thus, FDI in service industries will reduce the national economic identity. This is the 'intrusion hypothesis'. In consequence, the growth of services is and will be treated with greater suspicion than will growth in goods and will arouse more political resistance and economic barriers to dampen what may legitimately be perceived to be excessive penetration into service sectors (particularly in Third World countries).

As far as factor-embodied services are concerned, the cost-reductions in transportation costs will integrate the world economy in goods production but, except for countries which come to rely on potentially transitory manufacturing plants which flourish because of low wages, worker docility, and a lack of regulations on safety measures, the intrusion hypothesis will not hold. Transportation is a 'goods-related' genus of services and in that sense is more properly allied with trade in goods than with trade in services.

It is 'other services' that give the intrusion hypothesis validity: new management, data-processing, and information techniques allow the global systems to be knit together in areas in which perceived national interests and national values have been wont to stand unchallenged. Privacy of personal data, the reliability (robustness) of and the primacy of national concerns in the network of financial institutions, the ability to view actions within national boundaries as subject to the direction of the national economic policymakers are all accepted standards potentially weakened by incorporation from abroad of the technological advances in services.

It is these issues which will put the question of greater openness of international trade and (inward) investment in services at the forefront of a deep national consideration and debate. Greater openness of trade and investment (in goods and services) implies greater allocative efficiency and presumably greater real economic growth. This holds for the Third World as well as for the industrialized nations themselves. But it is probably also true to say that the prospect of freer involvement in service activities will detract from national stability-efficiency (because of the loss of independence). In other words, nations must see growth in the freedom of trade services in terms of the potential for economic growth as long as the system is well-behaved or tranquil, against the possibility of greater volatility in economic performance in times of turbulence. It may well be that the integration of service sectors is a necessary step along the progression toward 'one unified world'. That will represent a gigantic structural change which no one living today can realistically portray.

If the intrusion hypothesis has validity, and there is certainly an argument that it may, then integration in services should not be undertaken lightly, nor is it likely to be. Growth of output and trade in services will command an increasing share of the attention of policymakers, trade negotiators, economists, and political scientists for the rest of this century and beyond.

Appendix 5.A

Table 5.A.1 Employment in services in the United Kingdom (in thousands)

	1979	1981	1983	1985	1987
Total employed	23,173	21,891	21,067	21,504	21,802
Total in services	13,581	13,466	13,500	14,188	14,833
Wholesale	1,138	1,137	1,150	1,194	1,234
Retail	2,176	2,092	2,005	2,086	2,117
Hotels	943	943	963	1,061	1,111
Transport	1,056	987	912	911	900
Postal services	423	438	433	434	446
Finance	1,647	1,738	1,875	2,083	2,327
Government	2,002	1,899	1,918	1,962	2,034
Education	1,660	1,615	1,592	1,619	1,704
Health	1,233	1,293	1,294	1,308	1,309
Other services	1,303	1,324	1,358	1,530	1,651

Source: Monthly Statistical Review, June, 1988. See original for details on classifications

Table 5.A.2   Employment in services in the United States (in millions)

	1981	1983	1985	1987
Total non-agricultural employment	91.2	90.2	97.6	102.3
Total services	66.7	66.9	72.7	77.5
Transportation and utilities	5.2	4.9	5.2	5.4
Wholesale	5.4	5.3	5.7	5.8
Retail	15.2	15.6	17.4	18.5
Finance	5.3	5.5	6.0	6.5
Government	16.0	19.7	22.0	24.2

Source: *Survey of Current Business* (various issues)

Notes

1. Sauvant (1986b, Ch. V) presents an extremely good treatment of the way in which the knowledge-intensive industries in the United States exerted political pressure on the US government in order to have services placed on the Uruguay agenda.
2. Rugman (1988) argues that much of what is reported in balance-of-payments data as profits of multinationals is in reality a return on product and process technology transferred and other non-factor services provided by the parent to the subsidiary. There is undoubtedly a good case to be made for Rugman's thesis but much of the profits would still be a return on capital and the generality of the procedure depends upon the degree of ownership. Only if ownership is complete will a multinational corporation fail to unbundle such payments.

   Thus, 'investment income', an extremely important category of invisible trade, is a factor-service – except in so far as it needs qualification in line with Rugman's refinement.
3. This fact suggests that the task of negotiators in the Uruguay Round will be more than usually difficult.
4. Table 5.1 is given on the basis of data in current prices. Because prices of services have increased more quickly than those of tangible goods, it is possible that the data exaggerate the growth in importance of the services sector. This is by no means clear-cut, and similar computations in constant sectoral prices yield the same tendency. A greater tendency toward higher prices in a sector can result from a higher rate of inflation in that sector than in others, from a relative change in the mix of products toward more highly priced products, or from a relative improvement in the quality (and therefore the cost) of the products. Given the rapid rate of technological advance in services, the third explanation would seem to be important, so that current prices may be the more accurate measure.

5. For a description of the involvement of individual services in international trade, see Office of Technology Assessment (1986, Ch. 5).

6. While management/consulting probably involves a large amount of international travel (and, as such, is factor-embodied), it is also likely to include significant amounts of charges levied on subsidiaries by the head offices of MNCs for services rendered by head office in the normal course of operations.

7. The most obvious examples of service-embodied goods are the souvenirs of tourists and the (foreign) port expenditures on fuel and provisions of international carriers.

8. This section relies heavily on Sauvant (1986a, b).

9. Hindley (1982) explicitly recognizes the need for fiduciary regulation of the insurance industry and countenances special measures to control the ability of foreign-based firms to escape the regulatory network. Hindley is prepared to recommend the permitted entry of foreign firms in order that they might introduce their own product and process technologies but would forego the advantage which scale provides to insurance companies and would recognize the imposition of local capital requirements.

10. For an assessment of the difficulties encountered within the European Community – prior, of course, to the 1992 reforms – see Shelp (1981).

11. The existence of economies in intra-firm communication and the appropriability of proprietary technology, as well as the more traditional benefits of vertical integration, suggest that an 'owned' subsidiary may be particularly important for service industries.

12. Always provided that the agreement passes both legislatures.

13. Gray (1983) argues in favour of negotiating freer trade in services on the basis of mutual agreements among groups of nations and suggests that progress is likely to be made first among the industrialized countries.

14. The ability of a key-currency nation to finance current deficits by having the private financial institutions incur liabilities to non-residents allows the existence of huge indebtedness to appear as the simple desires of investors as expressed through the market and, in this way, to gloss over the problem of net indebtedness.

15. 'Total rate of return' is the product of the change in the value of the dollar in foreign exchange markets and the yield on the asset in dollars.

16. Levich (1988) provides a good account of innovations in international financial markets which may be said to have facilitated the financing of US deficits. This kind of innovation is complementary to, and almost equally as important as, the data-processing and communications technologies which were fundamental to the integrating of capital and money markets in the industrialized world.

17. This problem is accentuated by the huge debtor/creditor imbalance of the United States which precludes much in the way of constructive

measures being discussed, lest they trigger an abrupt and massive withdrawal of funds from dollar-denominated instruments.

18. Note that this aspect of FDI in services is different from the question of financial stability and national identity: this question involves a comparison of traditional economic considerations under the assumption of stability.

References

Bank for International Settlements (1987) Committee on Banking Regulations and Supervisory Practices, Basel: BIS Consultative Paper, December.

Bhagwati, Jagdish N. (1984) 'Splintering and disembodiment of services and developing nations', *The World Economy* 7: 133–44.

——— (1989) 'Is free trade passé after all?', *Weltwirt-schaftliches Archiv* (forthcoming).

Bryant, Ralph C. (1987) *International Financial Intermediation*, Washington: The Brookings Institution.

Feldstein, Martin (ed.) (1988) *The United States in the World Economy*, Chicago: University of Chicago Press for the National Bureau of Economic Research.

Giersch, Herbert (ed.) (1989) *Services in World Economic Growth*, Tubingen: J. C. B. Mohr.

Gray, H. Peter (1982) 'International transportation', in Ingo Walter and Tracy Murray (eds) *Handbook of International Business*, Section 11 New York: John Wiley & Sons.

——— (1983) 'A Negotiating Strategy For Trade in Services', *Journal of World Trade Law* 17: 377–87, October/November.

——— (1985) *Free Trade or Protection: A Pragmatic Analysis*, London: Macmillan.

Gray, H. Peter and Jean M. Gray (1981) 'The multinational bank: a financial MNC?), *Journal of Banking and Finance* 5: 33–63, March.

Grubel, Herbert. G. (1987) 'All traded services are embodied in materials or people', *The World Economy* 10: 319–30.

——— (1989) 'Modern service sector growth: causes and effects', in H. Giersch (ed.) *Services in World Economic Growth*.

Hill, T. F. (1977) 'On goods and services', *Review of Income and Wealth* 23: 315–38.

Hindley, Brian (1982) 'Economic analysis and insurance policy in the Third World', *Thames Essay No. 32*, London: Trade Policy Research Centre.

Kindleberger, Charles P. (1984) *Multinational Excursions*, Cambridge, Mass: MIT Press.

Levich, Ricard A. (1988) 'Financial innovations in international financial markets', in M. Feldstein (ed.) *The United States in the World Economy*, pp. 215–56.

McCulloch, Rachel (1988) 'International competition in services', in

Feldstein, M. (ed.) *The United Nations in the World Economy*,
pp. 367–406.
Office of Technology Assessment, U.S. Congress (1986) *Trade in Services:
Exports and Foreign Revenues – Special Report*, OTA-ITE-316, Wash-
ington, DC: US Government Printing Office, September.
Rugman, Alan M. (1988) '*Weltwirtschaftliches Archiv* (Heft 1).
Sauvant, Karl P. (1986a) *Trade and Foreign Direct Investment in Data
Services*, Boulder, Colo.: Westview Press.
——— (1986b) *International Transactions in Data Services; The Politics
of Transborder Data Flows*, Boulder, Colo.: Westview Press.
Schlesinger, James R. (1988) 'Domestic policies and international capital
flows', in M. Feldstein (ed.) *The United Nations in the World
Economy*, pp. 644–54.
Shelp, Ronald Kent (1981) *Beyond Industrialization*, New York: Praeger
Publishers.

Chapter Six

The growing internationalization of industry: a comparison of the changing structure of company activity in the major industrialized countries

John Cantwell

Introduction

No account of industrial change in recent years is complete without incorporating an assessment of the role of the growing internationalization of production. US manufacturing firms expanded their productive activities in Europe rapidly in the 1950s and 1960s, and they were already heavily internationalized by the early 1970s. Since this time European and Japanese companies have responded with a rapid expansion of their international networks as well. A system of oligopolistic interdependence has been created on a world scale. The changing structure of industry in any country now depends upon the global decisions of multinationals in the relevant sectors, which are linked to the relative competitive strengths and weaknesses of the individual firms concerned.

This chapter examines the factors which have underpinned the internationalization of the firms of each of the major industrialized countries. It sets out to show how the relative significance of such factors has varied across different national groups of firms. The rapid outward international expansion of Japanese firms in recent years has followed a rather different course compared to, for example, the continued international growth of British firms. The empirical part of the study focuses on the comparative performance of companies from the USA, West Germany, the UK, Italy, France, and Japan. It is concerned with shifts in the pattern of their total international economic activity, paying special attention to their international production (outside their home countries).

Economists have suggested various explanations for the recent internationalization of business. These explanations are often grouped together within a common theoretical framework; namely, the eclectic paradigm (Dunning 1981) or the internalization paradigm (Buckley and Casson 1985; Rugman 1981). Rather less has been written on the relative significance of different factors or explanations of internationalization as they affect the firms of a given country or industry over a given period of time. The empirical application of the theories of economists is still at an early stage.

This is for two reasons. First, the necessary data have often been lacking. Most countries do not publish information on the value of the international production of their firms, or on the value of domestic production controlled by foreign firms. Many countries provide data on foreign direct investment, but the industrial distribution of that investment is often not readily available. Even when the foreign direct investment statistics are suitably disaggregated, it is, in general, not easy to derive meaningful indicators of production from them. Recently, progress has been made in collecting data on foreign direct investment for a large number of countries in a comparable way (Dunning and Cantwell 1987), and in estimating international production and its sectoral distribution in the major industrialized countries (Cantwell 1989a).

The empirical section of this chapter makes use of these data on the international production of the firms of the leading industrialized countries. To measure the internationalization of production also requires data on the value of domestic production by indigenous firms in the country concerned. Data on indigenous firm exports from the major industrialized countries, and on the value of the production of foreign-owned affiliates which has been reported upon in the same source (Cantwell 1989a), is therefore used as well. The value of domestic production by indigenous firms within each country has been calculated by taking total industrial production in each sector and subtracting the production of foreign-owned affiliates. This can then be divided into indigenous firm exports and production for domestic markets.

The second reason why applied rather than theoretical work on internationalization is in shorter supply has to do with the problem of devising empirical measures or proxies that correspond to theoretical concepts. This is a familiar problem that is not confined to the field of international business. Macro-economists, for example, argue over the appropriate definitions of the money supply and unemployment, while Marxist economists disagree over whether the capital–labour ratio is a fair representation of the Marxian concept of the organic composition of capital. However, the problem is particularly acute in this area since the theory of multinationals is a relatively new branch of economics, and different authors have used central concepts such as 'ownership advantages' or 'internalization' in rather different ways.

This chapter develops an analytical framework that relates theoretical concepts widely used in the literature to empirical measures which can be constructed using the data that are now available. In particular, it suggests a way of discriminating between the various factors that are responsible for an increasing internationalization of business activity, and of assessing the relative empirical significance of each. The method proposed is designed to facilitate comparisons between groups of firms from different countries. For example, it seems reasonable to believe that the factors contributing to the recent rise in the internationalization of Italian firms are not identical to those that have affected British firms. By formulating observable measures of the factors involved, it is possible to quantify the contribution of each to the internationalization of the firms of a certain country *vis-à-vis* those of the rest of the world. The proportional change in the degree of multinationality of each group of firms can be decomposed into its constituent elements, and comparisons made between groups.

The theoretical explanation of the process of internationalization

The degree of internationalization of firms can be defined as the proportion of their total gobal sales that is accounted for by international production. Broadly speaking, there are four groups of reasons why the degree of internationalization may rise over time. These are concerned, first, with the ownership advantages of the firms in question; second, with the location advantages of production in different sites; third, with the efforts of firms whose international production is currently a small part of their operations to 'catch up' with their more multinational competitors, and fourth, a general trend towards internationalization which in recent years has been common to the firms of all countries. There has been some discussion of the relative significance of the first two factors (in the case of the UK, for example, by Dunning 1981), but there are as yet no empirical studies that satisfactorily integrate all four.

Ownership advantages

The ownership advantages of firms are the principal determinant of their ability to maintain or increase their share of the markets in which they compete. This is particularly the case when speaking of competition for international markets served by exports or international production rather than competition for domestic markets served by home-country production. A relatively weak company may survive for longer in its domestic market through consumer loyalty and government contracts, but these are less likely to be retained abroad. In the case of most manufacturing industries and many services, the strength or weakness of a company (the extent of its ownership advantages) depends mainly upon its capacity for innovation. Innovation relies upon both research and organizational change, which are mutually reinforcing.

Those firms who sustain the greatest capacity for innovation steadily accumulate ownership advantages (and most notably technological advantages) *vis-à-vis* their rivals. This accumulation of ownership advantages enables them to capture market shares and to grow faster than other firms in their industry. Growth is particularly rapid in international markets, and innovative firms tend to progress from export-led expansion to the establishment and extension of international production. Past a certain point, the scope for export growth may be diminished, especially if weaker firms abroad succeed in persuading governments to erect trade barriers in response, and the emphasis shifts away from domestic and towards international production. A further discussion of the relationship between technological advantages and the pattern of expansion of international economic activity can be found in Cantwell (1987a, 1989a).

This seems to be at least part of the explanation for the growth of international production in the post-war period. In the 1950s and 1960s it was innovative US companies that established production facilities in Europe. In the 1970s and 1980s it has been innovative Japanese and German companies that have supported their export strategies by expanding their production in the USA. To a lesser extent, and relying upon a rather less sophisticated form of technological accumulation, firms based in the newly industrialized countries have also embarked upon the establishment of international production. Ownership advantages enable firms to extend their operations more rapidly than the general rate of growth of markets, and this is especially so in the case of competition between the international production of different multinationals.

Consequently this element in the internationalization of business varies between different groups of firms. The most innovative groups of companies tend to have a faster rate of increase not only in their global sales, but also in their degree of internationalization. Of course, at the level of individual firms it may be difficult to distinguish the significance of such a factor, as the greater multinationality of the firm may in itself enable it to expand international production elsewhere (which comes into the third and fourth factors discussed below). At the level of an international industry, however, it is far easier to make this distinction, since the advantages that are due to the multinationality of firms are separable, except to the extent that they increase the firms' capacity for innovation (through, for example, the global co-ordination of research). The point remains that if, say, Japanese multinationals are growing faster than British firms that have already attained a high degree of internationalization, this may be attributable to the greater innovativeness of the Japanese companies, but not to a greater scope for global organization.

Location advantages

In any industry, shifts in location advantages will also affect national groups of firms very differently. If a country becomes an increasingly attractive site for production then this will favour domestic production for its own firms but international production for others. The degree of internationalization of firms will tend to rise where location advantages in their industry move against their home country relative to the rest of the world.

It might be envisaged that there is an inverse correlation between this factor and the first. In other words, a strong domestic industry based on an extensive indigenous research capacity will be associated with innovative domestic firms, but may also itself become an attractive location for the international research and production of other innovative multinationals (Cantwell 1987b). However, this depends upon the type of production under consideration. Assembly types of activity need not be supported by local research, and they may be attracted to lower-wage/lower-technology locations, in which indigenous firms have little capacity for innovation and outward investment of their own. A country can become more locationally advantaged and attractive to foreign firms without the ownership advantages of its own firms becoming any stronger. Equally, multinationals that originated from a location that was historically strong may retain their ground through their international production, even at a time when their home base is being gradually weakened as competing locations catch up.

Whether favourable shifts in location advantages are associated with a strengthening in the ownership advantages of the firms of the country in question will depend in part on the maturity of the internationalization achieved by that group of firms. Countries which establish themselves as new centres of innovation will initially be home to firms at a comparatively early stage of their development, for whom the growth of exports and international production go hand in hand. The location advantages of the home country steadily improve, and the rising degree of internationalization of its firms is to be explained as the means by which such firms can grow and capture market shares most rapidly. The dynamic factor underpinning internationalization is the ownership advantages of firms and certainly not an adverse movement in the location advantages of the home country. At the opposite extreme are countries which were powerful centres of innovation in the past but are no longer. Their firms are mature multinationals, and as location advantages have slipped away from the home country they have placed an increasing reliance upon their international operations. The driving force behind their most recent increase in internationalization may come more from their response to a shift in locational advantages than it does from the increasing competitive strength of the firms themselves.

The 'catching-up' factor

This leads into a discussion of what is termed here the 'catching-up' factor which seems to have become important in recent years. It has been suggested that where the degree of internationalization is rising at a similar rate amongst both mature multinationals and new multinationals the role played by ownership and location advantages may be very different in each case. In addition to this, it can be argued, other things being equal (with given ownership and location advantages), that the degree of internationalization will tend to increase faster for new multinationals than for the more mature, historically established multinationals. That is, there will be a catching-up effect.

This effect seems to have become significant in the last twenty years. The reason is that the ownership advantages of firms (including their capacity to innovate) have become increasingly interrelated with their degree of multinationality. Newer multinationals can therefore often increase their competitiveness *vis-à-vis* established multinationals simply by the device of a greater geographical diversification of their production. This allows them to take advantage of a reorganized international division of labour within the firm, specializing in particular activities in the most suitable locations. It enables them to co-ordinate a decentralized research strategy, increasing their capacity to innovate and to diffuse new technological advances more rapidly to all parts of their network. It also increases their ability to enter into coalitions with other innovative firms to their mutual benefit, as the pattern of their technological accumulation becomes more complementary.

Newer multinationals have therefore acquired a greater incentive to increase their degree of internationalization than have the more mature multinationals. The latter may be able to achieve a similar effect by moving towards a more global form of company organization, but this does not require an increased degree of internationalization as a precondition. To the extent that firms increase their capacity to innovate by adopting a more global strategy then this becomes an element in determining the strength of ownership advantages, the first factor referred to above. However, the catching-up factor is to be distinguished from the role of ownership advantages as separate influences on internationalization. Where firms successfully catch up with their more multinational rivals, the gain in ownership advantages is an effect rather than a cause; and the degree of internationalization is only one of a number of determinants of firms' overall ownership advantages or capacity to innovate. It may often be the case that a firm with little international production is more innovative than a mature multinational, despite the potential gains that the latter may obtain through internationalization.

The general trend towards internationalization

The final factor to be considered combines a range of other influences which have all tended to create a greater incentive to internationalize business activity, influences which in a given industry have affected the firms of all countries equally. This factor is the one that has been most widely discussed in the literature. A fall in the costs of transport and communications increases the scope for international specialization by encouraging intra-firm trade and the movement of personnel and other intangible assets across national boundaries. This helps to explain the general trend towards internationalization in both the pre-1914 and post-war periods (Wilkins 1970; Vernon 1971). It has also been associated with the organizational innovation that has developed during the twentieth century, lowering the costs of managing more complex multi-plant operations within the firm (Casson 1983).

In the past, the general trend towards internationalization has consequently been especially strong in periods of high innovation in the world economy (Schumpeterian upswings) such as 1890–1914 or 1950–70. This is also allied to the first factor underlying internationalization, since innovative leaders were particularly prone to establish multinational networks as a means of consolidating rapid growth (Cantwell 1989b). However, the general trend towards internationalization has continued since the early 1970s, despite the fall in world patenting activity and growth rates since that time. This is in large part due to the characteristics of the newly emerging technology paradigm (Freeman and Perez 1990) in which electronics plays a leading role. Although the wider application of the new technologies is still at an early stage, they have much more immediate effects in the communications and telecommunications sector. The costs of the transfer of information and international communications within the firm have continued to fall.

The new technologies and methods of work are more suited to a greater international dispersion of productive activity for another reason as well. Whereas the major technologies of the 1950s and 1960s were essentially scale-intensive in their applications in the chemicals, motor vehicles, metals, aircraft, and other manufacturing industries, the newer technologies need not be. By reorganizing themselves around the development of core skills, firms today have become much more dependent upon economies of scope, and less dependent upon economies of scale. This is particularly true of larger, multinational firms, and it has undermined the major economic motive for geographical concentration. In many manufacturing industries production is far more internationally mobile today than it once was.

A further reason why firms may prefer to move to smaller more dispersed production units is that it weakens the bargaining power of trade unions based on the organization of closed shops in large plants. The trend towards internationalization may therefore increase the share of profits in the total revenue of firms (Cowling 1984; Cowling and Sugden 1987). There are also political reasons why the pace of internationalization has not slowed down in the 1970s and 1980s in the way that it did in the inter-war period. The revival of nationalistic movements and protectionist pressures has been much more limited, such that the political risk associated with foreign investment has not changed very much, unlike in the 1930s.

Measures of the determinants of internationalization

There are various possible ways of measuring the factors outlined above as being responsible for the increasing internationalization of business. Measures are chosen here with the objective of decomposing the total change in the degree of internationalization, for a given group of firms, into its four major elements.

The raw data for each group of firms are comprised of the value of their international production (denoted by IP), domestic production for the domestic market (D), exports from the home country (X), and total global sales (S). Since these four variables are related by an identity $(S = D + X + IP)$, it is possible to work with just three of them, and D is not used explicitly in the calculations that follow. Four ratios are derived from IP, X, and S. Three of them are familiar from the work of Dunning and Pearce (1981, 1985); namely the foreign production ratio (FPR), the foreign content ratio (FCR), and the sourcing ratio (SR). They are defined as follows:

$$FPR = IP/S$$
$$FCR = (IP + X)/S$$
$$SR = IP/(IP + X)$$

The fourth ratio is the degree of internationalization (DOI), which differs from the foreign production ratio by being defined for the firms of any country (i) relative to the total position (T) for all firms in the world, or the sample. This is an important distinction, as while the general trend towards internationalization will increase the FPR of every group of firms, the other factors mentioned in the previous section of this chapter generate differences between groups in the rate at which their FPR rises. Thus:

$$DOI_i = FPR_i/FPR_T = (IP_i/S_i)/(IP_T/S_T)$$

The other feature of the data available is that they are calculated for particular years, so that is necessary to work with discrete changes in ratios over time. Hence, the proportional rate of change of the degree of internationalization is given by:

$$\Delta DOI_{it}/DOI_{it-1} = [\Delta(FPR_{it}/FPR_{Tt})]/(FPR_{it-1}/FPR_{Tt-1})$$

The first factor to be considered as an influence on this is the ownership advantages of firms from the country concerned. Where a group of firms have strong ownership advantages, it has been argued that they will capture international market shares, and that they will do so more rapidly than they capture domestic market shares. Strictly speaking, the condition for making gains in international competition is that ownership advantages in the current period are strong relative to the historical position; since an historically strong company will have made its gains in the past, and will simply maintain its present market share if its ownership advantages remain as strong as they were. If the ownership advantages of some group of firms relative to others are stronger today than they were historically, then their international sales $(X + IP)$ will grow especially fast compared to their domestic sales, since the former are the major means by which gains in international competition are achieved. The strength of the ownership advantages of each group of firms can therefore be measured by the relative rates of change of their foreign content ratios:

$$[\Delta(FCR_{it}/FCR_{Tt})]/(FCR_{it-1}/FCR_{Tt-1})$$
$$= (FCR_{it}/FCR_{Tt})/(FCR_{it-1}/FCR_{Tt-1}) - 1$$

This measure will be positive where the FCR of a given group of firms increases faster than average, and it will be negative where the FCR rises slower than average. Hence it is positive where firms have strong ownership advantages and negative where they are weak.

The internationalization trend, on the other hand, is assumed to affect all groups of firms in the same way, and not to influence relative shifts in their foreign production ratios. It can therefore be measured by the general trend in the foreign production ratio of all firms considered together:

$$\Delta FPR_{Tt}/FPR_{Tt-1} = (FPR_{Tt}/FPR_{Tt-1}) - 1$$

The influence of changes in location advantages and the catching-up effect have to be considered together. They both affect the foreign production ratio through their effect on the sourcing ratio. If the advantages of producing in different locations change, or if newer multinationals increase their international production as a means of moving towards a more global organization in serving international markets, this will be reflected in a changing balance between international production and exports. Shifts in the relative size of domestic and international markets are not the relevant issue in these cases, except to the extent that they are one of a number of influences on location advantages, and hence on the choice between exports and international production as a means of serving international markets. The combined locational and catching-up effect for the firms of any country can be measured by the change in their sourcing ratio relative to the change for the firms of all countries:

$$(\Delta SR_{it}/SR_{it-1}) - (\Delta SR_{Tt}/SR_{Tt-1})$$
$$= (SR_{it}/SR_{it-1}) - (SR_{Tt}/SR_{Tt-1})$$

The catching-up effect must be further related to the initial position of the sourcing ratio. It suggests that there will be a positive effect where the sourcing ratio is initially below average, and a negative effect where it is above average at the start of the period. That is, firms whose international production accounts for a low share of their international sales have an especially strong motive to increase the geographical dispersion of their productive activity. The measure of catching up must therefore be positively related to the difference $(SR_{Tt-1} - SR_{it-1})$. The greater the difference between these two sourcing ratios the greater the catching-up effect will be, and it can therefore be measured by:

$$(SR_{Tt-1} - SR_{it-1})[(\Delta SR_{it}/SR_{it-1}) - (\Delta SR_{Tt}/SR_{Tt-1})]$$

It can be seen that this measure works in a symmetrical fashion and thus allows comparison between groups of new and groups of mature multinationals. If the catching-up effect works in the way predicted then it will be positive for all groups of firms, irrespective of whether they start above or below the average sourcing ratio. Where SR_{it-1} $< SR_{Tt-1}$ then the catching-up term will be positive when the firms of the country in question succeed in narrowing the gap, but negative if they fall further behind and fail to achieve any catching up. Where $SR_{it-1} > SR_{Tt-1}$ then the measure will be positive when firms are caught up by those that lay behind them at the start of the period, and negative if instead they increase their lead. The catching-up effect can also be rewritten in the following way:

$$(SR_{Tt-1} - SR_{it-1})[(\Delta SR_{it}/SR_{it-1}) - (\Delta SR_{Tt}/SR_{Tt-1})]$$
$$= (SR_{Tt-1} - SR_{it-1})[(SR_{it}/SR_{it-1}) - (SR_{Tt}/SR_{Tt-1})]$$
$$= [(SR_{Tt-1} - SR_{it-1})/SR_{Tt-1}](SR_{it})$$
$$\cdot [SR_{Tt-1}/SR_{it-1}) - (SR_{Tt}/SR_{it})]$$
$$= [(SR_{Tt-1} - SR_{it-1})/SR_{Tt-1}](SR_{it})[-\Delta(SR_{Tt}/SR_{it})]$$

This shows the catching-up effect as the product of three terms. The final term measures the extent of the catching up that is actually achieved; where it is working (SR_T/SR_i) should move closer to one. The first term measures the share of the catching up actually achieved that can be attributed to a catching-up effect. That is, where SR_{it-1} lies further away from SR_{Tt-1} then the pressure on that group of firms to catch up, or the pressure on those that lie behind them to catch up will be greater. Finally, the second term indicates that the size of the effect is related to the magnitude of the country's sourcing ratio. Where the sourcing ratio is very small, a small absolute effect must be expected despite the large scale of the relative effect described by the first term.

This leaves the locational effect. Where locational advantages are moving away from the home country, then the sourcing ratio of its firms will tend to increase faster than that of firms based in the rest of the world. The influence of this shift in location advantages will be greater relative to the catching-up effect the greater is the initial value of the sourcing ratio of its firms. Hence the measure of the locational effect can be written:

$$(1 + SR_{it-1} - SR_{Tt-1})[(\Delta SR_{it}/SR_{it-1}) - (\Delta SR_{Tt}/SR_{Tt-1})]$$

In this measure, the first term varies around unity, such that firms that have already achieved a high degree of internationalization as measured by their sourcing ratio become more dependent upon locational influences relative to the catching-up effect. The second term measures the extent to which firms have actually shifted the location of their production for international markets, compared to the total sample of firms.

101

The decomposition of changes in the degree of internationalization

It now remains to demonstrate that the measures of the four factors discussed above add up to give a good approximation of the total change in the degree of internationalization of a country's firms over a given period of time. In this way they can be used to compare the relative significance of factors underpinning the internationalization of the firms of different countries.

Start by noting that the foreign production ratio is equal to the product of the foreign content ratio and the sourcing ratio:

$$FPR = IP/S = [(IP + X)/S][IP/(IP + X)] = FCR \cdot SR$$

This means that the degree of internationalization can be expressed in terms of FCR and SR rather than FPR as follows:

$$DOI_i = FPR_i/FPR_T = (FCR_i/FCR_T)(SR_i/SR_T)$$

From this comes an equation for the change in the degree of internationalization:

$$DOI_{it}/DOI_{it-1} = [(FCR_{it}/FCR_{Tt})/(FCR_{it-1}/FCR_{Tt-1})]$$
$$[(SR_{it}/SR_{Tt})/(SR_{it-1}/SR_{Tt-1})]$$

So:

$$1 + \Delta DOI_{it}/DOI_{it-1}$$
$$= [1 + \Delta(FCR_{it}/FCR_{Tt})/(FCR_{it-1}/FCR_{Tt-1})]$$
$$[1 + \Delta(SR_{it}/SR_{Tt})/(SR_{it-1}/SR_{Tt-1})]$$

Or:

$$\Delta DOI_{it}/DOI_{it-1} = \Delta(FCR_{it}/FCR_{Tt})/(FCR_{it-1}/FCR_{Tt-1})$$
$$+ \Delta(SR_{it}/SR_{Tt})/(SR_{it-1}/SR_{Tt-1})$$
$$+ \Delta(FCR_{it}/FCR_{Tt})/(FCR_{it-1}/FCR_{Tt-1})$$
$$\Delta(SR_{it}/SR_{Tt})/(SR_{it-1}/SR_{Tt-1})$$

This equation tells us that the proportional change in the degree of internationalization can be decomposed into three terms. The first term on the right-hand side measures the contribution of the relative strength of ownership advantages to the internationalization of the group of firms in question. The second term is related to the locational and catching-up effects, while the third is an unexplained component which will be small, provided that the changes in the degree of internationalization are not too large. It remains to examine further the second term, the proportional change in the sourcing ratio of the firms of country (i) relative to the international average.

The change in the relative sourcing ratio can be rewritten thus:

$$\Delta(SR_{it}/SR_{Tt})/(SR_{it-1}/SR_{Tt-1})$$
$$= (SR_{it}/SR_{Tt})/(SR_{it-1}/SR_{Tt-1}) - 1$$
$$= [(SR_{Tt-1}/SR_{Tt})(SR_{it}/SR_{it-1})] - 1$$
$$= [(SR_{it}/SR_{it-1}) - 1] + [(SR_{Tt-1}/SR_{Tt}) - 1](SR_{it}/SR_{it-1})$$
$$= (\Delta SR_{it}/SR_{it-1}) - (\Delta SR_{Tt}/SR_{Tt})(SR_{it}/SR_{it-1})$$
$$= (\Delta SR_{it}/SR_{it-1}) - (\Delta SR_{Tt}/SR_{Tt})$$
$$\quad - [(\Delta SR_{Tt}/SR_{Tt})(\Delta SR_{it}/SR_{it-1})]$$
$$= (\Delta SR_{it}/SR_{it-1}) - (\Delta SR_{Tt}/SR_{Tt-1})$$
$$\quad + (SR_{Tt} - SR_{Tt-1})\Delta SR_{Tt}/(SR_{Tt}SR_{Tt-1})$$
$$\quad - (\Delta SR_{Tt}\Delta SR_{it}/SR_{Tt}SR_{it-1})$$
$$= (\Delta SR_{it}/SR_{it-1}) - (\Delta SR_{Tt}/SR_{Tt-1})$$
$$\quad + \Delta SR_{Tt}(SR_{it-1}\Delta SR_{Tt} - SR_{Tt-1}\Delta SR_{it})/(SR_{Tt}SR_{Tt-1}SR_{it-1})$$

Now in this derived equation the first two terms on the right-hand side constitute the combined locational and catching-up effect, which both influence the relative change in internationalization through their impact on the relative change in the sourcing ratio. The final term is another comparatively smaller unexplained component. These elements can therefore be substituted into the equation for the change in the degree of internationalization. All that remains after that is to add in the general internationalization trend, measured by the change in the overall foreign production ratio. However, since the degree of internationalization is defined for the firms of any country relative to the world average, this general trend must also be subtracted to show how ownership and location advantages and the catching-up effect move the change in internationalization away from the overall trend.

The final equation is as follows:

$$\Delta DOI_{it}/DOI_{it-1}$$
$$= \Delta(FCR_{it}/FCR_{Tt})/(FCR_{it-1}/FCR_{Tt-1})$$
$$\quad + (1 + SR_{it-1} - SR_{Tt-1})[(\Delta SR_{it}/SR_{it-1})$$
$$\quad - (\Delta SR_{Tt}/SR_{Tt-1})]$$
$$\quad + (SR_{Tt-1} - SR_{it-1})[(\Delta SR_{it}/SR_{it-1}) - (\Delta SR_{Tt}/SR_{Tt-1})]$$
$$\quad + (\Delta FPR_{Tt}/FPR_{Tt-1}) - (\Delta FPR_{Tt}/FPR_{Tt-1})$$
$$\quad + \Delta(FCR_{it}/FCR_{Tt})/(FCR_{it-1}/FCR_{Tt-1})$$
$$\quad \Delta(SR_{it}/SR_{Tt})/(SR_{it-1}/SR_{Tt-1})$$
$$\quad + \Delta SR_{Tt}(SR_{it-1}\Delta SR_{Tt}$$
$$\quad - SR_{Tt-1}\Delta SR_{it})/(SR_{Tt}SR_{Tt-1}SR_{it-1})$$

This final equation enables an assessment to be made of the relative significance of the different determinants of the growing internationalization of business for the firms of each country. The measures of these determinants are added together on the right-hand side of the equation. The first term shows the contribution made by the relative strength of the ownership advantages of the firms in question. The second term is a measure of the importance of locational advantages, and the third reflects the strength of the catching-up effect. The first three components all explain variations in the movement of the foreign production ratio of the firms of a given country relative to the general world trend towards internationalization. This is what changes in the degree of internationalization refer to, since the degree of internationalization has been defined as the foreign production ratio of a given group of firms relative to all firms.

The fourth and fifth terms are measures of the general trend towards internationalization that affects the firms of all countries. They are included in the equation for the purposes of comparison, to see what weight should be given to this general trend compared to those factors which cause variations from the trend on the part of particular country groups. If the intention was to measure the proportional change in the foreign production ratio of the firms of a given country in absolute terms then it would not be necessary to subtract the general internationalization trend (the fifth term). It is subtracted in the version above to keep the analysis in relative terms (looking at changes in the degree of internationalization rather than the foreign production ratio itself). The final two terms of the equation represent an unexplained component which is not expected to be very large in magnitude.

This fundamental equation provides an analytical framework for use in empirical work on the determinants of the internationalization of firms. It is intended more for cross-country international comparisons rather than for individual country case studies. Leaving aside the general trend towards internationalization, variations between the firms of different countries have been created by the relative strength of their ownership advantages, by shifts in the locational advantages of different production sites, and by the requirements imposed by the needs of the less mature multinationals to catch up with their more global competitors. Using the data that is now available for the firms of the major industrialized countries, it is proposed to use the method outlined above to examine the relative importance of the factors underlying internationalization across different countries.

The evidence on recent comparative trends in internationalization

The empirical evidence considered relates to the period 1974 to 1982. The measure of the general trend towards internationalization (i.e. the proportional change in the foreign production ratio for the firms of the six major industrialized countries combined), is set out in Table 6.1. This shows that the overall foreign production ratio for manufacturing industries as a whole rose by about 8 per cent from 1974–82. This is perhaps rather less than might have been expected, and although large increases were recorded in the case of the chemicals, food products, and non-metallic mineral products (building materials) sectors, actual falls in the ratio were observed in the case of coal and petroleum products, motor vehicles, other transport equipment, and (just) rubber products.

There are two reasons for an apparently slow rate of growth of the foreign production ratio, both of which relate to the performance of US firms. The first is that, as shown in Table 6.2, the foreign production ratio of US companies fell on average by around 13 per cent over the 1974–82 period. The foreign production ratio of US firms declined in eight sectors out of twelve. This is despite a continued rise in the foreign production ratio of the largest US corporations (mainly multinationals) during the period in question

Table 6.1 The measure of the general trend towards internationalization over the period 1974–82

Food products	0.35
Chemicals	0.58
Metals	0.12
Mechanical engineering	0.03
Electrical equipment	0.04
Motor vehicles	−0.07
Other transport equipment	−0.17
Textiles	0.08
Rubber products	−0.01
Non-metallic	0.24
Coal and petroleum products	−0.30
Other manufacturing	0.09
Total	0.08

Source: For data on international production, Cantwell (1989a); for data on domestic industrial production, United Nations, *UN Yearbook of Industrial Statistics*, 1976, and *UN Industrial Statistics Yearbook*, 1984.

(see Dunning and Pearce 1985). This implies that other US firms, whose operations are more domestically based, grew in size relative to the sample of largest firms. This in turn is related to the increasing location advantages of producing in the USA since the mid-1970s.

The second reason for the relatively small increase in the overall foreign production ratio has to do with the dominant role of US firms in industrialized country production, such that what happens to them exercises a disproportionate influence on the average position of the firms of all six countries. US firms accounted for 50.6 per cent of the total world production of manufacturing companies from the six largest industrialized countries in 1974, and for 47.4 per cent in 1982. During the same period their share of international production fell from 67.8 per cent in 1974 to 60.0 per cent in 1982, their share of indigenous firm exports from home countries slipped from 27.7 per cent to 25.6 per cent, but their share of domestic firm production for domestic markets increased slightly from 50.6 per cent to 51.0 per cent. These figures, by indicating the relative buoyancy of US production for US markets, also help to show why it was that the foreign production ratio of US firms fell, contrary to the trend observed amongst the firms of all the other five major industrialized countries.

Most of the loss in the share of US firms in the total world manufacturing production or sales of companies from the six major

Table 6.2 The proportional change in the foreign production ratio of national groups of firms over the period 1974–82

	US	Germany	UK	Italy	France	Japan
Foor products	0.13	1.31	0.55	−0.35	0.53	0.79
Chemicals	0.34	0.81	1.28	0.53	0.02	1.34
Metals	0.16	0.47	−0.02	1.51	0.49	2.52
Mechanical engineering	−0.07	0.52	0.22	0.43	−0.33	1.57
Electrical equipment	−0.15	0.36	0.27	0.87	0.95	1.14
Motor vehicles	−0.15	0.05	0.12	1.23	0.40	1.10
Other transport equipment	0.99	−0.69	−0.54	0.26	0.24	4.26
Textiles	−0.23	0.76	0.39	0.41	1.07	0.50
Rubber products	−0.16	0.48	0.08	−0.16	0.00	0.28
Non-metallic	−0.11	1.39	0.14	1.12	0.73	0.66
Coal and petroleum products	−0.41	2.30	0.43	1.23	0.08	0.21
Other manufacturing	−0.05	0.19	0.58	0.77	0.88	0.76
Total	−0.13	0.64	0.51	0.53	0.44	1.19

Source: As for Table 6.1.

industrialized countries was captured by Japanese firm, which increased their share accordingly. Japanese companies accounted for 19.0 per cent of such total manufacturing production in 1974, but for 21.7 per cent in 1982. Japanese firms grew notably faster than average in their international production, their domestic exports, and their home production for domestic markets. However, their international production rose especially rapidly. The foreign production ratio (FPR) of all Japanese manufacturing firms, expressed as a percentage, climbed from 1.9 per cent in 1974 to 4.2 per cent in 1982. Over the same period the FPR of US firms fell from 19.4 per cent to 16.9 per cent, while the FPR of firms of other nationalities rose, in the German case from 11.9 per cent to 19.6 per cent, for the UK from 24.9 per cent to 37.6 per cent (the highest ratio of all), for the Italian group from 4.6 per cent to 7.0 per cent, and for French companies from 9.6 per cent to 13.8 per cent. The foreign production ratio of all manufacturing firms from the six countries combined increased from 14.5 per cent to 15.7 per cent.

These figures for the level of the foreign production ratio indicate that US firms already had a high degree of internationalization, and that it has remained high and is still above average despite the large size of the US domestic market. British firms have an extremely high foreign production ratio in both relative and absolute terms, while German companies are now also highly internationalized, and the degree of internationalization of French firms is only slightly below average. Japanese and Italian firms appear to be catching up quite fast. It seems reasonable, therefore, to think of the general trend towards internationalization as having gathered further pace since the early 1970s. This is because although the US position may have slipped back a little, due to the relatively faster growth of US firms that were initially more domestically oriented than the largest multinationals, the phenomenon of internationalization has become steadily more widespread and generally applicable to the firms of all the major industrialized countries.

Turning now to the underlying determinants of the process of internationalization, it is important to note that the procedure outlined in the previous section does not provide a measure of the relative significance of ownership advantages, location advantages, and the catching-up effect for any group of firms considered in isolation. It can only be used to assess the relative importance of these factors for a particular group of firms *vis-à-vis* others in the same sector. So, if the measure of ownership advantages comes out as a high value for firms of every nationality while the measure of location advantages is small in all cases, what really matters is the comparison between different national groups of firms in the relative size of these factors.

However, this does not mean that it is not possible for all three influences to be either positive or negative for a given group of firms. As an illustration, consider the case of Japanese firms which have witnessed a rapid rise in their degree of internationalization. Table 6.3 confirms this; for all manufacturing firms, the degree of internationalization of those of Japanese origin increased by as much as 102 per cent between 1974 and 1982. Now this suggests that the component parts of the change in the degree of internationalization, identified in the previous section, may all be large. Ownership advantages, location advantages, and the catching-up effect may all have been working in the direction of increased internationalization relative to the firms of other nationalities in this case.

The detailed structure of the proportional change in the degree of internationalization in twelve manufacturing sectors for the six different national groups of firms is set out in Table 6.3. Between 1974 and 1982 the degree of internationalization rose by 51 per cent for German firms, by 41 per cent for Italian firms, by 39 per cent amongst British companies, and by 33 per cent for the French. German firms increased their DOI most in food products, textiles, and coal and petroleum products; British firms did so in chemicals, coal and petroleum products, and other manufacturing; Italian companies saw an above average rise in their DOI in metals, electrical equipment, motor vehicles, other transport equipment, non-metallic mineral

Table 6.3 The proportional change in the degree of internationalization over the period 1974–82

	US	Germany	UK	Italy	France	Japan
Food products	−0.16	0.71	0.15	−0.52	0.13	0.32
Chemicals	−0.15	0.14	0.44	−0.03	−0.35	0.48
Metals	0.04	0.31	−0.13	1.24	0.33	2.15
Mechanical engineering	−0.10	0.47	0.18	0.38	−0.36	1.49
Electrical equipment	−0.18	0.31	0.23	0.80	0.88	1.07
Motor vehicles	−0.08	0.12	0.20	1.38	0.50	1.24
Other transport equipment	1.39	−0.63	−0.45	0.51	0.49	5.30
Textiles	−0.29	0.62	0.28	0.30	0.91	0.38
Rubber products	−0.15	0.49	0.09	−0.15	0.01	0.29
Non-metallic	−0.28	0.93	−0.08	0.71	0.40	0.34
Coal and petroleum products	−0.17	3.69	1.03	2.16	0.53	0.72
Other manufacturing	−0.13	0.10	0.45	0.63	0.73	0.62
Total	−0.20	0.51	0.39	0.41	0.33	1.02

Source: As for Table 6.1

products, coal and petroleum products, and other manufacturing; the equivalent sectors for French firms were electrical equipment, motor vehicles, other transport equipment, textiles, non-metallic mineral products, coal and petroleum products, and other manufacturing; while for Japanese firms the greatest increases in internationalization came in metals, mechanical engineering, electrical equipment, motor vehicles, and other transport equipment.

Perhaps the most unusual sector was other transport equipment (mainly aerospace, which has been displacing railways and shipbuilding in the industrialized countries), in which it was German and British firms rather than the Americans which suffered a decline in internationalization in both relative and absolute terms. Japanese firms seem to have experienced a dramatic increase in internationalization, but only from a very low base; from a foreign production ratio of under 0.1 per cent to one of 0.4 per cent. In other words, the higher degree of variation in this sector is a function of the weaker role of international production within it.

The evidence of Table 6.4, which shows the change in relative foreign content ratios, suggests that as a general rule all groups of non-US firms had stronger ownership advantages than US firms in the period in question, by comparison with the greater strength of US firms in the earlier part of the post-war period when they had made

Table 6.4 The estimated contribution of ownership advantages to the proportional change in the degree of internationalization over the period 1974–82

	US	Germany	UK	Italy	France	Japan
Food products	−0.12	0.57	0.24	0.00	−0.12	0.03
Chemicals	−0.01	0.07	0.19	−0.05	−0.07	−0.14
Metals	−0.04	−0.05	0.14	0.47	0.23	−0.16
Mechanical engineering	−0.17	−0.03	0.02	0.68	−0.14	0.63
Electrical equipment	−0.15	0.01	0.15	0.51	0.17	0.51
Motor vehicles	−0.18	−0.06	−0.03	0.16	0.06	0.29
Other transport equipment	0.01	−0.16	−0.06	0.01	0.51	0.01
Textiles	−0.20	0.20	−0.02	0.26	0.06	−0.13
Rubber products	−0.18	0.15	0.05	−0.05	0.08	0.21
Non-metallic	−0.23	0.15	−0.14	0.12	0.20	0.25
Coal and petroleum products	−0.17	1.69	0.89	0.43	0.53	0.16
Other manufacturing	−0.13	0.00	−0.03	1.14	0.31	0.21
Total	−0.18	0.14	0.22	0.34	0.12	0.18

Source: As for Table 6.1, and for indigenous firm exports, Cantwell (1989a)

their greatest gains in internationalization. For German and British companies strong ownership advantages made their greatest contribution to internationalization in food products and coal and petroleum products. For Italian and Japanese firms this effect came especially in mechanical engineering, electrical equipment, and other manufacturing. Ownership advantages made the largest contribution to the growing degree of internationalization of French firms in other transport equipment and coal and petroleum products.

On the whole, location advantages made a contribution to internationalization that was about as important as ownership advantages for German, British, and French firms, but which was more important for Japanese firms, and less important for US and Italian firms. This emerges from a comparison of Table 6.5 with Table 6.4, where each measure is calculated using the expressions defined in the previous two sections of this chapter. The figures for total manufacturing in Table 6.5 imply that locational advantages were shifting away from Europe and Japan towards the USA in the 1970s and early 1980s by comparison with the earlier post-war period, such that for US firms they acted to reduce internationalization (their contribution was negative). Table 6.5 also shows that it was Japanese, and to some extent German, firms that were especially attracted to the USA, while this changing locational advantage had a much smaller effect on the internationalization of US firms than did the weakening of their ownership advantages relative to firms of other nationalities.

However, the new pattern of location advantages does seem to have had an important influence on the international strategies of US firms in chemicals, and also in metals and other transport equipment in which they contributed to an increase in internationalization. Amongst non-US firms, location advantages were consistently more important than ownership advantages in explaining the change in internationalization in the motor-vehicle and other transport equipment sectors, with the possible exception of Japanese motor-vehicle companies. In the case of motor vehicles, location advantages exercised a positive influence on internationalization for the firms of all six countries, which is indicative of a switch towards other countries (particularly in Latin America) in the reorganization of the international industry during this period. Location advantages were also of widespread significance in affecting the international structure of corporate activity in the chemicals and metals sectors.

For German companies, location advantages also played a major role in increasing their degree of internationalization in mechanical engineering, electrical equipment, and non-metallic mineral products between 1974 and 1982. Locational influences were to the fore for UK

Table 6.5 The estimated contribution of location advantanges to the proportional change in the degree of internationalization over the period 1974–82

	US	Germany	UK	Italy	France	Japan
Food products	−0.04	0.07	−0.10	−0.31	0.17	0.29
Chemicals	−0.21	0.25	0.24	−0.02	−0.33	0.66
Metals	0.10	0.30	−0.32	0.33	0.07	1.71
Mechanical engineering	0.06	0.26	0.11	−0.07	−0.13	0.21
Electrical equipment	−0.02	0.22	0.07	0.10	0.39	0.20
Motor vehicles	0.11	0.13	0.22	0.65	0.29	0.34
Other transport equipment	1.03	−0.56	−0.46	0.36	−0.01	3.68
Textiles	−0.14	0.28	0.35	0.02	0.58	0.45
Rubber products	0.03	0.17	0.04	−0.10	−0.07	0.04
Non-metallic	−0.07	0.42	0.08	0.18	0.16	0.05
Coal and petroleum products	0.01	0.22	0.07	0.27	0.00	0.24
Other manufacturing	0.01	0.07	0.35	−0.13	0.18	0.25
Total	−0.03	0.23	0.15	0.03	0.13	0.39

Source: As for Table 4

firms in textiles and other manufacturing; for French firms in food products, electrical equipment, and textiles. With Italian firms, location advantages quite often favoured production in Italy, leading to a negative locational effect on internationalization in five out of twelve sectors, and most notably in food products. Location advantages made a major contribution to the growing internationalization of Japanese firms in food products and textiles, though the greatest quantitative impact came in chemicals, metals, and other transport equipment.

The catching-up effect in general contributed less to internationalization than did ownership and location advantages, as is apparent from Table 6.6. Only in the case of Japanese firms, who had most to catch up, did it make a major contribution in total manufacturing. Catching up played an important role for German firms in non-metallic mineral products and coal and petroleum products; for Italian firms in metals, motor vehicles, non-metallic mineral products, and coal and petroleum products; for French firms in food products, electrical equipment, and textiles; and for Japanese firms in chemicals, metals, mechanical engineering, electrical equipment, motor vehicles, other transport equipment, and coal and petroleum products.

This analysis of the changing international structure of activity amongst the firms of the major industrialized countries demonstrates

Table 6.6 The estimated contribution of the catching-up effect to the proportional change in the degree of internationalization over the period 1974–82

	US	Germany	UK	Italy	France	Japan
Food products	0.00	0.03	0.02	−0.25	0.14	0.02
Chemicals	0.04	0.02	0.03	0.00	−0.04	0.22
Metals	−0.02	0.07	0.10	0.18	0.01	0.95
Mechanical engineering	−0.01	0.06	−0.01	−0.04	−0.02	0.12
Electrical equipment	0.00	0.04	−0.01	0.07	0.13	0.12
Motor vehicles	−0.02	0.03	−0.02	0.24	0.05	0.28
Other transport equipment	0.08	0.10	0.13	0.05	0.00	0.61
Textiles	0.03	0.04	−0.07	0.01	0.16	0.09
Rubber products	0.00	0.11	0.00	0.00	0.01	0.02
Non-metallic	0.01	0.24	−0.01	0.34	0.00	0.02
Coal and petroleum products	0.00	0.50	0.00	0.91	0.00	0.23
Other manufacturing	0.00	0.02	0.09	−0.08	0.10	0.04
Total	0.00	0.08	−0.02	0.02	0.04	0.28

Source: As for Table 6.4.

the importance of paying close attention to the varying determinants of the internationalization of production. It would be interesting in the future to extend the discussion to a multi-period case, since the relative significance of ownership advantages, location advantages, and catching up in the continuing process of internationalization is likely to vary over time across different national groups of firms. It is also clear from the evidence that it is at least important to take account of why some groups of firms have internationalized their operations faster than others (which depends upon the three relative influences mentioned) as it is to consider the general trend towards internationalization. Although in recent years the international business literature has often focused on the question of why multinational firms in general grow relative to international markets, the empirical evidence for the 1970s and early 1980s suggests that a more relevant question is why it is that the international operations of some firms (the non-US group) have grown relative to those of other firms (the US group). In answering this, the favourable ownership advantages of European and Japanese firms compared to the earlier post-war period seem to have been critical.

References

Buckley, P. J. and Casson, M. C. (1976) *The Future of the Multinational Enterprise*, London: Macmillan.

Cantwell, J. A. (1987a) 'Technological advantage as a determinant of the international economic activity of firms', *University of Reading Discussion Paper in International Investment and Business Studies*, No. 105, October.

———(1987b) 'The reorganisation of European industries after integration: selected evidence on the role of transnational enterprise activities', *Journal of Common Market Studies* 26(2) December.

———(1989a) *Technological Innovation and Multinational Corporations*, Oxford: Basil Blackwell.

———(1989b) 'The changing form of multinational enterprise expansion in the twentieth century', in A. Teichova, M. Levy-Leboyer, and H. Nussbaum, (eds), *Historical Studies in International Corporate Business*, Cambridge: Cambridge University Press.

Casson, M. C. (1983) 'Introduction' in M. C. Casson (ed.), *The Growth of International Business*, London: Allen and Unwin.

Cowling, K. (1984) 'The internationalisation of production and deindustrialisation', *Warwick Economic Research Papers* 256.

Cowling, K. and Sugden, R. (1987) *Transnational Monopoly Capitalism*, Brighton: Wheatsheaf Books.

Dunning, J. H. (1981) *International Production and the Multinational Enterprise*, London: Allen & Unwin.

Dunning, J. H. and Cantwell, J. A. (1987) *The IRM Directory of Statistics of International Investment and Production*, London: Macmillan, and New York: New York University Press.

Dunning, J. H. and Pearce, R. D. (1981) *The World's Largest Industrial Enterprises*, Farnborough: Gower.

———(1985) *The World's Largest Industrial Enterprises, 1962–1983*, Farnborough: Gower.

Freeman, C. and Perez, C. (1990) 'The diffusion of technical innovations and changes of techno-economic paradigm', in F. Arcangeli, P. A. David, and G. Dosi (eds), *Modern Patterns in Adopting and Diffusing Innovations*, Oxford: Oxford University Press.

Rugman, A. M. (1981) *Inside the Multinationals: The Economics of Internal Markets*, London: Croom Helm.

Vernon, R. (1971) *Sovereignty at Bay*, Harmondsworth: Penguin.

Wilkins, M. (1970) *The Emergence of Multinational Enterprise: American Business Abroad from the Colonial Era to 1914*, Cambridge, Mass.: Harvard University Press.

Chapter Seven

Intra-industry foreign direct investment: a study of recent evidence

Jeremy Clegg

Introduction

Intra-industry forign direct investment (FDI)[1] and the theme of industrial restructuring are both topics which have attracted increasing interest in the 1980s. Two overlapping reasons can be identified which account for the growth in their appeal for economists and policy-makers.

First, the existence of widespread intra-industry FDI between developed countries would appear to be the conclusive stage in the process of the internationalization of firms and of economies. This stage has not yet been attained, but the empirical significance of international direct investment suggests that the trend is in this direction. In the course of this process the factors explaining the performance of multinational enterprises (MNEs) is held to owe more to the efficiency of firms' own extensive internal economic systems than to the characteristics of the countries from which they originated (Dunning 1981a; 1986).

Because such multinational firms are likely to have a significant proportion – even a majority – of their operations outside their mother countries, international rivals will in all probability have competing operations within similar sets of countries, and within the same regions. Such a scenario is implied by 'global competition'. It is this controlling of resources integrated within the firm, but in a number of locations, which leads multinationals to be prime agents of economic re-allocation. The question which arises from this is over the extent to which re-allocation via MNEs is distinctive from that via trade or via international contractual transfers.

The second reason for the attention afforded to the topics of intra-industry FDI arid restructuring is of more prominent relevance to policy. Intra-industry FDI is, in principle, cross-investment within the same industry. Such a principle enables each economy concerned to maintain both a domestic and a foreign foothold in what may be perceived to be key industries. While countries may become specialized in production within sections of industries, in an analogous fashion to intra-industry trade, restructing need not mean the elimination of whole industries if intra-industry FDI occurs. Foreign direct investment abroad is matched by inward FDI, with the expectation that the precise nature of the respective investments enhances the comparative advantage of each location. This process is underpinned by the increasing separability of vertically linked production stages, so enabling MNEs to engage in geographically dispersed but functionally integrated FDI.

Therefore, restructuring concerns the re-allocation of resources, and, for those industries concerned, country specialization through the relocation of certain activities. There are two distinct real-world dimensions to this relocation. The first concerns adjustment as between developed countries and the second as between developed countries and newly industrializing countries (NICs). In keeping with the theme of this book, this paper concentrates on the former subject, although it is a matter of fact that new entry by firms from NICs has formed a significant impetus for adjustment between developed countries.

To date the issue of intra-industry FDI as between developed countries and NICs has not arisen to a significant extent. However, the eventual generation of authentic competitive FDI by firms from NICs is most likely. In view of the foregoing the present argument centres around intra-industry FDI between developed countries, which as a group account for the bulk of global FDI.

Review of the theory

Much of the analysis familiar from received FDI theory remains relevant to the study of intra-industry FDI, although requiring clarification and development. To this extent, it is true to say that intra-industry FDI is not a new economic phenomenon in search of a theory, it merely highlights the inadequacies in the existing body of theory.

The current emphasis of mainstream theory lies on the adjustment of the extent of the firm in response to the ownership of intangible assets (broadly defined technology, expertise, and so on) which determine its competitiveness and therefore its performance (market share, profitability, etc.). Hence these are termed ownership-specific assets (Dunning 1977). The extent of the firm is simultaneously dependent upon the transaction costs of the intra-firm organization of business activities (based on such ownership advantages) relative to those of organization between firms. The latter is effected through the contractual sale of ownership assets (for example, licensing) and is regarded as the use of markets external to the firm. This analysis incorporates the internalization approach to the MNE (Buckley and Casson 1976), where the degree of internalization determines the extent of the firm. The location of production depends upon the comparative cost of immobile factors, influenced by impediments to trade and plant economies of scale.

Theory therefore allows any firm to compete internationally either by utilizing its own assets itself or by selling them for an appropriate return. It is only where a firm chooses to retain ownership itself and produce in a foreign location that foreign direct investment occurs, and direct exporting and non-affiliate contracting are in this instance precluded. This represents the basis of the dominant theory of the MNE, known as the eclectic theory, introduced by Dunning (1977) and elaborated in many subsequent works.

Some progress has been made in refining existing theory to deal with intra-industry FDI. However, the overwhelming impression is that such theory is as yet poorly equipped to explain the complexities of the international competitive process between firms, which must lie at the root of intra-industry FDI.

From inter-industry FDI to intra-industry FDI

The modern theory of the MNE is founded upon an approach originally devised to explain inter-industry FDI. This is one-way FDI from a source country a host country through the agency of a multinational firm operating in a given industry. Such FDI might be horizontal (import-substituting) or vertical (resource-based). The industrial organization approach to FDI was initiated by Hymer (1960) primarily as an explanation of US FDI in Europe. It was predicated upon the source country firms enjoying superiority in their production fuctions over host country firms. This superiority led to an absolute cost advantage deriving from what are now termed ownership advantages. This cost advantage was seen to compensate for the added costs of operating in a foreign environment – the host country – and so to explain FDI[2].

Hymer's approach therefore described events as they were. A generalization of the industrial organization approach can permit cross-FDI between countries, but this will be inter-industry (i.e. in non-competing industries). Intra-industry FDI could arguably be generated if there were a progression to outward FDI by firms indigenous to the host as economic development occurs. Given that the established foreign MNE does not disinvest in the industry concerned, intra-industry FDI can be generated.

Such an account as the above is what Caves (1986) has called a 'fall-out' explanation of intra-industry FDI: it does not specify the essential elements for intra-industry FDI to take place. There are other explanations of similar calibre, such as intra-industry FDI resulting from alternate over- and undervaluation of exchange rates. In a sense these explanations create intra-industry FDI by default, not through intent. It seems certain that such explanations are not sufficient to generate intra-industry FDI, though they may alter the timing of investment decisions, and the switch from exporting, licensing, and other competitive modes.

It is altogether more satisfactory to recognize the limitations of the industrial organization approach, which deals only with FDI, and work with a theoretical approach which allows exports and licensing as strategic choices for the firm competing in international markets. The question then becomes how to explain the choice of what will become intra-industry FDI among these options, which must logically include intra-industry trade and intra-industry licensing.

Renewed efforts to update theory to handle intra-industry FDI have followed three routes. Firstly, the reworking of the ownership advantage approach to allow differentiated advantages within the same industry. This permits firms to compete in a differentiated product industry, creating intra-industry FDI whenever firms from different countries, but in the same industry, choose FDI. The second approach is to emphasize economies of the firm, which cannot be sold contractually through the external market; such assets are firm-specific, so ownership can only be transferred through the sale of the entire firm. This causes foreign direct investment to be increasingly efficient as the means of international competition. The third approach has been to develop an argument put originally by Hymer (ibid.) as an alternative sufficient condition for inter-industry FDI. This concerns the existence of oligopolistic interaction between firms, causing oligopolistic rivalrous behaviour.

These three approaches constitute the current perspectives on intra-industry FDI. Each has different relevanace to particular industries, and different implications for the type of FDI which occurs and for policy. These approaches are now examined in some detail.

Asset advantages

As noted before, here firms own differentiated ownership advantages. Given that they face relatively imperfect external markets for the sale of these assets, and that there are impediments to trade, intra-industry FDI will result between countries. This approximates the proposal of

Caves (1986) for an analytical model of intra-industry FDI based on Chamberlinian monopolistic competition, where the technology represents a fixed cost of production, with production taking place under constant returns.

This model is neat and self-contained and has been suggested by Dunning (1981b) and Rugman (1985). However, its application is mainly to import-substituting FDI of a horizontal nature. It is appealingly symmetrical, in that firms from different countries in the same industry necessarily face the same international external markets for their technology advantages. If a key external market is notably imperfect in an industry, then intra-industry FDI will be intensive. It should be noted that the imperfections in the international market for technology in this model need be no more than those causing the transaction costs of contracting; that is, they are not caused by the structure of the market (e.g. oligopoly) *per se.*

An additional approach, which is essentially an internalization issue and may therefore be subsumed within the first approach to intra-industry FDI cited above, is the hypothesis based on geographical diversification to reduce risk and stabilize global profits. This may be a sufficient cause for intra-industry FDI in the presence of widespread market imperfections (Rugman 1985). This is an extension of a cause of FDI investigated by Rugman (1979) where firms internalize foreign operations to gain from imperfectly correlated disturbances in both product and factor markets (thus explaining the choice of FDI over exporting or contractual arrangements).

The asset advantage is held to be the particular portfolio of assets which the MNE comprises; this asset advantage is internalized as an MNE owing to the impediments to individual wealth-holders owning a similar portfolio; as a result the MNE enjoys relatively lower transaction costs. Such an approach generates intra-industry FDI when conditions create MNEs originating from different countries but in the same industry. It is evident that there must be some country-specific impediments preventing most individual wealth-holders from buying equity in one unified, geographically diversified MNE; however, if this is satisfied, intra-industry FDI is a consequence.

Despite its appeal, the asset advantage approach does not convey any of the complexities of the multinational firm. It appears best suited to single-product firms venturing abroad for the first time whose advantages reflect the character of the home country. Firm-specific factors have little place here, yet these are likely to be important, particularly for established MNEs, which contribute most to intra-industry FDI.

Economies of the firm

As noted earlier, these centre around efficiency which, although enjoyed by the firm as an advantage, cannot be disassociated from the firm and sold via the external market. A number of contributions have occurred under this broad heading. Concepts such as 'economies of scope' (Teece 1980; 1983) have been harnessed, notably by Kogut (1983). Economies of scope refer to the situation where there are economies arising from the use of shared inputs to produce multiple outputs and where this is likely to be under common ownership.

Dunning and Norman (1985; 1986) denote the same economies as 'transaction cost minimising advantages', implying that the internal economic systems of MNEs are continually able to co-ordinate activities at lower transaction costs than an external market. The importance of this approach, unlike the first, is that it is felt to apply well to established MNEs, which are collectively responsible for the bulk of intra-industry FDI. Thus it explains extensions to existing multinational firms, and decisions that depend on the context of the enterprise as a whole.

The aptness of describing these advantages or economies as invariably exploitable only within the firm is questionable. However, it is likely that nothing less binding than long-term co-operation between firms will be feasible, in a form such as a joint venture. The relevance of this general approach is that it helps explain both the movement towards rationalized production by established MNEs and the tendency towards internalization at the same time.

In the background of over-capacity and the seeking of efficiency in many industries, the rationalization of FDI can contribute to the growth of intra-industry FDI. Stopford and Dunning (1983) distinguish two types of rationalized FDI:

1. The specialization between the plants of an MNE in the production of similar final products. These are located in different countries, the outputs of which may then be traded (often within the firm) for sale in a number of final markets. This variant is typical of FDI in developed countries.
2. Vertical or process specialization in particular stages of the manufacturing process. This is akin to vertical FDI aimed at exploiting raw materials, with a somewhat more pronounced degree of process specialization, however, often to make use of low-cost labour. The outputs are typically exported to developed markets for further processing or sale. Such FDI is characteristic of that in less developed countries (LDCs).

The relevant type of rationalized FDI for the present purpose is Type 1. Conventional vertical FDI is clearly inter-industry in nature where it is orientated towards a specific resource, and the same is true of rationalized FDI in LDCs. However, rationalized FDI in developed countries is aimed at attaining efficient production through exploiting plant economies of scale. As Stopford and Dunning (1983) point out, such FDI thrives when impediments to trade are low; consequently this type of FDI is anticipated within customs unions and free trade areas. Greenaway and Milner (1986) identify the role of the same process in the generation of intra-industry trade.

The international organization of the MNE owes much to the type of economies enjoyed in each aspect of the production process. Multi-product economies of scale, which create the ability to spread overhead costs over a range of product varieties, will explain why, for example, the marketing function is replicated in each host country to market the full range of product varieties, including those imported from foreign plants and not produced locally. The scale economies in the production of each variety help explain the geographical diversity of specialized production.

Kogut (1983) has suggested that the economies-of-scope argument applies between the marketing and manufacturing functions. Such an argument would imply that inputs of information relevant to marketing will be location-specific and have additional use as feedback to manufacturing. Another approach which also emphasizes proximity to clients and customers is that of Cantwell (1987) structured around technological competition. Cantwell sees technological inputs as location-specific, promoting the decentralization of research and development facilities to foreign centres of innovative excellence to tap in to technological developments.

The intra-industry nature of FDI accordingly derives from the economies of uniting marketing and production with R&D and production for each firm, together with differentiated location-specific inputs. The location of the foreign affiliate in the host enhances the competitiveness of the MNE as a whole; as Cantwell (1987) notes, the role of the subsidiary is upgraded from a mere vehicle for the technological diffusion of parental technology to that of being itself a generator of new technology.

Rationalized FDI in developed countries will therefore generate intra-industry FDI when firms from different countries, producing competing products within the same industry, locate plant within each other's home economies. The above suggests that this type of intra-industry FDI will be most intensive where multi-product plant scale economies and economies of the firm such as economies of scope are significant. The principal industrial characteristics advocated as causes of scope economies between inputs and outputs are marketing and technology intensity.

An additional factor may be government's policies, designed to encourage established MNEs pursuing a rationalized FDI strategy to locate plant in their country.[3] The importance of this sort of intervention in creating intra-industry FDI is emphasized by Rugman (1985). Given that substantial sales take place in a market, government will be keen to have local production by the MNEs concerned, not simply to substitute for imports but to contribute to exports and local employment within the framework of rationalized investment. Incentives and subsidies may be offered, all of which will contribute to the positioning of specialized plants in a number of countries if competition between governments is keen for such foot-loose investment.

In summary it can be remarked that the rationalized investment account of intra-industry FDI makes no explicit mention of market structure. This will probably be oligopolistic, but within conditions of technological change rather than static technology. The appeal of the rationalized investment perspective is that it recognizes that foreign facilities are not set up to be slavish producers of single product lines, but rather to enquire, research and develop, manufacture, and sell numbers of lines and generations of products, including those not produced locally but imported from elsewhere within the enterprise. The type of firm indicated is explicitly more complicated and hence more realistic.

Oligopolistic rivalry

The final approach to explaining intra-industry FDI is to model such FDI as an exchange of threats between rival producers. Casson (1987) has gone furthest in modelling this account, which is a development of Hymer's (1960) explanation of inter-industry FDI as a consequence of oligopolistic interaction. For Hymer, the entry barriers causing oligopoly were innocent and structural, as opposed to strategic, and were therefore the result of the technical nature of the industry rather than the deliberate behaviour of firms.

With the substitution of strategic behaviour, this approach was used to explain US inter-industry FDI in Europe and the temporal clustering of US MNEs setting up subsidiaries (Knickerbocker 1973). The first use of this theme as an explanation of intra-industry FDI is by Graham (1974; 1978) using concentrated market structure and strategic entry barriers as the cause of FDI between the US and Europe.

Graham's thesis was that horizontal intra-industry FDI was used by oligopolists to reduce rivalrous conduct and stabilize the industry. This was held to be sufficient, if not necessary, for intra-industry FDI. Indeed, Graham argued that 'intuition suggests that it is unlikely that cross-investments would occur if the investments were motivated by industry-specific intangible assets' (Graham 1978: 88). Graham's empirical work on intra-industry FDI for nineteen industry groups yielded inconclusive results, and is open to criticism for not explaining why FDI was presumed to be superior to exporting, and for excluding locational factors in general. However, the message that oligopolistic market structure can influence FDI independently of ownership advantages is a valuable one.

The theme of Graham (1978) has been revised by Casson (1987) to present intra-industry FDI as a consequence of profit-maximizing behaviour in oligopoly rather than of oligopolistic uncertainty, as it remained in Graham's work. It is shown that a dominant firm seeking to expand its foreign market share following FDI may be restrained by a weaker firms, indigenous to the foreign market, using strategic FDI in the dominant firm's home market. The result is intra-industry FDI. The reason exporting is not chosen is because the credibility of the threat to damage the dominant firm's position in its home market is adequate only via FDI. It is evident that, while providing a plausible explanation of intra-industry FDI, this model does not, as it stands, elaborate on any internal or organizational features of MNEs, although it can be complemented by internalization theory (Casson 1987).

The question which remains is one of the empirical significance of the above and indeed all three accounts of intra-industry FDI. Certainly, their respective appropriateness will vary according to industry, and this renders it virtually impossible to disprove any one hypothesis if only aggregate data are available. The discussion in later sections of this paper places these three theoretical approaches in some empirical perspective. However, in summary of the above, we can note that the asset advantage approach consists of a rather abstract and simplified account of intra-industry FDI, and while it may be best suited to explaining pioneering FDI this must lessen its relevance to the greatest part of intra-industry FDI, as this is likely to be generated by established firms.

In this respect the oligopolistic rivalry hypothesis is somewhat similar, as it has no pretension to explaining the continued growth of intra-industry FDI, but merely attempts to trace the initial steps abroad. It seems likely that in the real world most intra-industry FDI consists of the general expansion of FDI in existing host countries, therefore the account based on economies of the firm probably contains the most empirical significance, with the inclusion of locational and governmental factors.

Intra-industry FDI and intra-industry trade

The previous section has considered the strands of theory advanced to explain intra-industry FDI. In general these are to be distinguished from those held to account for intra-industry trade. Some overlaps nevertheless do exist; for example, where there are firm-specific economies (e.g. in the branding of products) both intra-industry trade and FDI will have a common cause. This does not apply to plant scale economies, factor proportions, and similar accounts of intra-industry trade, where there is no direct relationship with factors causing the international extension of the firm.

Intra-industry FDI may have a range of impacts on trade, but these are possibilities rather than definite outcomes. Norman and Dunning (1984) approach the issue of intra-industry FDI from this wider perspective of intra-industry trade. From their analysis it is evident that the varying assertions made by a number of authors about the expected relationship between intra-industry trade and FDI are over-simplistic: the association (or absence of it) between the two depends crucially on the precise causes of intra-industry trade. The following discussion considers only the likely influence of intra-industry FDI on theoretically related intra-industry trade.

Horizontal or import-substituting intra-industry FDI will clearly have a negative relationship with intra-industry trade, in the sense that if impediments to trade rise, intra-industry FDI will also increase at the expense of trade. This is not to say that intra-industry FDI and trade will not both characterize some industries more than others. Here, differentiated product industries will be most significant. It is also crucial to note the time dimension, because if even a process so simple as the product cycle were to apply, at any given point in time new generations of similar products would characterize trade, while the mature generations would be produced in the foreign market. If this is a two-way process and FDI is universally chosen, both FDI and trade will be statistically positively correlated across industries, yet will reveal an inverse relationship for any specific generation of product in time series.

As an empirical question, import-substituting FDI is seen as primarily an issue of the first two decades after the Second World War, prompted by barriers to trade and the industrialization policies of governments. Rationalized FDI is, by contrast, of growing importance since 1970 (Stopford and Dunning 1983). It is unlikely that import-substituting intra-industry FDI (and therefore intra-industry trade-reducing) will occur between developed countries in the context of falling tariffs and transport costs. Where it may still persist is between the large trading units, such as the USA, Europe, and Japan, where both extensive production and sales occur, and trade barriers and other government-induced distortions are significant.

However, within the European market, intra-industry FDI and trade should be expected to exhibit the relationship suggested by rationalized FDI. This is the consequence of the separation of production stages already alluded to. Here, scale economies at the plant level favour the specialization of plants, which are likely to be in different regions. Intermediate products will be traded between plants in the MNE, and with the assumption that each variant of the final product can be sold in each of the host markets, so intra-industry trade will not only be generated as intra-firm trade between specialized plants and marketing outlets but also by the trade of competing MNEs.

In this way economies at the level of the firm in co-ordinating production help to create a positive relationship between intra-industry FDI and intra-industry trade, both within MNEs and indirectly between MNEs. However, it should be noted that observed intra-industry FDI and trade generally include upward bias resulting from categorical aggregation. This point is addressed further in the section on the definition and measurement of intra-industry FDI. Nevertheless, there are good reasons for believing that a relationship does exist between authentic intra-industry FDI and intra-industry trade.

Oligopolistic intra-industry FDI is most likely, in the first instance, to attenuate existing intra-industry trade. As export competition is held to be insufficient to retain market share, this must necessarily be so. However, if international rivals source foreign operations with similar intermediate products, then intra-industry (and intra-firm) trade will be created, of initially a lower value than that destroyed in final products. Nevertheless, the possibility of the subsequent export of final products to third markets cannot be ruled out, although this is not necessarily implied by the oligopoly account.

Only the rationalized investment account of intra-industry FDI necessarily implies an expansion of intra-industry trade. This would seem to account best for the observed simultaneous increase in the two, although this depends fundamentally on the reliability of the available data. Because of inadequate data on intra-industry FDI, notwithstanding the alternative theoretical accounts noted above, it has proven impossible to establish empirically a unique relationship between intra-industry FDI and intra-industry trade. Virtually no studies have found any unequivocal evidence of a clear statistical association (Dunning 1981b; Rugman 1985; Pugel 1985; Juhl 1985; Dunning and Norman 1986). This is unlikely to be because no such relationships exist, but rather a consequence of industrial and geographic aggregation, and the inaccuracy inherent in FDI data.

The industrial impact of intra-industry FDI

At the outset of this paper it was noted that one of the key features of intra-industry FDI was its policy aspects, and that competitive governmental bidding for footloose plant can create intra-industry FDI together with trade, if plant specialization takes place. This dispersion of FDI will occur mainly within naturally and commercially unified markets (such as the European Community). Between such markets, FDI will tend to substitute for imports to regions as a whole.

To this picture can be added the monitoring of individual MNEs' 'balance of trade' with individual economies. Firms with negative balances can be strongly encouraged by governments to locate new capacity locally. In these instances, the interests of firms will lie increasingly in the harmonization of distortions impeding the movement of goods within market regions.

As to the consequences of intra-industry FDI, each of the theoretical accounts has slightly different implications, although in practice the fixity of these differences is likely to prove illusory. Only the oligopolistic rivalry hypothesis suggests there need be no international transfer of technology, merely the extension of control. It is largely silent on implications for industrial impact; however, it is the least likely to generate intra-industry specialization. This is not surprising, as it best explains the prompting of intra-industry FDI. For the subsequent development, the other two accounts allow technology transfer. The differentiated-asset-advantage hypothesis is not formulated upon the gains from scale economies, and while it is unlikely to cause intra-industry specialization, local linkages in each host will be generated.

Intra-industry FDI caused by a rationalized investment strategy, in common with its near relation, vertical FDI, may tend to create fewer local linkages, but more intensive intra-firm trade. As scale economies are central to its rationale, intra-industry specialization by the economy will result, to a greater or lesser degree, depending on the diversity of products produced locally by plants or rival MNEs. As always, the disadvantage of rationalized FDI is the loss of local affiliate autonomy, together with the risk of industrial shocks or even drastic reductions in capacity in response to adverse market conditions external to the host.

There are strong reasons for not attempting to distinguish artificially between the hypotheses on intra-industry FDI, where the data are highly aggregate and cross-sectional in nature. Rationalized FDI will only follow some earlier form of FDI, perhaps best explained by the other two accounts. The existence of such a sequence means the hypotheses are not true alternatives, but part of the internationalization process. This may proceed further in some types of industries than others, but the nature of the available data preclude any scientific testing.

It can be noted that intra-industry FDI in raw materials and primary products is least probable, firstly because the uneven distribution of specific resources is least likely to generate intra-industry trade, and secondly because highly developed external markets for such commodities generally exist (Dunning 1981b; Norman and Dunning 1984). However, in manufacturing and services, similar conditions do not apply, and extensive disaggregation is essential to further investigation.

The definition and measurement of intra-industry FDI

Intra-industry FDI can be described as reciprocal FDI between two countries within the same industry, where the firms concerned are in competition. The intention of this definition is to draw attention away from intra-industry FDI as a statistical phenomenon – often inflated by the imprecise classification of an industry, causing upward bias attributed to categorical aggregation. Broad definitions of intra-industry FDI, especially those allowing substitutability in production to qualify (Erdilek 1985) will unnecessarily include much hidden non-competitive FDI.

If the above narrow definition of intra-industry FDI is adopted as that of 'authentic' intra-industry FDI, then it must be recognized that its correspondence with measures derivable from available data is a very tenuous one. Apart from industrial and geographical aggregation, the use of FDI data to gauge foreign activity is often unsatisfactory. FDI is a financial concept, itself often poorly evaluated and, as a partial input variable, far inferior to value-added as a measure of foreign involvement.[4] Moreover, as the method of financing foreign activity can vary systematically by country because of, for example, differences in the cost of borrowing, this distortion in FDI as a true measure will be compounded by the use of the index commonly used to gauge intra-industry FDI, as it is based on the overlap, or balance, of FDI.

The index generally adopted to represent intra-industry FDI (IIFDI for convenience) is obtained by analogy to the intra-industry trade index introduced by Grubel and Lloyd (1975):

$$\text{IIFDI} = \frac{(O_j + I_j) - |O_j - I_j|}{(O_j + I_j)} \times 100$$

where IIFDI = intra-industry FDI in industry j

O_j = outward FDI in industry j

I_j = inward FDI in industry j

This index shares the characteristics of its trade relation, including the undesirable ones discussed by Greenaway and Milner (1986, Chapter 5). In addition, FDI indices are particularly subject to two further distortions. First, as noted above, FDI data can systematically misvalue true foreign activity by country; the index depends on the balance of cross-FDI to impute IIFDI. Thus, if systematic distortions exist, much authentic IIFDI can be excluded. This will tend to depress the measure of IIFDI. In contrast, the higher industrial and geographical aggregation (more common with FDI data as compared to trade data) will act to bias measures of IIFDI upwards. There are no reasons to believe these various distortions will cancel each other out.

Intra-industry FDI is rarely disaggregated geographically. In the following section some attempt is made to do this where disaggregation is meaningful and the data permit.

Estimates of intra-industry FDI

In view of the many deficiencies in the available data on intra-industry FDI, this section is sparing in the inferences which it draws from the indices calculated for the USA, UK and Federal Republic of Germany. While much of the estimated IIFDI may not be authentic, Tables 7.1 to 7.4 demonstrate a further point: that in a large number of industries, what measured IIFDI there is lies in the hands of relatively few firms. This explains the many instances where data on outward and/or inward FDI have been suppressed to avoid disclosure (see footnote × in the tables). This does not necessarily mean that such suppressed IIFDI is truly competitive, because the industry classifications are so wide. However, it does reinforce the argument that IIFDI must be investigated at the level of the firm.

The frequency of suppressed data has forced the exclusion of a number of partner countries from the tables. Those which remain often provide no more than an indistinct outline. Appendix A

Table 7.1 Estimates of intra-industry foreign direct investment for the USA, 1980[a]

Industry group	World		Canada		Europe		Japan	
	IIFDI	Rank	IIFDI	Rank	IIFDI	Rank	IIFDI	Rank
Resource-based								
Agriculture, forestry, and fishing	85.8	5	81.0	4	7.4	28	80.0	3
Mining	40.0	20	38.2	7	8.8	27	–	–
Petroleum	35.1	23	28.9	11	65.1	12	×	–
Manufacturing	54.1	–	35.3	–	72.6	–	47.6	–
Food and related products	65.2	13	×	–	77.0	7 =	78.6	5
Industrial chemicals	81.4	7	3.7	18	76.7	9	54.4	8
Drugs	59.4	15	×	–	50.7	19	×	–
Soaps, cleaners, and toiletries	73.8	8	–	–	83.8	4	×	–
Agricultural chemicals	85.5	6	×	–	54.0	17	×	–
Other chemicals	30.7	25	0.6	19.	47.1	20	1.3	13
Rubber and plastics products	25.5	26	4.4	17	43.7	23	×	–
Primary metal industries	87.7	4	88.5	2	56.2	16	54.8	7
Fabricated metal products	41.7	19	30.7	9	62.4	14	×	–
Non-electrical machinery[b]	34.9	24	×	–	46.9	21	×	–
Instruments and related products	18.2	27	11.9	16	16.0	25	96.2	1
Electric and electronic equipment	72.7	9	×	–	77.0	7 =	79.7	4
Transportation equipment	15.3	28	×	–	35.1	24	×	–
Textile products and apparel	42.8	18	22.2	12	64.8	13	33.3	10
Lumber, wood, furniture, and fixtures	56.2	17	33.2	8	85.9	3	×	–

Paper and allied products	38.9	21	x	—	73.9	10	x	—
Printing and publishing	69.4	10	—	—	x	—	x	—
Stone, clay, and glass products	96.7	1	x	—	83.3	5	x	—
Banking and financial								
Banking	61.1	14	86.8	3	81.0	6	41.6	9
Finance	—	—	29.6	10	91.1	1	x	—
Insurance[c]	91.3	3	63.6	5	61.4	15	x	—
Other activities								
Construction	67.4	12	x	—	87.8	2	—	—
Wholesale distribution	68.2	11	54.2	6	71.7	11	57.9	6
Retail distribution	96.3	2	16.5	13	51.7	18	95.5	2
Transportation and communication[d]	58.3	16	96.4	1	x	—	x	—
Property owning and managing	16.8	29	14.9	14	12.7	26	3.8	12
Other services[e]	38.7	22	14.8	15	35.4	23	29.9	11
All industries	55.7	—	39.9	—	73.8	—	78.7	—
Aggregate outward/inward FDI %	259.3	—	401.6	—	171.0	—	155.6	—
Percentage of total FDI:								
Outward[f]	100.0	—	20.9	—	44.7	—	3.2	—
Inward[f]	100.0	—	13.5	—	67.8	—	5.3	—

Notes:

— Signifies that either or both outward and inward FDI are less than an absolute value of US$ 500,000.

x Signifies that both outward and inward FDI are greater than an absolute value of US$500,000 but that either or both have been suppressed to avoid disclosure of data on individual enterprises.

[a] Outward FDI data are for 1982.

[b] Includes computing equipment.

[c] Negative FDI positions are excluded.

[d] Includes public utilities.

[e] Includes services relating to hotels, business, films, engineering, architecture and surveying, health, and other services.

[f] The value of total FDI were US$M 207,320 (outward) and US$M 79,950 (inward).

Source: see Appendix B on pp. 139–40

provides some indication of the errors in the data by comparing alternative estimates of IIFDI calculated from reverse recorded data. The apparent stability in the rankings is somewhat misleading because so few industries are comparable between different countries' classifications. Table A(i) suggests some general agreement on IIFDI based on US and UK data. However, a great disparity in the valuation of cross-FDI between the two is demonstrated in the aggregate US outward/inward ratio, where this is substantially undervalued by UK data compared to US data. Similar discrepancies are evident in A(ii) and A(iii) for the other countries.

Somewhat more disaggregate data are available for the USA, but only for around the year 1980 (see Table 7.1). US data for other years and partner countries preclude the calculation of a comprehensive set of indices, although partner indices for the UK and Germany are presented in Appendix A (Table A).

The fact that stone, clay, and glass products rank first among the US–World IIFDI indices is a telling indication of the aggregation problem, as is the high ranking of lumber and affiliated products with Europe. Nevertheless, some pertinent observations can be made on these indices.

The first is that Canada, which receives 21 per cent of US FDI, and contributes 13.5 per cent to USA inward FDI, is very distinctive in its relationship with the USA. Canada records a significantly higher index with the USA than does Europe in the following industries: mining; agriculture, forestry, and fishing; transport, communications, and related industries; and primary metals. This effect of proximity with the USA is exceptional, as the conventional result with Europe is generally obtained, though not with Germany alone (see Table 7.3), in the case of a small quantity of cross-FDI in mining. Otherwise IIFDI with Europe is notably high in soaps, cleaners, and toiletries – a result probably best explained by mutual advantages in product differentiation. Conversely, the US transportation equipment index is notably low, reflecting the strong domestic market position of US producers, where European firms appear not to have made significant inroads via FDI.

Despite the expectation of low intra-industry FDI in primary product industries, a notably high index occurs for petroleum with Europe. This probably arises because of the gains from (real asset) geographical diversification, being particularly pronounced in the petroleum extraction industry, where it is advantageous for each firm to hold a portfolio of wells. Here, European MNEs own US wells and vice versa, reflecting the location of oil-fields in the USA and the North Sea.

In general, the distributive trades and services have higher than

Table 7.2 Estimates of intra-industry foreign direct investment for the UK 1974–81

Industry group	World 1981 IIFDI	Rank	World 1978 IIFDI	Rank	World 1974 IIFDI	Rank	USA 1981 IIFDI	Rank	USA 1978 IIFDI	Rank	USA 1974 IIFDI	Rank
Resource-based	N.A.	–	N.A.	–	N.A.	–	N.A.	–	N.A.	–	N.A.	–
Manufacturing	86.0	–	80.1	–	87.7	–	77.9	–	69.3	–	44.2	–
Food, drink, and tobacco	62.9	9	51.2	9	53.0	10	84.7	4	84.1	3	96.0	2
Chemicals and allied industries	69.3	5	61.2	7	78.2	5	92.8	2	97.5	1	46.4	6
Rubber	77.6	4	94.1	2	68.9	7	×		×		×	
Metal manufacture	65.8	6	81.8	3	98.2	1	26.6	11	×		×	
Mechanical and instrument engineering	63.7	8	56.8	8	66.9	9	35.8	10	18.9	9	×	
Electrical engineering	96.1	1	98.5	1	98.0	2	57.3	6	41.3	8	29.3	7
Motor vehicle manufacture	58.3	10	40.2	10	53.5	11	11.0	12	×		–	
Textiles, leather, clothing, and footwear	29.5	13	25.8	12	31.7	12	54.4	7	43.9	6	51.3	4
Paper, printing, and publishing	85.8	2	65.3	4	79.9	3	97.3	1	63.6	4	96.2	1
Other manufacturing industries[a]	65.0	7	65.2	5	79.5	4	80.2	5	34.2	7	16.3	8
Financial[b]	45.5	11	–		–		36.1	9	–		49.6	5
Other activities												
Construction	41.7	12	35.4	11	75.3	6	41.7	8	43.1	5	×	
Distributive trades	80.2	3	62.4	6	67.7	8	86.8	3	86.6	2	79.3	3
Total non-manufacturing	55.7		57.2		63.0		67.1		90.4		81.0	
All industries	74.5		72.6		78.9		91.0		73.2		51.6	
Aggregate outward/inward FDI %	168.3		175.5		153.6		83.5		57.7		34.8	
Percentage of total FDI:												
Outward[c]	100.0		100.0		100.0		28.0		19.6		12.6	
Inward[c]	100.0		100.0		100.0		56.4		59.5		55.6	

(Continued)

Table 7.2 (continued)

	Canada						European Economic Community (9)					
	1981		1978		1974		1981		1978		1974	
Industry group	IIFDI	Rank	IIFDI	Rank	IIFDI	Rank	IIFDI	Rank	IIFDI	Rank	IIFDI	Rank
Resource-based	N.A.	—	N.A.	—	N.A.	—	N.A.	—	N.A.	—	N.A.	—
Manufacturing	80.0		57.5		85.1		61.3		59.9		59.0	
Food, drink, and tobacco	81.6	2	52.1	5	91.1	2	39.8	9	50.1	2	18.0	9
Chemicals and allied industries	24.6	8	15.0	8	7.4	7	45.4	8	39.9	5	54.7	4
Rubber	—		—		—		58.6	5	×		×	
Metal manufacture	73.8	4	—		×		54.6	6	36.2	7	×	
Mechanical and instrument engineering	57.6	5	69.2	2	20.2	5	84.2	2	43.7	4	36.5	8
Electrical engineering	2.3	11	13.9	9	×		74.0	3	×		76.5	1
Motor vehicle manufacture	9.5	10	×		×		24.8	10	×		×	
Textiles, leather, clothing, and footwear	15.2	9	—		×		1.2	11	37.3	6	54.1	5
Paper, printing, and publishing	77.4	3	97.0	1	94.4	1	64.6	4	49.8	3	72.3	2
Other manufacturing industries[a]	38.9	6	29.1	7	13.4	6	45.7	7	33.1	8	39.5	7
Financial[b]	97.0	1	62.9	4	51.2	4	×		—		×	
Other activities												
Construction	—		30.5	6	×		×		×		42.1	6
Distributive trades	33.3	7	63.4	3	56.5	3	93.7	1	55.1	1	60.7	3
Total non-manufacturing	29.0		47.1		27.9		67.9		65.2		78.2	
All industries	63.8		54.2		61.9		64.0		61.8		66.1	
Aggregate outward inward FDI %	13.5		269.0		222.9		212.5		223.6		202.6	
Percentage of total FDI:												
Outward[c]	6.7		6.5		9.3		19.2		23.6		21.7	
Inward[c]	5.2		4.3		6.4		15.2		18.6		16.5	

Industry Group	FRG 1981 IIFDI	1981 Rank	1978 IIFDI	1978 Rank	1974 IIFDI	1974 Rank
Resource-based	N.A.	—	N.A.	—	N.A.	—
Manufacturing						
Food, drink, and tobacco	37.1	—	20.8	—	28.4	—
Chemical and allied industries	0.4	—	38.8	4	×	—
Rubber	43.0	—	—	—	×	—
Metal manufacture	×	—	×	—	68.4	2
Mechanical and instrument engineering	49.5	5	41.3	3	36.5	4
Motor vehicle manufacture	38.5	6	—	—	×	—
Textiles, leather, clothing, and footwear	69.3	2	×	—	54.6	3
Paper, printing, and publishing	3.2	7	4.2	6	33.3	5
Other manufacturing industries[a]	×	—	—	—	13.0	7
Financial[b]	—	—		—	×	—
Other activities						
Construction	80.3	1	62.7	2	93.8	1
Distributive trades	65.7	3	68.3	1	×	—
Total non-manufacturing	94.5	—	57.3	—	82.7	—
All industries	58.7	—	29.8	—	42.3	—
Aggregate outward/inward FDI %	240.9	—	571.0	—	372.5	—
Percentage of total FDI:						
Outward[c]	5.3	—	7.5	—	6.2	—
Inward[c]	3.7	—	2.3	—	2.6	—

Notes:

N.A. Not available.

— Signifies that either or both outward and inward FDI are less than an absolute value of £50,000.

× Signifies that both outward and inward FDI are greater than an absolute value of £50,000 but that either or both have been suppressed to avoid disclosure of data on individual enterprises.

[a] Includes shipbuilding.

[b] Excludes banking and insurance. Negative FDI positions are excluded.

[c] The values of total FDI were (for outward FDI) £M 28,545.1 (1981), £M 19,214.8 (1978), £M 10,117.8 (1974), and (for inward FDI) £M 16,962.0 (1981), £M 10,949.2 (1978) and £6,585.3 (1974), although certain of the earlier totals were later slightly revised by the UK Department of Trade and Industry.

Source: See Appendix B

Table 7.3 Estimates of intra-industry foreign direct investment for the Federal Republic of Germany, 1976–85

Industry group	World 1985 IIFDI	World 1985 Rank	World 1980 IIFDI	World 1980 Rank	USA 1985 IIFDI	USA 1985 Rank	USA 1980 IIFDI	USA 1980 Rank	European Community (9) 1976 IIFDI	EC 1976 Rank	EC 1985 IIFDI	EC 1985 Rank	EC 1980 IIFDI	EC 1980 Rank
Resource-based														
Mining and petroleum[a]	8.3	9	18.4	9	20.4	9	92.5	1	x	–	12.3	9	18.5	8
Manufacturing	83.2	7	97.1	–	95.7	–	67.6	6	N.A.	–	82.3	3	18.7	–
Chemical industry	53.9	3	63.3	8	49.2	6	61.6	8	87.3	1	63.5	1	62.1	4
Iron and steel production	68.9	4	84.9	3	58.0	5	29.7	8	x	–	99.5	6	37.3	7
Mechanical engineering[b]	67.0	5	96.8	1	78.7	4	87.4	3	30.0	4	55.3	8	89.1	1
Electrical engineering[b]	61.3	6	76.5	5	82.1	3	64.4	5	14.5	7	43.1	7	67.8	2
Road vehicle building	46.3	8	69.5	7	87.4	2	46.8	7	36.4	3	46.0	4	x	–
Banking and financial[c]	88.6	1	89.1	2	39.5	8	13.4	9	21.7	6	58.9	5	43.5	6
Other activities														
Distributive trades	66.9	5	80.0	4	47.3	7	91.4	2	29.2	5	55.4	2	67.8	2
Property administration[d]	71.2	2	69.9	6	98.2	1	81.3	4	48.5	2	66.4	5	57.0	5
All industries	74.8	–	91.9	–	86.4	–	76.4	–	40.9	–	74.0	–	88.7	–
Aggregate outward/inward FDI%	167.4	–	117.6	–	131.4	–	61.8	–	25.7	–	170.1	–	125.4	–
Percentage of total FDI:														
Outward[e]	100.0	–	100.0	–	30.3	–	21.6	–	13.7	–	30.7	–	33.9	–
Inward[e]	100.0	–	100.0	–	38.6	–	41.1	–	40.7	–	30.2	–	31.8	–

	UK					France					
	1985	1980		1976		1985		1980		1976	
Industry group	IIFDI	IIFDI	Rank	IIFDI	Rank	IIFDI	Rank	IIFDI	Rank	IIFDI	Rank
Resource-based											
Mining and petroleum[a]	—	—	—	—	—	×	—	×	—	×	—
Manufacturing	71.5	54.1	—	N.A.	—	48.0	—	49.4	—	N.A.	—
Chemical industry	80.0	91.1	1	87.2	3	34.0	5	34.0	7	41.8	4
Iron and steel production	25.6	73.2	3	×	—	79.9	2	91.3	1	90.6	1
Mechanical engineering[b]	44.3	77.0	2	98.7	1	20.7	8	40.2	6	40.6	5
Electrical engineering[b]	24.8	50.9	5	92.1	2	74.7	3	69.1	3	×	—
Road vehicle building	×	×	—	×	—	30.6	6	16.9	8	×	—
Banking and financial[c]	69.3	38.9	6	22.3	5	81.6	1	82.7	2	84.2	2
Other activies											
Distributive trades	50.1	59.4	4	41.3	4	49.3	4	56.4	4	26.4	6
Property administraation[d]	8.1	×	—	12.5	6	25.5	7	41.4	5	57.2	3
All industries	93.5	71.3	—	42.6	—	64.8	—	68.2	—	95.3	—
Aggregate outward/ inward FDI%	87.8	55.4	—	27.1	—	208.8	—	193.4	—	109.9	—
Percentage of total FDI:											
Outward[e]	4.8	3.9	—	2.8	—	7.9	—	10.3	—	9.7	—
Inward[e]	9.1	8.3	—	8.0	—	6.4	—	6.3	—	6.8	—

Notes:

N.A. Not available.

— Signifies that either or both outward and inward FDI are less than an absolute value of DM 500,000.

× Signifies that both outward and inward FDI are greater than an absolute value of DM 500,000, but that either or both have been suppressed to avoid disclosure of data on individual enterprises.

[a] Includes petroleum extraction but excludes petroleum processing.

[b] Prior to 1980 data-processing equipment (computing equipment) was included in electrical engineering, from 1980 it is included in mechanical engineering.

[c] Banks and investment companies only.

[d] Full description is 'Holding companies and other property administration'.

[e] The bases on which these outward and inward FDI data are assessed differ. Outward FDI includes both 'primary' and 'secondary' FDI, while inward FDI relates only to primary. Primary FDI refers to that directly controlled by a foreign parent, which may be fully consolidated and classified to country and industry. Secondary FDI is that maintained through holding companies of foreign investors, and can present consolidation and classification difficulties. The effect of this is to underestimate inward FDI; however this underestimation is less than 26% in aggregate in 1985. The values of total FDI in this table were (for outward FDI) DM M 147,794 (1985), DM M 84,361 (1980), DM M 48,516 (1976) and (for inward FDI) DM M 88,286 (1985), DM M 71,758 (1980) and DM M 63,531 (1976).

average IIFDI indices, partly reflecting the strongly market-orientated nature of these activities, with the same tending to be true in banking and finance. These tendencies recur in the data for other countries, indicating that the cause of IIFDI is industry-specific for these activities.

In Table 7.2 the UK indices for electrical engineering suggest substantial IIFDI. On disaggregation, this appears to be intra-European Community in nature, being more balanced with the EEC(9) than with Germany (or France) individually, and therefore may be evidence of rationalization as a cause of IIFDI within the EEC. A similar pattern seems to have developed in a rising UK–EEC index for mechanical and instruments engineering from 1974 to 1981.

A contrasting picture emerges for UK food, drink and tobacco, where relatively high IIFDI indices are recorded with the USA and Canada, but not with the rest of the EEC and especially not with Germany. This suggests IIFDI with North America based on similar tastes in final consumer products, and is more amenable to explanation by the assest advantage/impediments to trade account.

The least satisfactory data are for the Federal Republic of Germany (see Table 7.3), where the incomplete statistical consolidation of inward FDI causes an average underestimation of just less than 26 per cent in 1985. It seems clear, however, that Germany has rapidly increased its outward/inward FDI ratio over the period, especially with respect to the USA. By 1985 Germany was a net positive investor in the USA, across all the major industrial groups. Therefore, the trend away from balance in chemicals reflects this increase, while the growing balance in electrical engineering is part of the same process, but from a much lower IIFDI index. Again, this sort of development is more likely to reflect the growing asset advantages of German MNEs, together with the need to produce directly within the distant US market.

Within the EEC, German iron and steel production has the highest IIFDI index by 1985. If this reflects a rationalized investment pattern, then the relocation of production appears to have taken place away from the UK, where the IIFDI index fell markedly. The impression is that the dispersion of German manufacturing FDI within the EEC has not favoured the UK, although chemicals IIFDI remains high in the UK. This general picture is reinforced by both the mechanical and electrical engineering industries where, despite a classification change, IIFDI with the UK has fallen.

This pattern suggests that the UK may have been on the periphery of German rationalized FDI within the EEC, possibly owing to the net relative locational disadvantages of production within the UK. A contrast is evident in the banking sector, where IIFDI has increased with the UK.

Conclusions

The theoretical accounts advanced in this paper do seem to suit different industries, and different partner countries or regions. While it is evident that no hypothesis is supreme in explaining intra-industry FDI, the more simple asset advantage approach is best fitted to initial intra-industry FDI between the large trading units of the world: currently from Europe to the US (and possibly Japan to the US and Europe). However, within these continental markets, intra-industry FDI will increasingly be characterized by rationalized FDI. This process seems most advanced for FDI within the EEC (taken to be representative of Europe) both by native European firms and by US subsidiaries.

The asset advantage approach is likely to be a progressively incomplete description of intra-industry FDI; it helps to explain European FDI in the US but not US FDI in the EEC. Thus, the first two hypotheses are not true alternatives, and it is not surprising, therefore, that aggregate work to detect a single systematic relationship with intra-industry trade has not met with success. Because of the nature of the firms and industries concerned, and the geographical relationships between the partner countries, European and US FDI within Europe will tend to complement intra-industry trade. In the first instance, European intra-industry FDI in the USA may substitute for trade in final products. However, the European trade which is replaced may not be overwhelmingly intra-industry in nature because extensive US FDI in Europe is already in place.

Government policy on the parts of partner countries can act so as to increase intra-industry FDI. In the simplest case – local production requirements – regulations or any barriers to trade (specific to industries) can cause the substitution of intra-industry FDI for intra-industry trade. For those large established MNEs which have adopted world-wide sourcing policies, governmental monitoring of MNEs' individual balances of trade with hosts can also lead to further tendencies for intra-industry FDI to increase – in this case, together with intra-industry trade within the framework of rationalized FDI.

Although data on non-affiliate trade and licensing have not been included, it seems unlikely that these could have effectively substituted for intra-EEC, intra-industry FDI. The sort of restructuring generated via the MNE within continental markets is likely to be of this type. Between continental markets, intra-industry FDI may initially be substitutable, depending on the height of barriers to trade.

137

As MNEs become the prime agent in the transfer of production within Europe, competition between countries for inward FDI (or investment by their own native firms) is likely to intensify.

The inadequacies of the available data have been emphasized. To assess the true degree of authentic intra-industry competition via foreign operations, data at the level of the firm and specific product markets are required. This approach means surrendering the simultaneous coverage of all industrial sectors; however, this is already seen to produce unsatisfactory results. Only detailed research can establish the importance of the effect of market structure and, in particular, oligopoly, for foreign operations and, accordingly, the impact on industrial development.

Appendix 7.A

Table 7.A Concordance of the estimates of intra-industry foreign direct investment between the USA, UK and the FRG, 1980–1

i) *The USA and UK, 1980–1*

Industry group[a]	USA data		UK data	
	IIFDI	Rank	IIFDI	Rank
Manufacturing	58.9	–	77.9	–
Food and related products	88.4	2	84.7	3
Chemicals and allied products	99.1	1	92.8	1
Metal manufacture	66.7	5	26.6	7
Mechanical engineering[b]	39.7	7	35.8	5
Electrical engineering	68.5	4	57.3	4
Finance[c]	64.4	6	36.1	6
Distribution	84.3	3	86.8	2
All industries	64.7	–	91.0	–
Aggregate US outward/inward FDI %	209.0	–	119.8	–

ii) *The USA and FRG, 1980*

Industry group[a]	USA data		FRG data	
	IIFDI	Rank	IIFDI	Rank
Manufacturing	56.9	–	67.6	–
Chemicals and allied products	90.5	1	61.6	4
Metal manufacture	65.0	4	29.7	6
Mechanical engineering[b,d]	25.8	5	87.4	2
Electrical engineering[d]	70.7	3	64.4	3
Transportation equipment	22.3	6	46.8	5
Banking[e]	8.7	7	13.4	7
Distribution	89.0	2	91.4	1
All industries	65.2	–	76.4	–
Aggregate US outward/inward FDI %	207.0	–	161.8	–

iii) *The UK and FRG, 1980–1*

Industry group[a]	UK data		FRG data	
	IIFDI	Rank	IIFDI	Rank
Manufacturing	37.1	–	54.1	–
Chemicals and allied products	43.0	4	91.1	1
Mechanical engineering[c]	49.5	3	77.0	3
Electrical engineering[c]	51.9	2	50.9	4
Distribution	65.7	1	59.4	3
All industries	58.7	–	71.3	–
Aggregate UK outward/inward FDI %	240.9	–	180.5	–

Notes:
[a] Industry groups may differ significantly between countries despite similar names. The descriptions in this table have been simplified for intelligibility only, and the full titles remain as found in Tables 6.1, 6.2, and 6.3.
[b] US mechanical engineering includes computing equipment.
[c] UK finance excludes insurance.
[d] Prior to 1980 data-processing equipment (computing equipment) was included in FRG electrical engineering; from 1980 it is included in mechanical engineering
[e] US figure is for banking only while the German figure includes banks and investment companies.
Source: As for Tables 7.1, 7.2 and 7.3

Appendix 7.B

Sources of statistical data

USA

Department of Commerce, Bureau of Economic Analysis (1985) *US Direct Investment Abroad: 1982 Benchmark Survey Data*, December, Washington, DC: US Government Printing Office.
Department of Commerce, Bureau of Economic Analysis (1982) *US Direct Investment Abroad 1977–80*, updated material on computer printout from the *Survey of Current Business*, September, Washington, DC.
Department of Commerce, Bureau of Economic Analysis (1982) *Selected Data on US Direct Investment Abroad, 1950–76*, February, Washington, DC.
Department of Commerce, Bureau of Economic Analysis (1983) *Foreign Direct Investment in the United States*, 1980, October, Washington, DC: US Government Printing Office.
Department of Commerce, Bureau of Economic Analysis (1976) *Foreign Direct Investment in the United States, Volume 2: Report of the Secretary of Commerce: Benchmark Survey, 1974*, April, Washington, DC: US Government Printing Office.

UK

Department of Trade and Industry, Business Statistics Office (1984) *Business Monitor M A4, 1981 Supplement, Census of Overseas Assets, 1981*, London: HMSO.
Department of Industry, Business Statistics Office (1981) *Business Monitor M A4, 1978 Supplement, Census of Overseas Assets, 1978*, London: HMSO.
Department of Industry, Business Statistics Office (1977) *Business Monitor M4, 1974 Supplement, Census of Overseas Assets, 1974*, London: HMSO.

FRG

Deutsche Bundesbank (1987) *Die Kapitalverflechtung der Unternehmen mit dem Ausland nach Ländern und Wirtschaftszweigen 1979 bis 1985*, annex to *Statistical Supplements of the Monthly Report of the Deutsche Bundesbank, Series 3, Balance of Payments Statistics* 3, March.
Deutsche Bundesbank (1983) *Die Kapitalverflechtung der Unternehmen mit dem Ausland nach Ländern und Wirtschaftszweign 1976 bis 1981*, annex to *Statistical Supplements of the Monthly Report of the Deutsche Bundesbank, Series 3, Balance of Payments Statistics* 6, June.
Deutsche Bundesbank (1979) 'The level of direct investment at the end of 1976', *Monthly Report of the Deutsche Bundesbank* 31, 4 April: 26–40.

Acknowledgement

I am grateful to Dr Fred Meyer, University of Exeter, for helpful comments on a previous draft of this chapter.

Notes

1. Intra-industry FDI can be described as reciprocal FDI between two countries within the same industry, where the firms concerned are in competition. A discussion of this definition appears in the section on the definition and measurement of intra-industry FDI.
2. Hymer's approach presumed that licensing was precluded (see Clegg 1987, Ch. 2).
3. This also has implications for the relationship between trade and FDI, which is examined in the following section on intra-industry FDI and intra-industry trade.
4. The value of FDI is usually calculated as the share in the book value of the net assets of the foreign affiliate. Such a procedure is liable to

misrepresent the value of capital acutally controlled by the parent enterprise.

References

Aquino, A. (1978) 'Intra-industry trade and intra-industry specialisation as concurrent sources of international trade in manufactures', *Weltwirtschaftliches Archiv* 114, 2: 275–96.

Buckley, P. J. and Casson, M. C. (1976) *The Future of the Multinational Enterprise*, London: Macmillan.

Cantwell, J. A. (1987) 'Technological competition and intra-industry production in Europe', *University of Reading Discussion Papers in International Investment and Business Studies* 106, October.

Casson, M. C. (1987) *The Firm and the Market: Studies on Multinational Enterprise and the Scope of the Firm*, Oxford: Blackwell.

Caves, R.E. (1986) Review of Erdilek, A. (ed.) (1985) *Multinationals as Mutual Invaders: Intra-industry Direct Foreign Investment*, New York: St Martin's Press, In *Journal of International Business Studies*, Summer: 182–4.

Clegg, I. J. (1987) *Multinational Enterprise and World Competition: A Comparative Study of the USA, Japan, the UK, Sweden and West Germany*, London: Macmillan.

Dunning, J. H. (1977) 'Trade, location of economic activity and the MNE: a search for an eclectic approach', Chapter 12 in B. Ohlin, P.-O. Hesselborn, and Wijkman (eds), *The International Allocation of Economic Activity*, London: Macmillan.

—— (1981a) 'Explaining the international direct investment position of countries: towards a dynamic developmental approach', *Weltwirtschaftliches Archiv* 117, 1: 30–64.

——(1981b) 'A note on intra-industry foreign direct investment', *Banca Nazionale del Lavoro Quarterly Review* 139, December: 427–37.

——(1986) 'The Investment Development Cycle Revisited', *Weltwirtschaftliches Archiv* 122, 4: 667–76.

Dunning, J. H. and Norman, G. (1985) 'Intra-industry production as a form of international economic involvement: an exploratory analysis', Chapter 1 in A. Erdilek (ed.) *Multinationals as Mutual Invaders: Intra-industry Direct Foreign Investment*, London: Croom Helm.

——(1986) 'Intra-industry investment' in H. P. Gray (ed.), *Research in International Business and Finance*, vol. 5: *Uncle Sam as Host*, Greenwich, Conn.: JAI Press.

Erdilek, A. (1985) 'Introduction', in A. Erdilek (ed.), *Multinationals as Mutual Invaders: Intra-industry Direct Foreign Investment*, London: Croom Helm.

Graham, E.M. (1974) *Oligopolistic Reaction and European Direct Investment in the United States*, DBA thesis, Harvard Business School.

—— (1978) 'Transatlantic Investment by Multinational Firms: A

Rivalistic Phenomenon?', *Journal of Post Keynesian Economics* I, 1, Fall: 82–99.

Greenaway, D. and Milner, C. (1986) *The Economics of Intra-Industry Trade* Oxford: Blackwell.

Grubel, H. G. and Lloyd, P. J. (1975) *Intra-Industry Trade: The Theory and Measurement of International Trade in Differentiated Products*, London: Macmillan.

Hymer, S. H. (1960) *The International Operations of National Firms: A Study of Direct Foreign Investment*, PhD thesis, MIT, 1960, Cambridge, Mass.: MIT Press, 1976.

Juhl, P. (1985) 'The Federal Republic of Germany', Chapter 4 in J. H. Dunning (ed.) *Multinational Enterprises, Economic Structure and International Competitiveness*, Geneva: Wiley/IRM.

Knickerbocker, F. T. (1973) *Oligopolistic Reaction and Multinational Enterprise*, Boston: Harvard University Press.

Kogut, B. (1983) 'Foreign direct investment as a sequential process', in C. P. Kindleberger and D. Audretsch (eds) *The Multinational Corporation in the 1980s*, Cambridge, Mass.: MIT Press.

Norman, G. and Dunning, J. H. (1984) 'Intra-industry foreign direct investment: its rationale and trade effects', *Weltwirtschaftliches Archiv* 120, 3: 522–40.

Pugel, T. A. (1985) 'The United States', Chapter 2 in J. H. Dunning (ed.) *Multinational Enterprises, Economic Structure and International Competitiveness*, Geneva: Wiley/IRM.

Rugman, A. M. (1979) *International Diversification and the Multinational Enterprise*, Lexington, Mass.: D.C. Heath.

—— (1985) 'The determinants of intra-industry direct foreign investment', Chapter 2 in A. Erdilek (ed.) *Multinationals as Mutual Invaders: Intra-Industry Direct Foreign Investment*, London: Croom Helm.

Stopford, J. M. and Dunning, J. H. (1983) *Multinationals: Company Performance and Global Trends*, London: Macmillan.

Teece, D. J. (1980) 'Economies of scope and the scope of the enterprise', *Journal of Economic Behaviour and Organisation* 1: 223–47.

—— (1983) 'Technological and organisational factors in the theory of multinational enterprise', Chapter 3 in M. C. Casson (ed.) *The Growth of International Business*, London: Allen & Unwin.

Chapter Eight

Restructuring among the largest firms: changing geographical and industrial diversification, 1977–82

Robert D. Pearce

Introduction

The substantial, and in many respects unpredicted, changes in the structure of international comparative advantage over the past quarter century have been extensively documented and closely analyzed. Also well recognized is the fact that the broadly based potential benefits from such an evolution in the distribution of international competitiveness cannot be fully realized without substantial structural adjustments within the traditional industrial economies. The latter point frequently develops into the discussion of, adjustment to, or protection against, the rise of major new forces in international trade as the operative alternatives facing the established industrial economies. In an important contribution to the latter debate, Franko (1981) argues that the ease of such adjustment in OECD countries (and by implication the likely degree of pressure for protection) depends on five principal characteristics of an industry's structure in these developed economies (see Franko 1981: 488). Two of these characteristics in fact relate to particular attributes of the leading firms in the industry; these being, in essence, what we refer to in this chapter as their level of geographical and industrial diversification.

It may be argued that the greater the degree of multinational spread of a firm's existing productive activity, the greater the scope that exists for intra-firm adjustment to forces that challenge particularly vulnerable parts of the group's operations. Where an enterprise has an extensive geographically dispersed range of productive units, it is likely to have the option of expanding at a site that retains competitiveness, whilst retreating in those that do not.[1] It could further be argued that firms with an established, globally dispersed, production network are likely to have developed, in acquiring that network, an expertise in evaluating locations and implementing changes which enhances their willingness to choose the route of intra-firm adjustment. A familiar example of such adjustment exists where MNEs have transferred parts of their production processes to the newly industrializing countries which have been prominent in the changing structure of international comparative advantage. Where such adjustments are viable, the implication is that the established *firms* retain certain competitive assets (ownership advantages), but find their established *locations* increasingly uncompetitive as bases for realizing their potential.

By an analogous line of argument, firms with an existing range of industrial activities might find an internal adjustment of the balance in this 'portfolio' a viable, and preferable, response to the problems of part of the range, as compared to the pursuit of artificial protection.

The analysis in this chapter focuses on the performance over the years 1977–82 of samples of the world's leading enterprises,[2] with respect to the geographical and industrial diversification of their activity. The information available does not allow us to evaluate the diversification performance of the enterprises covered in terms of the potential available to them. Nor can we draw any conclusions with respect to the extent to which the achievements in diversification did mitigate any protectionist pressure which might have emanated from these firms, had such routes for growth not been available. Nevertheless, it is hoped to document certain important aspects of the performance of major enterprises during a period when they were faced with continuing pressure from the evolution of a 'new international division of labour', and also by the emergence of a period of general recession.

Broad aggregates indicate increasing diversification by leading enterprises between 1977 and 1982. Thus a sample of 355 firms had 24.4 per cent of their sales outside their main industry in 1982, compared with 22.8 per cent in 1977.[3] Similarly, a sample of 308 firms had 33.6 per cent of their production outside their parent country in 1982, compared with 31.2 per cent in 1977.[4] Less notably, a sample of 232 firms exported 19.9 per cent of parent country production in 1982 compared with 19.5 per cent in 1977.[4] The purpose of the ensuing analysis is to attempt to discern the extent to which these broad aggregates reflect significant pervasive tendencies at the firm level, and to investigate other firm-level aspects of diversification performance.

Change in industrial diversification ratio

It is the purpose of this section to seek to detect significant trends in the industrial diversification of leading enterprises during the period 1977 to 1982. The sample consists of 355 firms for which 'the industrial diversification ratio' (IDR) was available for both 1977 (IDR_{77}) and 1982 (IDR_{82}). The IDR is defined as the percentage of a firm's total sales which consist of goods or services from an industry other than its main industry.[5]

The dependent variable tested is the 'change in industrial diversification ratio' (CIDR) between 1977 and 1982, i.e. $IDR_{82}-IDR_{77}$. In the first phase of our analysis, we simply test to see if, across the 355 firms, the behaviour of CIDR fulfils certain criteria which we consider to constitute evidence of a significant general tendency towards increasing or decreasing industrial diversification over the period covered. Since CIDR takes the form of the number of percentage points change in IDR, we would suggest that strong evidence of, for example, a generalized increase in IDR between 1977 and 1982 would require a positive relationship between CIDR (as the dependent variable) and IDR_{77} as an independent variable. Thus we expect larger values of CIDR for firms with larger established levels of IDR. However, since this may be considered a particularly exacting criteria for firms with very high values of IDR_{77}, the equation is also run in a quadratic form to allow for a possible weakening of any relationship between IDR_{77} and CIDR at higher values of IDR_{77}. Since IDR_{77} is the only independent variable, it is also possible to interpret significant values of the intercept in terms of the relationship between IDR_{77} and CIDR. Thus, in this phase, the two regressions run are equations 1.A.1 (linear) and 1.A.2 (quadratic), with IDR_{77} as the sole independent variable.

In the second phase, dummy variables are added for industry (twenty industries are covered) and for area/nationality (five area/nationalities are covered). This serves two purposes. First, by normalizing for industry and area, the relationship between IDR_{77} and CIDR becomes that within industries and within areas, with the influence of inter-industry or inter-area differences removed. Second, the results for the dummy variables themselves provide evidence of significant industry or area influences on CIDR. In the case of industry, 'electronics and electrical appliances' is the omitted dummy, so that significant positive or negative coefficients on other dummies suggest significantly higher or lower values of CIDR for those industries compared with 'electronics etc.'. Similarly, for areas significantly positive or negative, coefficients are interpreted relative to the omitted area, i.e. USA. The two equations incorporating IDR_{77} and dummies are designated as 1.B.1 (IDR_{77} linear) and 1.B.2 (IDR_{77} quadratic). Since IDR_{77} is still the only non-dummy variable included, it remains (as with the first phase equations) possible to interpret significant values of the intercept.

In the third phase, we add two more variables to the equations,

145

which may help explain CIDR. The first of these is the size of the firm in 1977, i.e. total sales in 1977 (TS_{77}). This is hypothesized to have a positive relationship to CIDR for fairly conventional reasons. The larger a firm is, the more likely it is to seek to diversify industrially, due to approaching saturation of its established markets, or in some cases a feeling that substantial further expansion in its main activity might involve competitive measures that could destabilize existing oligopolistic balance in undesirable ways. Further, the larger a firm the more likely it is to have the resources (financial; managerial; marketing, technological) to facilitate industrial diversification.

The second additional explanatory variable is the rate of growth (1977/82) of the firm's main activity (RGMA), i.e. the growth rate of its sales in its main industry. This is likely to be related to CIDR in a number of ways, which provide us with an hypothesis of a negative relationship between RGMA and CIDR. First, a firm with below average RGMA and some existing industrial diversification may well find CIDR increasing, without any positive decision or action being taken to encourage this. Thus, if the firm's existing diversified activities are into industries with generally healthier growth performance, these 'outside' activities are likely to grow faster than 'mainstream' activities, thus providing a rise in CIDR. This type of influence may be reflected both at the industry and firm level. Generally, other things being equal, rising CIDR would be expected to be more visible in industries with poor growth in their mainstream activities than in those with predominantly healthier performance. This may be detected in the industry dummy variables in equations 1.B.1 and 1.B.2, i.e. before RGMA is included at the firm level. Moreover, within industries, we would also expect those firms with below average RGMA to have a higher CIDR than those with above average RGMA.

The second reason for predicting a negative relationship between RGMA and CIDR is simply that we would expect those firms with the least healthy performance in their established mainstream activities to make the greatest deliberate efforts to encourage their diversified lines, and to enter new areas providing potentially better prospects. A third factor which needs to be considered concerns the nature of the firm's strengths or weaknesses. The lines of argument pursued above have tended to assume that above or below average RGMA is determined predominantly by factors relating specifically to these mainstream activities, i.e. product-line-specific factors. Where diversified activities provided the potential for better growth performance, the firm was assumed to be capable of taking up such opportunities. However, if poor performance in mainstream activity reflected firm-wide weaknesses, e.g. general financial vulnerability or poor top management, it is unlikely that diversified activities would perform any better. Indeed, where firm-level weaknesses, especially management, predominate, it may be the diversified lines that are most affected, possibly because they may be the ones with which management is least familiar, and also because they are likely to be the most vulnerable if a weakness in co-ordination is a particular manifestation of an uncompetitive top management. Thus, the more important are firm-wide strengths or weaknesses, compared to those at the product-line level, the weaker is likely to be our predicted negative relationship between RGMA and CIDR.

The equations adding TS_{77} and RGMA are designated as 1.C.1. (all non-dummy variables in linear form) and 1.C.2. (all non-dummy variables in quadratic form).

The results in Table 8.1 suggest that there has been a significant tendency amongst the largest industrial enterprises towards increasing industrial diversification, though not in precisely the form projected in our hypotheses. Amongst the statistically significant results, only equation 1.A.2 provides the positive relationship between IDR_{77} and CIDR. Even in that case, the relationship is not linear and the coefficients indicate a turning point well within the range of values taken by IDR_{77}, though CIDR is likely to remain positive for most values of IDR_{77}. This result, taken with the existence in other equations of significant positive intercepts but negative signs for IDR_{77}, suggests that, generally, industrial diversification increased amongst the largest firms between 1977 and 1982, but that this proved easier to achieve for those firms with lower levels of diversification at the start of the period. Firms already substantially committed to industrial diversification found it relatively hard to achieve further diversification.

Firm size (TS_{77}) had no significant influence on CIDR. The results do provide strong support for our hypothesis of a negative relationship between RGMA and CIDR; although both terms are significant in the quadratic, so that the relationship weakens at high values of RGMA.

An explanation may be suggested for this non-linear result for RGMA. In terms of the hypotheses introduced earlier with respect to RGMA, the strong negative relationship at low values of RGMA implies that firms with poor performance in their mainstream activities nevertheless possess the ability to realize the potential for higher rates of growth in other, diversified, lines of activity. By contrast it may be that those firms with notably above average RGMA, where the negative relationship with CIDR has become much weaker, only achieve this exceptional performance by backing a distinctive strength in their main product lines with a general firm-

147

Table 8.1 Regressions with CIDR as dependent variable

Equation	1.A.1	1.A.2	1.B.1	1.B.2	1.C.1	1.C.2
IDR_{77}	−0.32777; D-1 (−1.6246)	0.11402* (1.7077)	−0.46655; D-1** (−2.1984)	0.88841; D-1 (1.2762)	−0.34950; D-1* (−1.6874)	0.10359 (1.5552)
IDR^2_{77}		−0.2472; D-2** (−2.3050)		−0.22751; D-2** (−2.0427)		−0.24280; D-2** (−2.2767)
RGMA					−0.38386; D-1*** (−4.8371)	−0.10068*** (−5.6968)
$RGMA^2$						0.26741; D-3*** (3.9326)
TS_{77}					−0.48515; D-4 (−0.65264)	−0.18268; D-3 (−1.0285)
TS^2_{77}						0.29188; D-8 (0.76326)
Food[a]			−3.1416 (−1.5887)	−3.0897 (−1.5698)	−3.4426* (−1.7929)	−3.6355* (−1.9383)
Paper and wood products			−3.8420* (−1.6978)	−3.7687* (−1.6732)	−5.1045** (−2.3017)	−5.7960*** (−2.6513)
Industrial and agricultural chemicals			−2.5441 (−1.3606)	−2.6051 (−1.3997)	−3.5206* (−1.9275)	−4.1847** (−2.3319)
Petroleum			−6.2966*** (−3.0096)	−6.5671*** (−3.1476)	3.3817 (−1.5416)	3.0182 (−1.3926)

	(1)	(2)	(3)	(4)	(5)	(6)
Rubber			−3.9278	−4.8210	−6.0300	−8.9311**
			(−0.9691)	(−1.1883)	(−1.5260)	(−2.2819)
Motor vehicles			−1.9591	−1.9314	−2.6156	−3.7946**
			(−0.9857)	(−0.9764)	(−1.3473)	(−1.9771)
Aerospace			−6.2226*	−5.6396*	−5.2268*	−4.3202
			(−1.9396)	(−1.7593)	(−1.6775)	(−1.4150)
Industrial and farm equipment			−5.9518***	−5.6453***	−5.8646***	−7.2966***
			(−3.0115)	(−2.8618)	(−3.0486)	(−3.7686)
Pharmaceuticals and consumer chemicals			−3.9456*	−4.4857**	−3.8254*	−4.3238**
			(−1.8757)	(−2.1258)	(−1.8691)	(−2.1306)
UK			4.1052***	3.9549***	4.4083***	4.6913***
			(2.7079)	(2.6182)	(2.9965)	(3.2548)
Rest of the world			−2.7289	−3.0107	−1.9208	−3.7855**
			(−1.3841)	(−1.5306)	(−1.0015)	(−1.9706)
Intercept	2.4475***	1.3391	5.1758***	4.2936**	7.4164***	9.2726***
	(3.6967)	(1.6430)	(3.1663)	(2.5509)	(4.3920)	(4.9831)
R^2	0.0074	0.0222	0.1239	0.1349	0.1823	0.2288
F	2.639	3.992**	1.944***	2.051***	2.813***	3.325***

Notes: In the notation D·X, X is the number of noughts to be inserted after the decimal point, e.g. 0.2472; D·2 reads 0.002472.
Figures in parentheses are t values.
* = significant at 10 per cent; ** = significant at 5 per cent; *** = significant at 1 per cent.
ᵃOnly dummy variables significant at 10 per cent, or better in at least one equation are reported.

wide managerial and organizational strength. This firm-level strength makes it possible to obtain a level of performance among diversified activities comparable to that in main activities. Thus, high RGMA does not imply low CIDR to the same extent as low RGMA implies high CIDR. A further implication of this interpretation of the non-linear relationship between RGMA and CIDR is that the differences in growth performance among the world's largest enterprises seem to stem more from specific strengths and weaknesses relating to their major established product lines than from more basic firm-level factors, e.g. top management.

In equations 1.B, five industries have significant negative coefficients, indicating a lower increase in CIDR than the omitted industry, 'electronics and electrical appliances'. Two of these, 'petroleum' and 'aerospace', were industries with average RGMA well above that of 'electronics etc.', so that this may be suggested as an explanation of their low CIDR. The diminished significance of these dummies (especially petroleum) in equations 1.C, where RGMA is incorporated independently at the firm level, tends to support this suggestion. Of the other industries two, 'paper and wood products' and 'industrial and farm equipment', had low CIDR despite average RGMA well below that of 'electronics'. Here other influences limit their ability to diversify effectively, a possibility being that the low R&D intensity of these industries, compared to electronics, may generate less knowledge applicable to other industries as a basis for diversification. The possible forces behind the low CIDR for 'pharmaceuticals and consumer chemicals' are less easily suggested. This industry's average RGMA is very similar to that for electronics, but whilst it is an industry notable for its high R&D, the specialized and consumer-oriented nature of this R&D may make it less likely to provide offshoots with diversification potential than some other industries.

Four industries ('food', 'industrial and agricultural chemicals', 'rubber', 'motor vehicles') become significantly negative in equations 1.C.1 and/or 1.C.2. All of these were industries with below average RGMA, an influence conducive to high CIDR which appears to have offset other factors encouraging lower CIDR in equations 1.B. Once RGMA is allowed for at the firm level, the influences against industrial diversification in these industries predominate.

The most notable result for the nationality/area dummies is the persistently positive coefficient for the UK, indicating a higher CIDR for UK firms than for the omitted nationality, i.e. USA. The regression results provide no strong suggestion as to the factors encouraging industrial diversification among UK firms. Thus the dummy remains strongly positive when RGMA is included as an independent variable, whilst the inclusion of industry dummies removes any possible influence of the industrial composition of the UK sample.[6]

Regressions 1.B and 1.C were re-run, omitting the industry dummies. F-tests on the difference in explanatory power of the restricted and original regressions were significant at either 5 per cent or 10 per cent. This suggests that inter-industry differences were a significant influence on CIDR. The fact that the F values were of similar significance when testing for exclusion of industry dummies from 1.B (when RGMA was not included in the regression) and 1.C (with RGMA in the equation) suggests that inter-industry differences in average growth rates was not one of the more influential industry characteristics. When a similar procedure was adopted with respect to nationality/area, omitting these dummies from regressions 1.B and 1.C was significant in F-tests at 1 per cent or 5 per cent. The results also suggested that differential growth rates were not among the more crucially influential of the nationality/area characteristics influencing CIDR.

The regressions were also run for sub-samples of US, UK, and other European firms. In all three cases, the results suggested some tendency towards increased industrial diversification. For the US, significantly positive intercepts combined with negative signs on IDR_{77}, in a manner which indicated positive CIDR over the range of values taken by IDR_{77}. For both UK and other European sub-samples, IDR_{77} was never significant, but evidence of increasing industrial diversification was found in positive intercepts.

TS_{77} was not found to be significant in any of the sub-samples. RGMA was significantly negatively related to CIDR for both US and UK firms, but was not significant for the sub-samples for other European firms.

For the US sub-sample, a number of industry dummies are significant, though, as for the full sample, this is often dependent upon the composition of the rest of the equation. Only 'industrial and farm equipment' remains significantly negative when RGMA is either included or excluded from the equation. Petroleum is significantly negative when RGMA is excluded, but becomes insignificant when RGMA is included at the firm level. By contrast 'paper and wood products' only becomes significantly negative when RGMA is included; this also applies to 'industrial and agricultural chemicals' and 'rubber', but only in the quadratic equation – the dummies remaining insignificant in the linear version. None of the industry dummies are significant in the UK regressions. In the sample of other European firms, petroleum is marginally significantly negative (at 10 per cent) in equation 1.B.1, and just misses significance in other equations. The fact that the petroleum dummy is virtually unaffected by the inclusion or exclusion of RGMA from the equation (by contrast with the full and USA sample) is further indication that differential rates of growth of main activity have less influence on changing industrial diversification for continental European firms. F-tests on the industry dummies proved insignificant for all these area/nationality samples. This was so, whether the test related to the addition of industry dummies to an equation including or excluding RGMA.

The regressions were run separately for each of the eight industries[7] for which more than twenty observations were available. A significant positive trend towards increased diversification was found in one industry, 'electronics and electrical appliances', whilst a tendency towards lower IDR was indicated in 'industrial and farm equipment' and 'petroleum'. No statistically significant tendency was discerned in the other industries. In only one industry, 'industrial and agricultural chemicals', was TS_{77} significantly related to CIDR, the positive sign indicating that larger firms were more successful in industrial diversification than smaller ones. RGMA was found to be significantly negatively related to CIDR in 'food', 'metal manufacturing and products', 'industrial and agricultural chemicals', and 'pharmaceuticals and consumer chemicals'. Two of the industries where RGMA was not significant, 'motor vehicles' and 'industrial and farm equipment', were industries of generally low growth in mainstream activity, which should (as in the case of 'food', 'metals', and 'industrial and agricultural chemicals') have permitted the firms with lowest RGMA to have achieved higher values of CIDR through subsidiary operations in faster-growing sectors. As suggested in our earlier hypothesizing with respect to RGMA, the fact that this did not happen in 'motor vehicles' and 'industrial and farm equipment' may indicate pervasive firm-level (rather than, or in addition to, main-product-specific) weaknesses in these industries, which limit the ability to achieve and co-ordinate potential diversifications. In the case of 'electronics and electrical appliances' a different explanation for the insignificance of RGMA may be suggested. Since this is, generally, an industry of average RGMA performance, the notably strong trend towards increased industrial diversification seems likely to reflect other industrial characteristics; perhaps the creation of a healthy number of potential opportunities for diversification through the industry's notable commitment to R&D and innovation. Such strong influences on industrial diversification appear, in the case of 'electronics and electrical appliances', to overwhelm the influence of growth rates of mainstream activity, leaving RGMA insignificant. In the case of 'petroleum', RGMA is consistently positively signed and in equation 1.C.1 approaches significance. Thus, though we suggest that the very high growth rates of main activity which predominate in this industry contribute to the tendency to low or declining industrial diversification, *within* the industry those firms with the highest RGMA also seem to possess the highest CIDR.

Change in overseas production ratio

In this section we analyze trends in the internationalization of production by leading enterprises during the period 1977 to 1982, using procedures similar to those adopted in our discussion of changing industrial diversification. The sample consists of 308 firms for which the 'overseas production ratio' (OPR) was available for both 1977 (OPR_{77}) and for 1982 (OPR_{82}). The OPR is defined as the percentage of a firm's total production which is carried on outside its home country.

The dependent variable tested is the 'change in overseas production ratio' (COPR) between 1977 and 1982, i.e. $OPR_{82}-OPR_{77}$. As was the case for CIDR, our analysis develops through three phases. In the first of these, we simply seek to test for evidence of a significant tendency towards increasing or decreasing internationalization of production, with OPR_{77} serving as the only independent variable. Significant trends in OPR may be detected in the intercept and/or in significant relationships between OPR_{77} and COPR. The two regressions run in this phase are 2.A.1 (OPR_{77} linear) and 2.A.2 (OPR_{77} quadratic).

In the second phase, dummy variables are added for industry and for area/nationality; with 'electronics and electrical appliances' serving as the omitted industry, and USA as the omitted area, in the regressions. Significant coefficients on industry dummies therefore reflect a greater or lesser tendency towards increasing OPR compared to that for 'electronics and electrical appliances', and, for significant area/nationality dummies, a similar larger or smaller tendency compared to USA. With the proviso that values now reflect behaviour within industries and areas, we can still interpret results for OPR_{77} and the intercept in terms of general trends in changing internationalization of production. The two equations incorporating OPR_{77} and dummies are designated as 2.B.1 (OPR_{77} linear) and 2.B.2 (OPR_{77} quadratic).

In the third phase, we add two further variables – in this case with the hope that they may contribute to explaining the behaviour of the dependent variable COPR. Our hypothesis with respect to the first of these, TS_{77} (the firm's total sales in 1977), is that it would be positively related to COPR. The larger the firm, the more likely it is to have outgrown its home market and to be seeking to expand productive activity in other areas. Further, the greater resources available to larger firms should make it easier for them to implement any such desired spread of productive assets.

The second explanatory variable added in the third phase is the firm's rate of growth of production in its home country between 1977 and 1982 (RGHP). The lines of argument relating to the potential relationships between RGHP and COPR are closely analogous to those discussed in some detail earlier with respect to RGMA and CIDR, and again lead to an hypothesis of a negative relationship. If a firm already has some existing overseas productive operations, then, the lower is RGHP, the more likely it is that, even without conscious encouragement or stimulation, overseas production will grow faster than that at home thus causing OPR to rise. This type of influence may also be visible in equations 2.B.1 and 2.B.2, i.e. before growth of home production is incorporated at the firm level. In that case, areas where below average values of RGHP predominate would be expected to reveal higher values of COPR.

Further, firms with below average RGHP will be those most likely to deliberately seek to expand overseas production as an alternative route to growth. Indeed, expanding overseas production could be the *cause* of the low RGHP, if firms decide that a switch to overseas production sources has become a more profitable means of supplying a given market. Once again, this influence may also contribute to explaining any significant nationality/area dummies in equation 2.B. The negative relationship between RGHP and COPR, implied by the arguments just developed, may not emerge if the RGHP predominantly reflects firm-level strengths or weaknesses rather than explicit home-market performance. If, for example, low RGHP is caused by sources of vulnerability which will affect all the firm's operations, wherever located, then COPR may not rise in response. The equations adding TS_{77} and RGHP are designated as 2.C.1 and 2.C.2.

The regression results, reported in Table 8.2, are generally indicative of a significant trend to increasing internationalization of production among the world's largest enterprises. However, this result does derive from positive intercept values, and is not supported by our more strict criterion of a positive relationship between OPR_{77} and COPR. Indeed, the results indicate a negative relationship between COPR and OPR_{77}, though, taken in conjunction with the intercept values, the implication is of positive values of COPR over the range of OPR_{77}.

Table 8.2 Regressions with COPR as dependent variable

Equation	2.A.1	2.A.2	2.B.1	2.B.2	2.C.1	2.C.2
OPR_{77}	−0.47706; D-1** (−2.5502)	0.40971; D-1 (0.7726)	−0.77060; D-1*** (−3.5122)	0.76273; D-2 (0.1217)	−0.76896; D-1*** (−3.4386)	0.18958; D-2 (0.0299)
OPR^2_{77}		−0.11976; D-2* (−1.7863)		−0.10985; D-2 (−1.4430)		−0.11170; D-2 (−1.4290)
RGHP					−0.21955; D-1*** (−3.1033)	−0.42941; D-1*** (−3.7549)
$RGHP^2$						0.49915; D-4** (2.4027)
TS_{77}					0.72187; D-4 (0.9779)	−0.11841; D-3 (−0.6647)
TS^2_{77}						0.43028; D-8 (1.1681)
Paper and wood products[a]			−2.8845 (−1.3806)	−2.6592 (−1.2716)	−3.5214* (−1.7038)	−4.0346* (−1.9445)
UK firms			2.0389* (1.7940)	2.0517* (1.8087)	2.8462** (2.4348)	2.7700** (2.4348)
Other European firms			2.6432** (2.5137)	2.9222*** (2.7383)	2.6751*** (2.5882)	3.2145*** (3.0419)
Intercept	3.0840*** (5.0556)	2.1012** (2.5628)	3.3796** (2.3177)	2.0903 (1.2240)	4.7572*** (3.0959)	5.3574*** (2.8335)
R^2	0.0208	0.0308	0.1248	0.1312	0.1628	0.1859
F	6.504**	4.871***	1.681**	1.704**	2.101***	2.189***

Notes: In the notation D-X, X is the number of noughts to be inserted after the decimal point, e.g. 0.11976; D-2 reads 0.0011976. Figures in parentheses are t values.
* = significant at 10 per cent; ** = significant at 5 per cent; *** = significant at 1 per cent.
[a] Only dummy variables significant at 10 per cent, or better in at least one equation, are reported.

Size of firm (TS_{77}) was never significantly related to COPR. By contrast, the hypothesized negative relationship between RGHP and COPR is found consistently and strongly. Thus, even though both terms are significant in the quadratic, the coefficient values imply the persistence of the strongly negative relationship over the range of values taken by RGHP. This significant negative relationship may suggest that, in the main, the world's leading enterprises have the firm-level ability to realize the potential flexibility stemming from the internationalization of operations. Where home country production is particularly vulnerable (low RGHP), overseas activity can be stimulated (above average COPR) as an alternative, but when conditions are more favourable in home country production, this can be substituted for overseas activity (low COPR).

Only one industry dummy, 'paper and wood products', with a negative sign in equations 2.C, was found to be significant. The indication from this (that inter-industry differences have little influence on COPR) was confirmed when regressions 2.C were re-run, omitting the industry dummy variables. F-tests on the difference in explanatory power of the original and restricted regressions were not significant. By contrast, two of the nationality/area dummies, for UK and other Europe, were consistently positively significant. Our regressions provide no indication as to the factors enouraging the above-average trend towards internationalization of production by European firms. The average RGHP for both UK and other European sample firms was similar to that for USA firms, so this was unlikely to be an important influence. This tends to be confirmed by the fact that the dummies are relatively unaffected by the inclusion or exclusion of RGHP from the regressions. F-tests on these dummies are significant, indicating that inter-area differences are an important influence on OPR.

The regressions were re-run for sub-samples of USA, UK and other European firms. In each case, there is statistically significant evidence of a trend to rising OPR, though this is only found through positive intercepts; OPR_{77} is either insignificant or negative. TS was insignificant for UK and other European firms, but was significantly positive for US firms in equation 2.C.1. RGHP was only significantly negative for UK firms, though for US and other European firms it was consistently negatively signed and approached significance (at 10 per cent). There were few significant industry dummies, with 'petroleum' being negative for US firms, 'building materials' negative for UK firms, and 'motor vehicles' positive for other European firms. As this would have tended to indicate, F-tests on the explanatory power of the industry dummies were never significant in these area samples.

Change in parent firms' export ratio

In the light of the evidence of a fairly pervasive tendency to an increased internationalization of production, we proceed to investigate another possible contribution to changing internationalization of sales – namely, exports from the parent country. The sample consists of 232 firms for which the 'parent export ratio' (PER) was available for both 1977 (PER_{77}) and 1982 (PER_{82}). The PER is defined as the percentage of the firm's parent country production which is exported. In view of the tendency towards an increased importance of overseas production amongst leading enterprises, two possibilities may be distinguished with respect to exporting performance.

If the rise in overseas production predominantly reflects an initial aim of expanding overseas sales, then exporting, as an alternative means of achieving this end, may also rise in importance. If, however, firms see themselves as operating in a context of limited market growth, then the rise in overseas production may reflect a relocation of productive activity in search of the most competitive sources. Where this is so, the expanded overseas production may substitute, in particular, for home country exports, so that, alongside a rising OPR, the PER may be falling.

The dependent variable is the 'change in parent's export ratio' (CPER) i.e. $PER_{82}-PER_{77}$. The analysis proceeds in the usual three phases. Thus, equations 3.A.1 and 3.A.2 incorporate PER_{77} as independent variable in linear and quadratic form respectively. Equations 3.B.1 and 3.B.2 add industry and nationality/area dummies to equations 3.A.1 and 3.A.2. The additional independent variables added in the third phase are the size of the firm's parent-country operations (i.e. parent-country production in $1977 = PP_{77}$), and the rate of growth of the firm's home-country sales between 1977 and 1982 (RGHS).

In Table 8.3 the significant intercept in equation 3.A.1 is indicative of a general tendency to a rising PER. However, in equation 3.B.1, where we normalize for the industry and area composition of the sample, the significant values suggest that, whereas CPER was positive for firms with lower initial commitment to exporting, those with higher values of PER_{77} (above approximately 20 per cent) suffered a fall. The size of home-country operations (PP_{77}) was found to have no significant influence on changes in exporting performance. However, a clear negative relationship was found between RGHS and CPER, indicating that those firms with below-average sales-growth at home were, to some degree, able to compensate through exporting.

Table 8.3 Regressions with CPER as dependent variable

Equation	3.A.1	3.A.2	3.B.1	3.B.2	3.C.1	3.C.2
PER_{77}	−0.17121; D-1 (−0.9555)	0.71629; D-1 (1.3445)	−0.12774*** (−4.8593)	−0.97514; D-1 (−1.4532)	−0.10673*** (−4.1477)	−0.53831; D-1 (−0.8143)
PER^2_{77}		−0.12871; D-2* (−1.7679)		−0.38479; D-3 (−0.4898)		0.67190; D-3 (−0.8695)
RGHS					−0.32812; D-1*** (−4.3991)	−0.42363; D-1*** (−2.7273)
$RGHS^2$						0.40738; D-4 (0.6184)
PP_{77}					−0.13836; D-3 (−1.3856)	−0.24730; D-3 (−1.1420)
PP^2_{77}						0.30970; D-8 (0.5577)
Food[a]			−3.0871* (−1.8825)	−2.8769* (−1.6943)	−3.6698** (−2.3176)	−3.3960** (−2.0689)
Tobacco			3.6347 (1.2485)	3.7802 (1.2894)	4.5836 (1.6353)	4.9740* (1.7555)
Building materials			−2.6507 (−1.3575)	−2.4613 (−1.2343)	−3.9660** (−2.0847)	−3.8782** (−1.9841)
Metal manufacturing and products			2.9285* (1.9229)	2.9976* (1.9564)	1.2556 (0.8319)	1.1593 (0.7559)
Motor vehicles (including components)			2.8886* (1.6772)	2.8632* (1.6587)	1.5078 (0.8776)	1.1996 (0.6852)
Industrial and farm equipment			3.2157** (2.0065)	3.1995** (1.9923)	1.7234 (1.0932)	1.3933 (0.8636)
Other European firms			5.6028*** (4.2927)	5.4477*** (4.0492)	4.8527*** (3.8380)	4.6285*** (3.5369)
Rest of world			7.0888*** (3.1593)	6.9480*** (3.0659)	5.4181** (2.4779)	4.9075** (2.1970)
Intercept	1.6959*** (3.1335)	0.93852 (1.3635)	2.2780* (1.8417)	1.9884 (1.4481)	4.8864*** (3.6200)	4.9509*** (3.1905)
R^2	0.0040	0.0174	0.2204	0.2213	0.2886	2939
F	0.913	2.023	2.686***	2.571***	3.500***	3.144***

Notes: In the notation D-X, X is the number of noughts to be inserted after the decimal point. Figures in parentheses are t values.
* = significant at 10 per cent; ** = significant at 5 per cent; *** = significant at 1 per cent.
[a] Only dummy variables significant at 10 per cent or better in at least one equation are reported.

Amongst the industry dummies we find three cases, 'metal manufacturing and products', 'motor vehicles', and 'industrial and farm equipment', which are significantly positive in equations 3.B.1 and 3.B.2. These were industries with notably below-average RGHS, and it may be suggested that this, in conjunction with the ability to do at least somewhat better in export markets, made a strong contribution to the positive result. This is supported by the failure of each of the industries to achieve significance in equations 3.C.1 and 3.C.2, when RGHS is incorporated at the firm level. In the case of the two industries with significantly negative coefficients, the result seems likely to reflect specific problems or policies relating to exports. In 'building materials' the average RGHS is notably low, so that the negative CPER indicates that problems that were widespread throughout the firms hit exports harder than home sales. This interpretation is supported by the fact that the negative coefficent on 'building materials' is only significant when RGHS is included in the equation (3.C.). In food, the influence of problems or policies specific to exports is again suggested by the fact that the industry's RGHS is slighty below average, and also by the relatively small influence on the results of the inclusion or exclusion of RGHS. F-tests on the explanatory power of the industry dummies proved to be significant; at 5 per cent in equation 3.C.1 and at 10 per cent in equation 3.C.2.

Amongst the area/nationality dummies 'other European firms' and the 'rest of the world' are significantly positive, i.e. have a significantly higher increase (or smaller decrease) in PER than USA. These areas were the ones with the lowest average RGHS, but the influence of this on their CPER seems to be limited, since both dummies remain significant in equations 3.C.1 and 3.C.2. F-tests on the explanatory power of nationality/area dummies in equations 3.C.1 and 3.C.2 were significant at 1 per cent. This indicates that inter-area differences (other than growth rates of home-country sales) made a significant contribution to an explanation of CPER.

The regressions were run for USA, UK, and other European sub-samples. The strongest evidence of a general positive trend to increasing PER was found for other European firms. For the USA, the significant relationship was one of positive CPER for firms with low PER_{77} (below approximately 20 per cent), and negative for those with higher PER_{77}. There was no significant evidence of any trend in PER for UK firms. RGHS was significantly negatively related to CPER for USA and (in the linear equation only) for other European firms, but was not significant for the UK. The size of parent country operations (PP_{77}) was only significant in one case, when it took a negative value, in the quadratic equation only, for the UK sub-samples. Metal manufacture and products, with a negative sign, was the only significant industry dummy for USA, whilst tobacco and industrial and farm equipment were significantly positive for UK. In each of these cases the relationship varied little between the equation in 3.C. (RGHS included at the firm level) and those in 3.B. For other European firms, food was strongly negative in equations 3.C only, while motor vehicles was significantly positive in 3.B only. F-tests on the explanatory power of industry dummies were never significant.

Change in industrial diversification ratio and change in overseas production ratio

Having verified in earlier sections the presence of a tendency among leading enterprises towards increases in both industrial and geographical diversification, we now pursue a further speculation – namely, the relationship between these routes to expansion at the firm level. Are an expanding range of industrial activities and an extension of international production complementary in firms pursuing diversification as a basis for growth? Or do these routes tend to be mutually exclusive substitutes, with firms pursuing one or other route whilst perhaps even increasing concentration (on a more limited range of activities, or fewer production sites) in the other?

The samples used in the earlier tests of CIDR and COPR were found to have 225 firms in common, these then providing us with the sample for the tests of the relationship between these two variables. In the equation tested, CIDR serves as the dependent variable, with COPR as the independent variable of central interest. However, to normalize for other influences on CIDR, the equations also include IDR_{77}, OPR_{77}, TS_{77}, RGMA, and dummy variables for industry and nationality/area. We are thus, in effect, testing to see if there is a statistically significant relationship between CIDR and COPR for firms with the same initial levels of CIDR and OPR, of the same initial size, with the same rate of growth of main activity, and from the same industry and aera.

As Table 8.4 shows, for the full sample of 225 firms, there is no evidence of any statistically significant relationship between CIDR and COPR. Changes in industrial diversification do not seem to be either complementary with, or alternatives to, changes in overseas production. When the tests are re-run for sub-samples of USA firms, all non-US firms, and European firms, the relationship between CIDR and COPR remains persistently insignificant.

The sample of 225 firms was also subdivided into those firms with overall growth rates above the average for their industry[8] (101 firms), and those with below-average growth rates (124 firms). As Table 8.4

Table 8.4 Regressions with CIDR as a dependent and COPR as an independent variable

Equation[a]	Full sample	High-growth sample	Low-growth sample
IDR$_{77}$	− 0.62993; D-1**	− 0.84135; D-1**	− 0.46912; D-1
	(− 2.2162)	(− 2.0911)	(− 1.3748)
TS$_{77}$	− 0.84898; D-4	− 0.71305; D-3*	0.34765; D-4
	(− 0.84671)	(− 1.6894)	(0.36475)
RGMA	− 0.67906; D-1***	− 0.90697; D-1***	− 0.17822***
	(− 5.5114)	(− 4.9018)	(− 7.9967)
COPR	0.57662; D-1	0.28310**	− 0.11163
	(0.56769)	(2.2576)	(− 0.80793)
OPR$_{77}$	0.54462; D-2	− 0.22361; D-1	0.86138; D-2
	(− 0.1555)	(− 0.42772)	(0.21469)
Intercept	11.674***	20.107***	9.1172***
	(4.6944)	(5.8337)	(2.8859)
R^2	0.2665	0.4506	0.5747
F	2.543***	2.334***	4.585***

Notes: In all the regressions reported here industry and nationality/area dummy variables were included but are not reported.
[a] In the notation D-X; X is the number of noughts to be inserted after the decimal point, e.g. 0.54462; D-2 reads 0.0054462.
Figures in parentheses are t values
* = significant at 10 per cent; ** = significant at 5 per cent; *** = significant at 1 per cent.

reports, a statistically significant positive relationship now emerged for those firms with above-average overall rates of growth. Thus, for this sub-sample of firms, those with the greatest tendency to extend their range of industrial activity were also the ones with the greatest relative increase in overseas production. This would imply that, among firms which achieved an above-average overall growth performance between 1977 and 1982, quite a systematic distinction may be perceived. This being between those firms which achieved their growth by pursuit of new dimensions to their operations, both in terms of new activities and extended internationalization of production, and those which were able to perform well whilst retaining a strong focus on their existing pattern of industrial and geographical diversification. For the low-growth sample, the sign on COPR is negative, but does not approach statistical significance.

Conclusion

The broad conclusion of the analysis is that, in our samples of leading enterprises, the significant pervasive tendency has been towards increased diversification, both in terms of the geographical spread of production and of the range of industrial activity. It is notable, ￢

however, that the results indicate that the ability to achieve such diversification, as routes to growth, has not been by any means the monopoly of firms with an extensive existing commitment to such a dispersion of operations. It may be suggested, from the results, that if increasing spread of activity (geographically or industrially) is part of the secret of survival of leading enterprises, then the ability to achieve this may be accessible to a majority of the firms, and not just those with an established tradition in diversification. This may be considered to be an encouraging conclusion if it is true that, where firm-level adjustment is viable, pressure for protectionism is mitigated.

Appendix A

Data sources

The samples used in the various sections of the paper are all sub-samples from an original sample which comprised the 792 largest industrial enterprises in the non-communist world in 1982. This sample was derived, in a manner described in detail in Part 1 of Dunning and Pearce (1985), from an analysis of the *Fortune* data on the largest 500 US and largest 500 non-US industrial enterprises. The samples analyzed in the paper then constitute all the firms from the 792 for which data was available, from the sources listed below, on the particular ratios for both 1977 and 1982

Industrial diversification ratio

The following sources were used to obtain information on the extent of industrial diversification:

1. Company reports and accounts
2. J. M. Stopford (1983) *The World Directory of Multinational Enterprises 1982–83*, London: MacMillan.

Overseas production ratio and parent firms' exports ratio

The following sources were used to obtain information on the extent of overseas production and parents' exports:

1. Special surveys carried out by J. H. Dunning and R. D. Pearce in 1979 and 1983.
2. Company reports and accounts.
3. J. M. Stopford (1983) *The World Directory of Multinational Enterprises 1982–83*, London: MacMillan.

4. United Nations Centre on Transnational Corporations (1983) *Transnational Corporations in World Development–Third Survey*, annex Table 11 – 31, New York: United Nations.
5. 'The 50 leading exporters', *Fortune*, 8 August 1983.

Notes

1. This, of course, provokes another area of discussion; namely the extent to which such adjustment by MNEs constitutes 'export of jobs' from certain countries. Though this is clearly a controversy of considerable relevance it is not the point at issue here, where we are more concerned with the potential of such intra-firm adjustment as a factor mitigating possible pressure for protection emanating from leading firms.
2. See Appendix A for details of the derivation of the samples and the data sources used.
3. See Dunning and Pearce (1985: 88–91, and Table 5.9). The industry classification used is described in Dunning and Pearce (1985, Appendix 1).
4. See Dunning and Pearce (1985: 139–40, and Table 7.8).
5. See Dunning and Pearce (1985, Part V).
6. The UK contribution to the sample of world's largest enterprises tends to be somewhat biased towards low R&D industries, which might be expected to lead to limited potential for industrial diversification. In fact, when subsidiary regressions are run omitting the industry dummies, the positive UK coefficient rises modestly, opposing the suggested industry composition effect.
7. Electronics and electrical appliances; food; metal manufacturing and products; industrial and agricultural chemicals; motor vehicles (including components); pharmaceuticals and consumer chemicals; industrial and farm equipment; petroleum.
8. The average growth rates used to classify sample firms were those for the larger sample from which the samples used in this paper were derived (see Dunning and Pearce 1985, Part VI).

References

Dunning, J. H. and Pearce, R. D. (1985) *The World's Largest Industrial Enterprises 1962–1983*, London: Gower.
Franko, L. (1981) 'Adjusting to export thrusts of newly industrialising countries: an advanced country perspective', *The Economic Journal* 91 June: 486–506.

Part Three

Policy and structural change

Chapter Nine

Japanese manufacturing investment and the restructuring of the United Kingdom economy

John H. Dunning

Introduction

The United Kingdom has always been an attractive location for foreign-based manufacturing companies. The first American ventures by Colts, North British Rubber, and Singer date back to the 1850s and 1860s. The most recent influx of Japanese investors include such companies as Nissan, Sharp Electronics, and Komatsu. Both groups of firms chose Britain for the same reasons: the prospect of good and expanding markets; political and economic stability; a well-educated and productive labour force; a first rate legal, commercial, and communications infrastructure; a cordial business and pleasant living environment; and, not least, their familarity with English – the leading language of international business.

The United Kingdom is now the largest European recipient of both US and Japanese direct investment; foreign-owned subsidiaries account for about one-fifth of all the goods produced in British factories and provide one in seven of the jobs in manufacturing industry.

Even before the Industrial Revolution, Britain was a veritable 'open house' to foreign technology, skills, ideas, and entrepreneurship; indeed, such trade has been a two-way street for many a century, and has been of enormous benefit to world peace and prosperity. In our modern age, however, it is the multinational enterprise which is the main vehicle for the commercial dissemination of new products, technology, and skills. Probably four-fifths of all industrial research and development activities is undertaken by these firms. Increasingly, in their search for new markets, manpower, and materials, enterprises have had to look beyond their national boundaries. Today, the billion-dollar industrial companies straddle the world and produce about one-third of their output outside their home countries. The service companies – the banks, advertising agencies, management consultancies, air lines, and hotel chains – are following hard on their heels (UNCTC 1988).

More and more companies are preaching and practising the virtues of globalization. The world-wide operations of such companies as IBM, ITT, Philips, and Royal Dutch Shell are well known; but these are just the tip of the iceberg. Thousands of large and medium-sized companies of all nationalities are looking for a presence in the rich triad markets of the USA, Europe, and Japan – for it is there where three-quarters of the world's wealth is currently produced and consumed. The Europeans were the first to go overseas in the search for new trading routes, raw materials, precious metals, and territories. The Americans followed, as modern industry spread outwards from the USA. In the last twenty years, the Japanese have entered the global arena, first by trade and more recently, and increasingly, by foreign production.

The Japanese presence in the UK

In 1960, Japanese companies accounted for less than 1 per cent of the world's foreign direct capital stake. By 1985 this proportion had risen to nearly 12.0 per cent. According to the UN Centre on Transnational Corporations (UNCTC 1988), between 1980 and 1985, the Japanese invested some $47 billion overseas – half as much again as the USA. By the end of 1989, if not sooner, Japan will have replaced the UK as the second largest foreign direct investor in the world.

And this is only the start of the story. For, on average, still less than 10 per cent of the output of the leading Japanese industrial companies is currently produced outside Japan – it is rather higher in the consumer electronics industry;[1] while only about 35 per cent of their foreign investment is directed to the USA and the EEC – the heartland of the western industrial world. By contrast, 35 per cent of the output of European and US industrial multinationals is supplied by their foreign subsidiaries, and nearly three-quarters of this is within OECD countries. Bringing the statistics nearer home, for every £1 spent by the UK consumer on manufactured imports from the USA in 1986, £3.50 was spent on goods made by American firms in the UK; whereas for every £1 spent on Japanese imports, only 10p and 12p was spent on goods actually made by Japanese manufacturing affiliates in Britain.

Of course, in some industrial sectors, noticeably the CTV industry, a large portion of the goods marketed by Japanese firms are produced at least partly, in the UK – and the proportion is increasing all the time. For the most part, however, investment by Japanese multinationals in Europe, and in the UK in particular, is targeted to a select group of industries, in which the Japanese perceive themselves to have a competitive edge over western firms, and which, until recently were mainly located in Japan.

The contemporary figures tell us little about the likely future of the Japanese corporate presence in the UK, save to emphasize that it is increasing rapidly and the potential for more growth is tremendous. Between 1969 and 1983, twenty-four Japanese manufacturing affiliates were set up in the UK; and by the end of 1983, they employed about 6,000 people. In the following three years another twenty-six plants were established or acquired. But according to the Invest in Britain Bureau, between 1 January 1987 and 25 February 1988, twenty-eight new Japanese companies began production or announced they were to manufacture in the UK. Nevertheless, although the UK accounts for one-third of Japanese-owned manufacturing assets in Europe, worth over $1 billion, the 20,000 or so people employed by the sixty-five Japanese manufacturing plants currently in operation, represent only about 2 per cent of those employed in all foreign subsidiaries, and a minute fraction of the total manufacturing labour force. And, as we have already suggested, these activities are highly concentrated. Apart from the 2,500 people employed by the Sumitomo Rubber Company in the ex-Dunlop plants, two-thirds of the labour force in Japanese factories is in consumer or industrial electronics. Contrary to what is commonly supposed, most manufacturing affiliates are quite small; in mid-1987, for example, there were only eighteen Japanese-owned factories which employed 300 or more people; and only four with more than 1,000 employees.

The regional distribution is also highly skewed, with a heavy concentration of Japanese factories in Wales – which, at the latest count, had twenty plants – Scotland, Northern England, and also in some of the thriving newer industrial conurbations of the South Midlands. All these facts and figures point to a selective participation and limited economic impact of the Japanese corporate investment in the UK.

Limited and selective – yes; but also highly visible. This is partly because many of the goods produced in Japanese plants – CTV sets, VTRs, typewriters, and motor vehicles – have a high 'awareness' factor among consumers; and partly because of the widespread (and often justifiable) publicity given to Japanese managerial philosophy and work practices. It is this philosophy and these practices which help to explain the very distinctive economic impact of the Japanese presence the UK economy, which has spread well beyond the gates of their factories.

Japan's predecessors: US subsidiaries in the UK

In the mid-1950s, the present author undertook a survey on the role of American-based manufacturing subsidiaries in the UK economy. The results obtained (as set out in Dunning 1958), which have been broadly confirmed by later studies,[2] may be summarized as follows. Compared with UK firms, US affiliates were concentrated in high-growth, high-productivity, and technology-intensive industrial sectors. Their contribution to Britain's balance of payments, regional development, technological capability, industrial training, and international competitiveness, was found to be very positive; and this was primarily the result of their managerial professionalism, marketing skills, entrepreneurial drive, emphasis on careful corporate planning and budgetary control, and their speedy application of the most advanced production methods. The spillover effects of the US corporate presence on the rest of UK industry – for example, on their suppliers, competitors, and customers – was found to be generally beneficial, and particularly so in those sectors in which there was already a strong indigenous technological capability.

By the mid-1970s, most American firms had become household names and fully integrated into the UK economy. The productivity gap between British (and other European) and US firms had narrowed; some of the early euphoria which had greeted such companies as IBM, Ford, Honeywell, Caterpillar Tractor, and Merck Sharpe and Dohme in the 1960s, had all but disappeared. Indeed, by the later 1970s, the mighty American industrial machine was itself being challenged, partly by a technologically revitalized Europe (or, perhaps more correctly, European-owned firms such as Philips, ICI, Siemens, and Fiat) but more so – although again very selectively – by the Japanese phoenix.

The competitive advantages of Japanese firms

The competitive weapons employed by the Japanese to penetrate the markets of the west have been well documented in the literature.[3] First by price, then by quality and reliability, and most recently by product improvement, adaptation, and innovation, they quickly won the hearts (and the pockets) of European and US consumers. Why? Simply because, somewhere along the line, American and European manufacturers had lost their ability or willingness to give consumers full satisfaction for their money. For most of the post-war period, the west had been spoiled by easy and expanding markets, and a complacent consumer who could easily be guiled into believing that the latest product was always the best, and that some faults or failures – the Friday-afternoon-car syndrome – were only to be expected. But when the novelty of the new electronic toys and the bigger-than-ever motor cars lost their appeal, when growth declined and the recession started to bite into employment and incomes, the consumer was ready for a change.

It was at this point that the Japanese began to emerge as serious competitors, offering to the western consumer a new deal – a low-priced, reliable, and (comparatively) fault-free product, which usually needed much less after-sales servicing, maintenance, and repair than those produced by European and US competitors.

The question then is, how did they do it? The story is already well known and has been told elsewhere, e.g. Kidd and Teremato (1981), Marsh (1983), and Trevor (1983). My own findings, as set out in Dunning (1986), revealed that the chief executives of Japanese manufacturing affiliates in the UK perceived their main advantages over their UK competitors to be threefold, as follows:

1) product reliability, which is achieved by an integrated and detailed system of quality control and testing procedures, embracing both outside purchases and in-house activities;
2) a flexible manufacturing and work system; and
3) an ability to foster and sustain a maximum commitment to the goals of enterprise by workers and management alike.

We came across only a few examples of a unique product or even production processes being identified as the key competitive advantage; rather it was the way in which the resources, human talents, and experience were packaged together to achieve mutually agreed objectives by management and workforce alike, which most marked off Japanese firms from their competitors. If American firms introduced new products to the UK, and helped promote the most modern production techniques, the Japanese have taught (or perhaps we should say retaught) UK industry how to produce efficiently, how to economize on materials and inventories, how to get the best out of the work force, and how to best interpret and meet the needs of the consumer. If the Americans stimulated their UK competitors to become more professional managers, and underlined the virtues of aggressive marketing, the Japanese have reminded us of the value of establishing and maintaining good and trusting relationships with suppliers, work force, and customers; and of approaching production as a team effort in which all participants have a common stake in success.

There is no Japanese miracle (and never has been); neither have Japanese firms sought to bribe the best out of their labour force by offering huge monetary incentives. Rather they have practised a dedicated and uncompromising application of well-tested managerial and personnel procedures, an assiduous attention to detail, and a total refusal to settle for second best. In addition, they have steadfastedly adhered to the belief that, in the long run, at least, the consumer is king. We should, perhaps, add that it *is* the long run in which the Japanese are interested; not the rate of return on capital earned this or next year – or even over the next five years.

Will these competitive advantages last?

The question now arises, to what extent have the qualities which have made it possible for the Japanese to establish manufacturing bridge-heads in Europe and the USA – in spite of all the disadvantages of producing in an unfamiliar environment – likely to persist in the future; and, if they do, how far will they allow Japanese firms to make further inroads into European and US industry? We link Europe and the USA together because we think the reasons for Japanese invest-ment in both areas are similar; moreover, what the Japanese are doing in the USA today may be seen as a good predictor of what they are likely to be doing in Europe tomorrow.

First, we would make a general point. Contemporary technolog-ical and organizational advances are extending the territorial bound-aries of firms. They are also encouraging the formation of cross-border alliances in such areas as product innovation and develop-ment, production, and marketing (Contractor and Lorange 1988). It is the very sectors in which the Japanese industrial machine has achieved its greatest commercial success which are becoming the most global in their orientation. There are several reasons for this, but the most important is the rocketing cost of technological innovation. R&D costs in such industries as micro electronics, pharmaceuticals, biotechnology, and optic fibres are no longer measured in millions but in billions of dollars. And yet, in an increasingly competitive international environment, maintaining a technological cutting-edge is not a luxury but a necessity. To recoup these costs, large – very large – markets are essential. Hence the imperative for firms from each of the leading industrial countries to sell their goods in their competitor's backyards. Second, firms are finding that, however much they may be in competition with each other, they need to form alliances to undertake certain tasks which, by themselves, they could not afford to do. There are literally hundreds of examples of Japanese collaborating with European and American firms to exploit comple-mentary technologies and capture new markets even if they may be bitter rivals in other directions. Researchers believe this trend will accelerate in the 1990s (Contractor and Lorange 1988).

Our first point is, then, that the world is becoming a global village, in which the interpenetration of domestic markets by companies of different nationalities will continue; this is occurring fastest in the sectors in which Japanese industry and Japanese multinationals have established an international comparative advantage.

Our second observation concerns the competitiveness of the Japanese economy. Historically, countries with the strongest outward investment thrust have been those in the van of technological progress and international competitiveness. However, they have also been those whose domestic market growth has lagged behind that of foreign markets, and those with strong, and often undervalued, real exchange rates. If one takes the period from the mid-1950s to the mid-1970s and compares the Japanese and US economies, one notices that while the latter exhibited all of the characteristics just described, together with a non-restrictionist policy of the US government towards outward investment, Japanese firms had little inducement and no encouragement from their government to look overseas for their markets, let alone to substitute foreign for domestic production.

The situation in the mid-1980s is totally different. While the appreciation of the yen (it rose by 35 per cent against most European currencies between September 1985 and March 1988) is a reflection of the underlying strength of the Japanese economy, it is reducing the competitiveness of Japanese exports. At the same time, expenditure on R & D by Japanese firms has mushroomed, while the proportion of patents registered in the USA by Japanese companies doubled between 1970 and 1985. In their efforts to restructure the Japanese economy towards high-technology sectors, and to lessen trade frictions with Europe and the USA, the Japanese government has deliberately encouraged outward investment by its companies to manufacture products in the later stages of their product cycles. By contrast, in the last ten years, there has been a sharp decrease in the rate of new US outward investment as the dollar has depreciated and opportunities for domestic investment have improved. In the 1970s, the US economy lost some of its technological hegemony, and took a relaxed attitude to investment in industrial research and development. In this scenario not only did US multinationals retrench some of their foreign operations, but there was an upsurge of European and Japanese investment in the USA. The USA is now by far the largest recipient of inward direct investment, and by far the largest net debtor on the international investment account. By contrast, in 1986, Japan was the world's largest creditor nation.

Some alternative scenarios

What then of the future? Let us consider just two possible scenarios. The first is that the Japanese competitive advantage may be only a temporary phenomenon. US and European competitors have learned, or are learning, from their mistakes; they are doing what the Japanese are doing and fighting back to reclaim lost markets. The renewed attention now given to industrial restructuring, quality control, industrial relations, and cost-saving measures is now paying off. The 'quality' gap between Japanese and western goods is falling. No longer do the Japanese have quite the edge they used to in such products as consumer electronics, cameras, and motor vehicles.

Moreover, so the argument continues, the falling value of US and European currencies is eroding Japanese competitiveness, both in Japan and abroad. While this is being partially compensated by offshore production by Japanese multinationals elsewhere in Asia and in the major industrial markets, there is some doubt as to whether the Japanese can move as quickly as they would like to to counteract the resurgence in western competitiveness; or whether the reasons for their success in the first place – and particularly those to do with the organization of work, the attention given to quality control, the close relationships established with suppliers and customers, and the constructive interaction between government (mostly MITI) and private industry, can be satisfactorily translated to a western culture and business environment. Finally, as the Japanese people become more exposed to western goods, values, and work practices; as they begin to taste the fruits of wealth and leisure; as the pace of domestic growth slows down; and as a new generation of well-travelled and western-educated Japanese workers emerges, the question arises as to whether the institutions, relationships, and loyalties, which have been an integral part of Japanese economic success, will remain intact.

This, then, is the so-called 'convergence' hypothesis. Just as the UK and the USA have gone through their cycles of economic hegemony, relative decline, and partial recovery, so it is argued (somewhat wistfully one feels) that Japan will eventually catch the western disease of complacency and resting on its economic laurels, and switch the emphasis of its values away from those of a creative and entrepreneurial society to those more geared towards economic security and social and environmental welfare.

The alternative scenario is that the Japanese are themselves fully aware of the situation just described and will aim to counteract it by upgrading their technological capacity and human capital, so as to compete with Europe and the USA as product innovators in the 'cutting-edge' industrial sectors. To achieve this, it is argued that Japanese firms will need to increase their foreign production in two directions. The first is that involving products in which the Japanese comparative advantage is declining, but which can be economically produced in other countries – under Japanese management; these include relatively mature products in the motor-vehicle and consumer-electronics sectors. The second is in the technologically advanced sectors where a global strategy is necessary, both to cover R & D costs – this is why cross-border alliances are most likely to be favoured – and to be in close proximity to the main centres of the industry's R & D activities. This might be called the 'keeping-one-step-ahead' type of Japanese scenario.

Which of the two scenarios described will materialize remains to be seen. Our own feeling is that the cross-penetration of the major industrial markets is inevitable, with the leading participants each developing their own particular set of strategic competitive advantages. For the UK, however, as it seeks to evolve its own policy towards inward investment and industrial restructuring, we perceive the two scenarios to be complementary to, rather than in conflict with, each other. A strategy which helps its own multinationals to be competitive, while welcoming inward direct investment wherever it strengthens its domestic technological base, seems to be consistent with the growing needs of Japanese investors and the strengthening of UK international competitiveness.

The locational attractions of the UK

But what of the other side of the coin? Assuming that Japanese firms continue to pose a strong competitive challenge, what are the chances of the UK providing a satisfactory production base for her European activities? First, we wish to make another general, but important, point. The forces influencing the international location of production are undergoing profound changes. It can be said that fifty, or even twenty, years ago, raw material, labour, and transport costs were the main determinants of the siting of manufacturing activities. With the dramatic reduction in material and labour content of most goods and the tremendous advances in international transport, these items are no longer as relevant as once they were. Over the past decade, the average labour content of a motor-vehicle assembling operation has dropped from 25 per cent to 7 per cent. In the mid-1980s Japanese industry was consuming only 60 per cent of the raw materials to produce the same volume of production as it did in the early 1970s (Drucker 1986).

Instead, international firms are increasingly searching for two things in a foreign location. The first is stability in government economic policy and reliability in business relationships. The second is a good supply and technological capability. Stability in government macro- and micro-economic strategy and reliability in industrial relations, component supplies, and final goods markets are regarded as vital prerequisites to maintaining a consistent flow of high-quality intermediate products from the supplier through to the customer. The other necessities are an adequate supply of a well-motivated and trained labour force, and a first-class national and international transport and communications infrastructure. It is a quite mistaken belief that foreign-owned firms in high-technology sectors wish to invest in a weak economy or an uncompetitive industry; for this usually means that the supply capabilities they need are not available. This is particularly the case where the intention is to engage in R & D or to produce goods and services for the export market, and where the host government encourages foreign affiliates to buy a high proportion of their inputs from local sources.

Let us give just two examples of what we mean. Though there have been some impressive inward investments in the UK motor-vehicle industry in the last twenty years, until the advent of Nissan the UK was not an attractive European location for foreign companies. Take one very telling set of statistics. The UK content of cars sold in the UK by the multinational producers fell from 88 per cent in 1973 to 46 per cent in 1984 in the case of Ford, 92 per cent to 42 per cent in the case of Talbot and 89 per cent to 22 per cent in the case of General Motors. More generally, over the same period in trading terms, the motor-vehicle industry experienced the greatest deterioration of any British manufacturing sector; between 1978 and 1984, for example, vehicle exports rose by 13 per cent (in value terms) while imports increased by 118 per cent. In volume terms, the exports of all the major UK producers fell quite dramatically in the early 1980s. Britain's share of the global R&D expenditure by motor vehicle firms (which was always lower than her production, and substantially lower than her consumption, of vehicles) has slumped even further since the mid-1960s. Until the mid-1980s, at least, the motor industry was not one of Britain's success stories.

Moreover, as inward investment fell, and became less directed to high-value activities, this further weakened the industry's ability to compete. Multinationals were choosing not to produce in Britain because the supply capabilities were perceived as inadequate, while the environmental stability (especially in terms of industrial relations) was thought to be inferior to that offered by continental competitors. Only the most generous of incentives and the most persuasive efforts of UK government ministers induced companies like Ford to make the huge new investments they did in Wales and the North West. The fact that Nissan and, more recently, Honda and Toyota, have expressed their faith in the British economy and British work force has undoubtedly been a shot in the arm for the British car industry. Maybe it will see a turning of the tide.

By contrast, the tale of the pharmaceutical industry is one of almost uninterrupted vitality and vigour. From the early 1950s, foreign producers have acted as a competitive challenge to an already quite strong indigenous sector. The reputation of the UK scientific community, its professional system of drug registration, its patent system, and its clinical testing procedures are all excellent. Its industrial relations and contacts with universities and the medical profession are second to none; and the government, through the PPBS scheme, has offered a stable and fair reward system for the pharmaceutical companies, as well as providing them with good incentives to engage in innovatory activities.

The results are shown in a variety of indices. First, the pharmaceutical industry (a substantial net contributor to the UK balance of payments) in 1986 exported nearly twice the amount it imported. Second, the UK is one of the two or three leading centres for pharmaceutical research and development in the world. At the end of the 1970s, it was estimated that, while only 3.5 per cent of the world's drugs were bought by UK consumers, 5 per cent of the world's production was undertaken in the UK, as also was 11.5 per cent of the industry's global research and development (Dunning 1988). Success breeds success: though foreign companies account for about 45 per cent of the drugs supplied by the National Health Service, this figure has remained fairly constant over the year. British multinationals are among the world's leading drug producers and in the forefront of technological advances. Between them, foreign and domestically owned firms have generated a critical mass of physical and human innovatory capacity, which, separately, neither could have ensured. The agglomerative economies so gained are in total contrast to those lost in the motor-vehicle industry.

Government and the restructuring of the UK economy

To our mind these two case studies encapsulate the conditions necessary for successful foreign investment. We are all rehearsed in the reasons why Japanese firms are investing in Europe, and we also know why they choose (or do not choose) the UK as a European location. What, perhaps, is not as well appreciated, is the value placed by Japanese (and other) investors on a strong and vibrant industrial economy; *and* the crucial role which government has to play in bringing this about. Inter-country differences in wage, raw-materials, and transport costs no longer are the crucial locational factors. These have been replaced by an efficient macro-economic management, and an educational, technological, and industrial policy which promotes entrepreneurship, innovation, and efficiency; a realistic and positive attitude of mind towards work, rewards, and competitiveness; and a unity of commercial and social purpose. These are all important influences which will determine, for example, how much R&D companies like Sony, NEC, Sharp, and Nissan will eventually undertake in the UK. Equally to the point, they are shaped, if not directly determined, by the actions or non-actions of governments.

There is a lot of misunderstanding about the role of government in a modern industrial economy. All schools of thought seem to agree that governments have a responsibility to set the right economic climate, and that there are some functions which only governments can perform. But as soon as one talks about industrial strategy, the positions diverge. The free market protagonists preach 'let the discipline of the market decide'; governments are not technically competent to make the right decisions on who should produce what; much better leave it to those who know and are prepared to bear the consequences for their action. The opposing view is that imperfections and distortions in the market system, and differences between private and social benefits and costs, require some intervention by governments in the allocation of resources. A third school of thought – the structuralists – argues that the market mechanism as conceived by the non-interventionists is inherently incapable of dealing with many of the demands of the modern economy, and particularly with the high transaction costs associated with uncertainty and co-ordinating interrelated activities.

The fact is that, in today's global economy, many firms, and particularly those supplying markets dominated by international oligopolists, cannot compete effectively unless they are able to reap the full economies of scale and scope of their activities. At the same time, the costs of structural adaptation to new patterns of consumption and technological advances are often too great for individual firms to bear.

The principle of comparative advantage and the invisible hand was initially based on the assumption that the wealth or assets of a country consisted of its natural resources. But, increasingly, the prosperity of modern industrial economies rests in their ability to create new technology and human capital, and to provide the appropriate institutional machinery and incentives to foster wealth-creating activities. These are not things which a *laissez-faire* philosophy or 'hands-off' approach to resource enrichment or allocation can readily do. The provision of adequate education; transport and telecommunications infrastructure; laws, rules, and regulations which affect human and physical capital formation and technology development; the promotion of an efficient market system, taxes, and incentives; policies which affect savings, consumption and investment patterns, and industrial relations are, at the very least, the responsibility of both government and the private sector, and some would argue the major onus lies with government.

History suggests that almost every industrial country has needed, and still needs, the active support of its government for its economic restructuring. The instruments used range from protectionism of one kind or another to well-defined and holistic industrial strategy, within which firms (who are still the main arbiters of resource allocation) produce. If the Japanese have taught the west anything at all, it is the need for a unity of purpose and strategy between the various contributors to the value-added process – workers and managers, suppliers and customers, the private sector, and governments. The European country whose government promotes the type of macro- and micro-economic policies which ensures domestic and foreign investors the right environment for growth will, most likely, be the one which will both attract the bulk of inward Japanese and (especially) investment in the 1990s and benefit most from it.

Conclusions

Let us summarize our argument. Japanese participation in British manufacturing industry is still in its infancy; but it is growing fast. The opportunities and likelihood of a major increase in the Japanese presence in the 1990s are very real – particularly in high-value activities. The rising yen and the increasing pressure towards globalization are the main driving forces, together with some protectionist sentiments towards Japanese imports.

A recent survey of Japanese manufacturers in the UK confirms that the great majority are both contemplating major expansion plans in Europe and are likely to buy more of their purchases from local sources (JETRO 1988).[4] At the time they set up their affiliates in the UK, the Japanese companies sourced about 35 per cent of their inputs from Britain and the EEC; by 1987 this had risen to 45 per cent; by 1990 it is expected to be over 70 per cent. In addition, most Japanese affiliates are enlarging their range of products. Companies like NEC, Toshiba, Yuasa Battery, and Alps Electric are all expanding their UK operations faster than they had originally planned; and some like Sony are starting up their R & D laboratories. It seems likely that, by the end of the 1980s, around 25,000 people will be employed by Japanese factories in the UK; but a series of major

179

take-overs in the last two years of the decade could easily double this figure.

But it is in the 1990s where the real impact of Japanese investment in the UK is likely to occur. We have estimated that if, by the turn of the century, the Japanese manufacturing affiliates in Britain produced a volume of goods equal to that *currently* imported from Japan, their employment would rise to 60,000. However, if the ratio of their UK production to imports were to reach that of the US subsidiaries in the UK in the 1980s, the labour force would rise to 250,000. Even this figure could be a conservative one, as most Japanese companies are coming to the UK to supply the *European* market, which is four times bigger than that of the UK.

If the unified European market – or anything like it – comes about in 1992, not only should this strengthen the individual European economies, but increase Europe's attractiveness as a whole to Japanese investment. For its intention is to facilitate the cross-border movement of goods, assets, and people; if successful, this will considerably enhance the gains to be had from the Japanese corporate presence. The USA, which is currently the largest integrated market in the world, but with a population of 85 per cent of the enlarged EEC, was home to 837 Japanese manufacturing subsidiaries in 1988 (JETRO 1989). Between them, these subsidiaries directly employed 180,000 people, and, indirectly, many thousands more.

This chapter has not sought to evaluate the costs and benefits of Japanese direct investment in the UK. We will, however, offer just one observation. It is this. We do not believe it is in the UK's best interest to have her major key industrial sectors completely owned or controlled by foreign firms. We sense this to be even more the case in the 1980s than in the 1950s, as multinationals, particularly in high-technology sectors, are increasingly pursuing global strategies, rather than seeking to advance the interests of their individual affiliates. We accept that a country may prefer to accept inward investment on these terms, rather than see it go to its competitors, but we would also argue that the long-term interests of both the UK and investing firms are best served if there is a strong indigenous technological sector. For this to happen, however, there must be reciprocity in trade and investment. If Europe and the USA open their borders to Japanese investors in high-technology industries, so must the Japanese not add hindrances to the normal commercial difficulties faced by foreign firms breaking into the Japanese market.

There are many success stories of European and US affiliates producing in Japan – indeed, more goods are produced in Japan by US and European multinationals than are exported to it from US and

European factories (Ohmae 1987), but rightly or wrongly, western businessmen perceive there are a variety of non-tariff barriers – some of which are government-supported –which inhibit their presence in that country. On this issue, there remains a good deal of ignorance and misunderstanding. But a statement by the US Ambassador to Japan that 'The Japanese market is not as closed as foreigners might believe but not as open as the Japanese might think' indicates that the real problem may lie in the perception gap between the trading partners about each other's expectations and capabilities.

There seems little doubt that inward investment from Japan *could* play an important – if not crucial – role in the restructuring and upgrading of British industry, in a similar way as the US multinationals did twenty or thirty years earlier. However, unless the UK is simply to become simply an industrial satellite of Japan, this cannot be achieved without healthy indigenous competition and a strong supply capability; to achieve and sustain this, the UK government as well as the private sector has a positive role to play. We do well to remind ourselves that governments of advanced economies (on behalf of their constituents), like firms, are now competing with each other for jobs and investment; and that the battle is not lost or won by the incentives offered to, or the performance requirements imposed on, foreign companies, but by the gamut of economic and institutionally related policies which, directly or indirectly, affect the profits of enterprises, be they foreign or domestically owned. To this extent, the future of Japanese investment in UK industry lies as much in the hands of UK policy-makers and industrialists as anything which the Japanese multinationals might plan to do, or global economic trends might dictate. This is a responsibility which must not be taken lightly, as both the rewards of success and the penalties of failure are high.

Notes

1. Examples of higher than average foreign production ratios include Sony (25 per cent), Matsushita (12 per cent), and JVC (14 per cent) (see *The Economist* 1988).
2. See, especially, Dunning (1985).
3. See, for example, Dunning (1986); Ozawa (1985); Franko (1983).
4. The question of local content is currently a particularly sensitive issue in the European Economic Commission. See *The Economist* (1988).

References

Contractor, F. J. and Lorange, P. (eds) (1988) *Coporate Strategies in International Business*, Lexington, Mass.: Lexington Books.

Drucker, P. F. (1986) 'The changed world economy', *Foreign Affairs* 64: 768–9.

Dunning, J. H. (1958) *American Investment in British Manufacturing Industry*, London: Allen & Unwin.

—— (ed.) (1985) *Multinational Enterprises, Economic Structure and International Competitiveness*, Chichester: John Wiley.

—— (1986) *Japanese Participation In British Industry*, Beckenham (UK): Croom Helm.

—— (1988) *Technology, Multinationals and Competitiveness*, London: Allen & Unwin.

The Economist (1988) 'Walkman factories don't walk', *The Economist*, 12 March: 66–7.

Franko, L. G. (1983) *The Threat of Japanese Multinationals*, Chichester: John Wiley.

JETRO (1988) *Japanese Direct Investment in Europe. A Recent Survey*, London: JETRO.

—— (1989) *JETRO White Paper on World Direct Investments*, Tokyo: JETRO.

Kidd, J. B. and Teremato (1981) *Japanese Production Subsidiaries in the United Kingdom: A Study of Managerial Decision Taking*, University of Ashton Management Centre Working Paper no. 203 (May).

Marsh, F. (1983) *Japanese Overseas Investment*, London: Economist Intelligence Unit (May).

Ohmae, K. (1987) *Beyond National Borders*, Homewood, Illinois: Dow-Jones-Irwin.

Ozawa, T. (1985) 'Japan', in J. H. Dunning (ed.) *Multinational Enterprises, Economic Structure and International Competitiveness*, Chichester: John Wiley.

Trevor, M. (1983) *Japan's Reluctant Multinationals*, London: Francis Pinter.

UNCTC (1988) *Transnational Corporations and World Development*, New York: United Nations.

Chapter Ten

Trade liberalization and specialization in manufactured goods

Chris Milner

Introduction

Empirical evidence suggests that a substantial proportion of trade
in manufactures in general, and between industrialized countries in
particular, is now of a two-way or intra-industry nature. This
stimultaneous exchange of similar products has also increased in
empirical significance over the post-war period. There is a substantial
theoretical literature which provides 'natural' explanations for the
phenomenon (see Greenaway and Milner, 1986) – explanations in
terms of the demand for variety, decreasing costs, and international
oligopolistic rivalry, for instance. There is also a substantial amount
of empirical validation for these 'natural' explanations (Greenaway
and Milner, 1984). Nevertheless, some commentators have expressed
the belief that the observed phenomenon is to a considerable extent
'man-made'; induced either by the idiosyncracies of official trade
classifications (e.g. Finger 1975; and Pomfret 1979 and 1985) or by
the conduct of commercial policy on the process of *inter*-industry
specialization, (e.g. Hufbauer and Chilas 1974; and Tumlir 1979).
Given that it has been asserted on several occasions that adjustment
to trade expansion is likely to be smoother in a setting of *intra*- as
opposed to inter-industry trade (e.g. Balassa 1966; Aquino 1978),
then it is important that the nature and extent of 'man's' influence
on specialization patterns and structural adjustment problems is
properly understood.

The issue of 'categorical aggregation' has been dealt with extensively elsewhere (Greenaway and Milner 1983 and 1985). Substantial
levels of intra-industry trade (IIT) have been identified in numerous
studies of different countries at alternative levels of aggregation, in
official and re-grouped data and using a range of different indices.
Observed IIT may remain a somewhat uncertain mixture of genuine
IIT and measurement error at the individual industry level, but there
is a consensus that IIT is not merely a 'statistical artefact'.

The aim of this chapter will be to concentrate on the impact of commercial policy instruments and the conduct of commercial policy on specialization patterns. It will examine the empirical robustness of apparently competing hypotheses. In a Heckscher-Ohlin world, trade barriers restrict (absolute) net trade balances; as a result, trade liberalization is expected to encourage the growth of *inter*-industry trade. Under alternative conditions where both inter- and intra-industry trade simultaneously occur for 'natural reasons', then trade liberalization may be expected to encourage the growth of all types of trade. If trade liberalization takes the form of bilateral swaps of tariff concessions on a selective basis and between 'similar' economies, then liberalization may encourage the growth of intra-industry trade only. Thus, trade liberalization might be viewed alternatively as a constraint on intra-industry specialization, a stimulus to intra-industry specialization (only), or as a simultaneous source of inter- and intra-industry specialization. Given the possibility of greater similarity in factor intensities within rather than between industries, the nature and extent of structural adjustment problems associated with further trade liberalization depend critically on which of these commercial policy influences predominate. Moreover, if adjustment pressures do vary with the 'type' of trade expansion, this in turn may encourage bilateralism.

Patterns of intra-industry trade and specialization

There has been a range of documentary studies[1] for different types of economies and at different stages of development, from which it

Table 10.1 Average[a] levels of intra-industry at the third digit level in the UK (selected years)[b]

SIIC Section	1959	1964	1970	1977	1980
(0) Food and live animals	0.23	0.22	0.31	0.35	0.38
(1) Beverages and tobacco	0.26	0.28	0.27	0.35	0.43
(2) Crude materials	0.18	0.19	0.36	0.40	0.34
(3) Mineral fuels	0.30	0.35	0.26	0.58	0.59
(4) Animal and vegetable oils	0.41	0.29	0.25	0.50	0.48
(5) Chemicals	0.42	0.56	0.59	0.69	0.69
(6) Manufactured goods	0.44	0.52	0.56	0.69	0.71
(7) Machinery and transport equipment	0.38	0.51	0.60	0.69	0.68
(8) Miscellaneous manufactured goods	0.66	0.75	0.79	0.80	0.80

[a]Arithematic averages.
[b]The number of 'industries', i.e. third digit groupings, in each section varies between years as the classification changes.
Source: Calculated from third digit indices for 1959 and 1964 from Grubel and Lloyd (1975); calculated from *Overeas Trade Statistics of the UK* for other years.

Table 10.2 Cross-country comparison of average levels* of intra-industry trade at the third digit level, 1980

No. of j	USA	Japan	Belgium-Luxenburg	Denmark	France	W. Germany	Ireland	Italy	The Netherlands	UK
(0) (34)	0.31	0.15	0.59	0.40	0.48	0.48	0.36	0.32	0.61	0.38
(1) (4)	0.36	0.06	0.51	0.41	0.32	0.53	0.57	0.54	0.68	0.43
(2) (33)	0.39	0.08	0.47	0.40	0.51	0.38	0.29	0.22	0.49	0.34
(3) (7)	0.23	0.10	0.45	0.32	0.44	0.45	0.21	0.24	0.51	0.59
(4) (4)	0.22	0.63	0.74	0.68	0.67	0.59	0.24	0.52	0.52	0.48
(5) (25)	0.59	0.64	0.72	0.56	0.75	0.66	0.49	0.74	0.72	0.69
(6) (53)	0.59	0.35	0.67	0.52	0.77	0.72	0.53	0.57	0.72	0.71
(7) (45)	0.63	0.31	0.69	0.63	0.72	0.52	0.53	0.66	0.70	0.68
(8) (28)	0.53	0.49	0.63	0.62	0.77	0.69	0.67	0.51	0.67	0.80
(9) (6)	0.40	0.36	0.64	0.43	0.44	0.48	0.37	0.43	0.66	0.59

* arithmetic average of industry (j) levels where $IIT_j = I - \dfrac{|X_j - M_j|}{(X_j + M_j)}$.

Table 10.3 Average[a] levels of intra-industry trade[b] for country types 1978

	Total trade	Trade with DMEs only	Trade with all LDCs	Trade with NICs only
Industrial countries (DMEs)	0.59	0.64	0.21	—
Non-NIC developing countries (LDCs)	0.15	0.10	0.22	—
Newly industrialized countries (NICs)	0.42	0.48	0.38	0.31

[a]Arithmetic average across countries of the Grubel and Lloyd summary index.
[b]For trade in manufactures.
Source: Adapted from Havrylyshyn (1983).

is possible to suggest certain 'stylized facts' about the characteristics of intra-industry trade. Consider Tables 10.1 to 10.3. The post-war growth of *per capita* incomes in the developed market economies has increased the demand for variety and scope for product differentiation. This has resulted in the growth in the share IIT in total trade, especially in trade in manufactures and in trade between high-income, industrialized or developed market economies. IIT seems to be more pervasive, therefore, in economies where market size or physical/cultural distance from similar high-income markets does not act as a constraint on within-industry specialization and non-H-O type trade. On the basis of this type of casual empiricism, however, it is difficult to separate 'natural' influences from 'policy' influences. Are the generally higher levels of IIT for EEC countries than for the USA and Japan (see Table 10.2) due to some kind of integration or commercial policy effect, or are 'natural' factors such as demand similarity and proximity correlated with characteristics of integration? Existing econometric evidence does not allow us to disentangle easily the separate 'natural' and 'policy' influences.

'Natural' sources

Winters (1987) concludes that trade policy matters at the detailed level, but that on present evidence it can no longer be considered a major factor behind the broad patterns of international trade in manufactures. This conclusion is based on an evaluation of the accumulated knowledge on the testing of traditional theories (see Deardorff 1984, for a survey), and on Leamer's study (Leamer 1984) of the sources of comparative advantage. In the case of the latter, factor endowments differences (or H-O factors) explain quite a large proportion of the cross-section variance of net trade patterns in ten aggregates of goods (including four 'types' of manufacturing goods). This is at a high level of aggregation and does not negate the possibility of non-H-O factors (simultaneously and at lower levels of aggregation) influencing trade patterns.[2] Indeed, there is consistent evidence from the econometric studies of IIT thus far published that inter-industry and country differences in IIT levels at the approximate level of the 'industry' are systematically related to the country characteristics of trading partners and to industry characteristics (see Greenaway and Milner [1987]). Thus the presence of decreasing costs or scale factor of some form, and of scope for horizontal or vertical product differentiation, for instance, do appear to have significant and symmetric influences on the levels of both exports and imports at the detailed commodity or 'industry' level.

It must be recognized also that aggregate or macroeconomic developments may influence the (average) intensity of IIT, in the short to medium term in particular. The UK's net overall trade balance on manufactures was affected significantly over the 1970s, for instance, by trend factors (e.g. secular influences on productivity and competitiveness, cyclical factors (e.g. adjustments to exchange rate changes), and erratic shocks (e.g. the oil shocks induced by OPEC price rises). Inter-temporal comparisons of measured IIT have therefore to be undertaken with some caution. The dangers of bias are more serious, however, when comparing single summary statistics on an economy-wide basis than when comparing on an industry-by-industry basis.

Policy influences

In tems of the analysis of inter-industry trade-flows, the conventional view is that industrial countries' tariffs are now (given the progressive post-war lowering of rates) a relatively unimportant factor in the broad pattern of world manufactured trade.[3] However, these judgements are based in general on the aggregate trade effects of a relatively uniform lowering of the existing structure of tariffs. The measurements are relative to prevailing patterns of trade rather than a (hypothetical) antimonde. The differential treatment of products and of suppliers (industrial and non-industrial) in country 'concessions' in tariff negotiations and the increasing and selective use of non-tariff barriers may significantly disturb specific trade flows (defined by exporter, importer, and commodity or tariff line). However, much of the available information is rather impressionistic and incomplete in coverage (see Winters 1987).

In addition, some of the existing evidence on the impact of trade policy on trade patterns is contradictory or difficult to reconcile. Robson (1984) and Winters (1986), for instance, report large 'integration' or EEC effects on trade patterns in manufactures – up to half of actual trade with any individual partner country in 1979 could have been due to integration. This evidence is difficult to reconcile with the suggestion above that the broad/aggregate effects of tariffs are relatively small. It has been suggested that integration positively stimulates intra-industry trade rather than inter-industry trade. Although this is confirmed by some econometric studies of intra-industry trade (e.g. Loertscher and Wolter 1980; Havrylyshyn and Civan 1983), it may be that the integration effect in these studies is capturing other effects of proximity omitted from the regressions. It is of interest to note, for example, that an 'EEC' dummy is not significant in the case of the study by Balassa (1986) when other proximity dummies are included.

There is clearly a need for more careful and systematic analysis of the impact of trade policy on the detailed pattern of trade flows. We turn therefore to an examination of the impact of trade liberalization on intra- and inter-industry trade and specialization.

Specialization and trade policy: alternative hypotheses

There is some confusion to be found in existing econometric studies of intra-industry trade over the expected impact of trade restrictions. Consider, for example, some of the following quotes:

> 'Trade liberalisation generally encourages both inter- and intra-industry trade.' (Bergstrand 1983: 225)
> 'Intra-industry trade among countries is intense if barriers to trade are low.' (Loertscher and Wolter 1980: 283)
> '...the lower and more similar the trade barriers between countries the higher should be the level of two-way trade.' (Pagoulatos and Sorenson 1975: 460)

Trade barriers are represented as discouraging both intra- and inter-industry trade, *however measured*. In fact, all three studies quoted above use a Grubel and Lloyd-type index of the *share* of intra-industry trade (B) or matched trade in gross trade, and apply this measure on a cross-sectional, industry (j) basis. But the relationship expected between trade barriers and the *proportion* of IIT and between trade barriers and the *absolute amount* of IIT may not be identical, even for a given model of the determinants of exports (X) and imports (M) (see Milner, 1988). If:

$$(X_j + M_j) \quad = |X_j - M_j| + [(X_j + M_j) - |X_j - M_j|] \quad [10.1]$$

$$\left\{ \begin{array}{ll} \text{gross trade} & = \text{net or} \quad + \text{the absolute level of} \\ & \quad \text{inter-} \quad\quad\quad \text{intra-industry trade} \\ & \quad \text{industry} \quad\quad (IIT_j) \\ & \quad \text{trade} \end{array} \right\}$$

and

$$1 = \frac{|X_j - M_j|}{(X_j + M_j)} + \left[1 - \frac{|X_j - M_j|}{(X_j + M_j)} \right] \quad [10.2]$$

$$\left\{ \begin{array}{ll} \text{total share} & = \text{share of} \quad + \text{share of intra-} \\ & \quad \text{inter-} \quad\quad\quad \text{industry trade} (B_j) \\ & \quad \text{industry} \\ & \quad \text{trade} (T_j) \end{array} \right\}$$

then IIT_j and B_j are not necessarily directly related. This problem is, in fact, recognized by Caves (1981):

> Countries 1 and 2, which initially carry on some two-way trade in product A, both cut their tariffs in half. In the long run, producers in each country find export opportunities sufficient to attain the same proportional expansion of exports. The *amount* of intra-industry trade will have increased, but the *proportion* (our dependent variable) will remain the same. Why should trade liberalisation bring about faster growth of the (initially) smaller trade flow – necessary to bring about a proportional and not just absolute expansion of intra-industry trade?
>
> (Caves 1981: 213)

Given such ambiguity, it is hardly surprising that studies employing tariff and non-tariff independent variables against *a specific share measure of intra-industry trade* should produce inconsistent results. Some previous results are as follows:

Study	Tariff barriers	Non-tariff barriers
Pagoulatos and Sorenson (1975)	– ***	– [a]
Caves (1981)	+ [a]	
Toh (1982	+ [a]	– [a]
Bergstrand (1983)	– [a]	

*** Denotes 1 per cent level of significance.
[a] Statistical significance not reported.

There is therefore a clear need to specify more carefully the

189

hypothesized relationship between trade patterns and trade policy, and to test the hypothesis more carefully.

Trade liberalization as a constraint on intra-industry specialization (Case A)

Full tests of international trade theory should combine empirically the three components of the H-O model: factor intensities, factor endowments, and the direction of trade (see Leamer and Bowen 1981). Although Leamer (1984) does not employ factor-intensity data, he does show that in a simple multi-good and factor H-O model, countries' net trade vectors are linearly related to factor endowments. We would therefore expect that (symmetric multilateral) tariff imposition would lower net trade balances (where the sign on the trade balance is unaltered). For a given industry (j), we would also expect non-symmetric expansion of trade ($|\Delta X_j| > |\Delta M_j|$, if $X_j >$

Table 10.4 A schema of possible effects of trade liberalization on trade and specialization indices

Indices[a]	Case A	Case B	Case C
(1) $[X_j + M_j]$	+	+	+
(2) $|X_j - M_j|$	+	constant	+
(3) IIT_j	−	+	+
(4) T_j	+	−	constant
(5) B_j	−	+	constant
(6) $\dfrac{|X_j - M_j|}{Q_j}(M > X)$	+	constant	(?) + (for constant consumption)
(7) $\dfrac{|X_j - M_j|}{Q_j}(X > M)$	−	constant	−
(8) $\dfrac{IIT_j}{Q_j}(M > X)$	+	+	(?) + (for constant consumption)
(9) $\dfrac{IIT_j}{Q_j}(X > M)$	−	+	−

[a] = Statistical significance.
[b] Q_j = net production.

M_j, or $|\Delta M_j| > |\Delta X_j|$, if $M_j > X_j$) to result from symmetric trade liberalization. The implications of this for alternative trade and production indices for the case where M_j or X_j declines in absolute terms (the classic inter-industry specialization case for constant consumption patterns) are set out in Table 10.4 (Case A).

Under this schema, trade liberalization increases gross (1) and net (2) trade in industry (j) and reduces the absolute level of intra-industry trade (3) as exports/imports increase and imports/exports decrease in absolute terms. The share of inter-industry trade (4) increases and the share of intra-industry trade decreases (5). For those industries where exports increase and imports decrease (and $X_j > M_j$), total production increases. Therefore the share of IIT_j in production (9) declines, and the share of inter-industry trade in production (7) is likely to decline (given the increase in the denominator). For those industries where imports increase and exports decrease (and $M_j > X_j$), total production falls. Therefore, the share of inter-industry trade in production (6) in these cases rises, and the share of intra-industry in production (8) is likely to rise.[4]

Trade liberalization as a stimulus to intra-industry specialization (Case B)

Gross trade $(X_j + M_j)$ in manufactures has expanded in the post-war period at a far faster rate in general than net trade $(|X_j - M_j|)$. Thus, Hufbauer and Chilas (1974) argue that there has not been any significant increase in inter-industry specialization over this period, despite the progressive reduction in tariff barriers.[5] Their explanation for this is that: 'GATT may be viewed as the Western vehicle for ensuring "balanced trade" in manufactured goods among the major industrial powers' (Hufbauer and Chilas 1974: 6–7). Given the political ascendancy of producers over consumers, then the GATT formula has fostered the swapping of tariff concessions. It has been easier to secure one industry's consent for lower tariff barriers if the same industry also stands to gain from reciprocal concessions abroad. (Even better are mutual concessions which increase export potential for the firms whose domestic sales are threatened.)

In a stylized representation of this pattern of trade liberalization (Case B), we would expect symmetric liberalization to result in symmetric expansion of both imports and exports (i.e. $\Delta X_j = \Delta M_j$), so as to leave net trade (2) and total production unaltered. (Indices (6) and (7) are therefore unaltered.) All the other indices must increase, except for the share of inter-industry trade in gross trade (4) which must fall.[6]

Trade liberalization as a stimulus to both inter- and intra-industry specialization (Case C)

In a world where both H-O factors and non-H-O or Linder-type factors may simultaneously influence levels and patterns of trade, trade liberalization may encourage the simultaneous growth of both inter- and intra-industry trade in absolute terms (indices (2) and (3) in Case C of the schema) without altering the relative importance of particular factors, and therefore shares, of each type of trade (indices (4) and (5) remain constant). This would result from an equal proportionate increase in both exports and imports $(\Delta X_j/X_j = \Delta M_j/M_j)$.[7] The production effects (for a constant level of consumption) depend, therefore, on the sign on net trade. Where $X_j > M_j$, trade expansion will increase domestic production, and the shares of inter- and intra-industry trade in total production (indices (7) and (9)) are likely to fall (given the increase in the denominator). For a given level of consumption on j, then proportionate trade expansion where $M_j > X_j$ will lower domestic production. In this case, the shares of inter- and intra-industry trade in total production should rise. In a world of Linder-type influences, however, imports of differentiated products may not displace existing domestic production. Consumption of j is likely to increase as the demand for variety is satisfied. Thus, even in industries where $M_j > X_j$, proportionate trade expansion may be accompanied by production growth. In which case the effect of trade liberalization on indices (6) and (8) is uncertain for Case C.

Some evidence for trade liberalization and specialization

Problems of formal testing

Formal econometric testing of the hypotheses set out in the previous section is seriously data-constrained. Time-series modelling of inter-industry changes in levels of intra- and inter-industry trade and specialization would require time-series information on 'natural' and commercial policy variables. Information on factor endowments and intensities, or on Linder-type influences such as the scope for product differentiation and scale economies, is not comprehensively available on a continuous and industry basis. Measurement and proxy problems also abound; and, in any case, it is not at all obvious what the implications of changing technological and market conditions should have for the *inter-industry* pattern of trade and specialization. The same can also be said for the implications of inter-temporal changes in the inter-industry pattern of commercial policy variables.

For instance, a 50 per cent reduction of import tariffs on products x and y will have very different consequences if there is a differential amount of 'water-on-the-tariff' in the case of the two products. It is not the case, in any event, that the reduction of nominal tariff rates unambiguously equates with trade liberalization. Where the nominal tariff is measured by the revenue incidence of tariffs on imports (i.e. an ex-post measure), then this is an average of duty-free and dutiable imports for a given industry. Any change over time, therefore, is the outcome of changes in duties on product lines within an industry, and/or in the proportion of duty-free imports. A fall in the average tariff could therefore be accompanied by a rise in duties or a decrease in the amount of duty-free imports (though not both). Even if falling nominal tariffs could be unambiguously interpreted, there would still be a need to measure the impact of non-tariff trade barriers and the combined effects of all trade barriers on both final products and intermediate inputs for effective rates of protection before the restrictiveness of commercial policy could be accurately quantitifed.

Similar difficulties confront cross-section (only) analysis in this area. Even if the impact of 'natural' influences can be captured appropriately on a cross-sectional basis, and this is not unproblematic, it is not obvious why inter-industry variations in possible dependent variables, such as the absolute level or share of intra-industry trade, should be systematically related to inter-industry variations in rates of protection (however measured). Given these constraints on formal empirical testing, it will be more useful for the present purpose to adopt a more informal empirical methodology.

Some informal evidence

Rather than seek formally and accurately to 'explain' inter-industry variations in trade and specialization patterns, the present task will be to draw inferences from the consistency of actual episodes in post-war trade liberalization experienced by the UK, with the three stylized cases outlined in the previous section.

Trade liberalization episodes

The periods or episodes chosen are 1970–3, 1973–8 and 1979–84; post-Kennedy Round, transition to EEC membership, and post-Tokyo Round periods respectively. The justification for this selection and the characteristics of each period can be made with reference to Table 5. This table gives summary or aggregate information on the share of duty free imports (column (1)) and the average rate of duty paid on dutiable imports (column (2)) and on all imports (column (3)) for UK manufactured imports for the years between 1967 and 1985 (inclusive).

The Kennedy Round of GATT negotiations ended in agreement in May 1967. Table 10.5 shows the marked fall in revenue incidence on dutiable imports between 1967 (16 per cent) and 1973 (8.7 per cent). There was no immediate effect on the broad direction of UK imports – the share of duty-free imports (from EFTA in particular) did not fall until 1970. After 1969, however, there was a marked decline in the share of duty-free imports. Multilateral tariff liberaliz-ation may therefore be viewed as exposing the UK to greater competition from non-EFTA industrial countries. The post-Kennedy-Round period (1970–3) will seek to capture the effects of this multilateral liberalization. By contrast, the period 1973–7 covers the transition to EEC membership – tariff revenue incidence on dutiable imports fell somewhat further, and, towards the end of the transition period, the share of duty-free imports rose sharply. The period 1973–8 will therefore seek to capture the effects of a substantial regional trade liberalization. (The average duty paid on all manu-

Table 10.5   Tariffs on manufactured imports in the UK, 1967–85

| Year | *Total manufactures (SITC 5–8)* | | |
	(1) Share of duty-free imports *(%)*	*(2)* Tariff revenue incidence on dutiable imports	*(3)* 'Ex-post' tariff average on all imports
1967	63	0.160	0.059
1968	66	0.126	0.043
1969	64	0.126	0.045
1970	59	0.114	0.047
1971	56	0.100	0.044
1972	50	0.095	0.048
1973	53	0.087	0.041
1974	54	0.080	0.037
1975	53	0.071	0.033
1976	50	0.058	0.029
1977	64	0.069	0.025
1978	79	0.101	0.021
1979	79	0.100	0.021
1980	79	0.093	0.020
1981	76	0.096	0.023
1982	77	0.089	0.021
1983	77	0.086	0.020
1984	77	0.083	0.019
1985	77	0.083	0.019

Source: Adapted from Jones (1987)

factured imports fell from 4.1 per cent to 2.1 per cent between 1973 and 1978.) Since 1978, the share of duty-free imports has remained fairly stable (at about 77 per cent of all manufactured imports). However, the Tokyo Round of GATT negotiations (completed in 1979) resulted in relatively small tariff reductions which could be phased in over eight years from 1 January 1980. (The revenue incidence on dutiable UK manufactured imports only fell from 9.3 per cent to 8.3 per cent between 1980 and 1985.) Indeed, this episode of tariff liberalization might be viewed as being especially likely to encourage intra-industry specialization (in line with the Hufbauer–Chilas type of argument). It might be argued that tariff reductions (even if relatively small on average) were only agreed upon by industrialized countries because non-tariff interventions were by this time more pervasive, and because 'sensitive' items (e.g. textiles, footwear, etc.) were exempt from, or subject to below-average, tariff reductions. This period (1979–84) of so-called multilateral trade liberalization will therefore seek to capture the effects of the 'new protectionism', rather than the effects of the dismantling of the 'old protectionism'. Jones (1987) shows that the share of UK manufactured imports subject to non-tariff restraints remained, in fact, relatively constant between 1980 and 1983 (at around 10 per cent of extra EEC trade). But this hides the fact that a fall in one specific area – i.e. in restraints on textiles and clothing from 'Mediterranean' suppliers such as Greece, Portugal, and Spain – offset a large rise in voluntary restraints on a number of other products (cars, video recorders, televisions, footwear, pottery, cutlery, etc.).

Changes in UK trade and specialization, 1970–84

Each of the indices set out in the earlier schema were calculated at the 'industry' level (SIC digit 3) for the years 1970, 1973, 1978, 1979, and 1984. For the first three of these years, 100 manufacturing industries, according to the pre-1980 SIC classification, were identified. In 1979 and 1984, ninety-six industries, according to the 1980 SIC classification were used.[8] Frequency distributions and overall averages for three of the indices – the share of intra-industry trade in total trade (B_j) and the indices of inter- and intra-industry trade – are set out in Tables 10.6, 10.7, and 10.8, respectively. (Given the change in classification between 1978 and 1979, comparisons between these two years must be undertaken cautiously.) For the present exercise, it was also necessary to compare these indices for the beginning and end of each of the periods identified in the last section. Table 10.9 summarizes the frequency with which all the indices increased or decreased over the periods 1970–3, 1973–8, and 1979–84.

Table 10.6 Industry indices of share of intra-industry trade in total trade,[a] 1970–84

	% of industries with index in range				
	1970	1973	1978	1979	1984
0–10	2	1	0	1	2
11–20	2	2	4	3	2
21–30	9	6	4	7	6
31–40	13	4	5	6	6
41–50	11	11	8	6	7
51–60	13	12	13	14	6
61–70	17	18	13	8	14
71–80	11	9	13	18	8
81–90	11	20	12	15	27
91–100	11	17	28	22	21
Overall average[b]	59	66	69	66	69

[a]B_j as defined in text ($\times$ 100).
[b]Arithmetic average.

Table 10.7 Industry indices of inter-industry specialization,[a] 1970–84 in percentages

	% of industries with index in range				
	1970	1973	1978	1979	1984
0–0.10	29	33	30	32	28
0.11–0.20	18	21	12	13	11
0.21–0.30	15	13	20	14	15
0.31–0.40	8	8	12	14	10
0.41–0.50	7	3	5	0	5
0.51–0.60	2	4	3	9	2
0.61–0.70	3	0	4	0	2
0.71–0.80	2	3	1	1	4
0.81–0.90	4	2	2	2	1
0.91–1.00	1	2	1	2	2
Over unity	11	11	10	14	19
Overall average[b]	0.42	0.39	0.39	0.86	0.91

[a]$\dfrac{[X_j - M_j]}{Q_j}$ as described in text.
[b]Arithmatic average.

Several distinctive features of the data should be noted before analyzing it in detail. First, it should be noted that intra-industry trade has been pervasive throughout this period, even when measured at this level of disaggregation. Even in 1970, when IIT was at its lowest overall average level, its share in total trade was over 50 per

Table 10.8 Industry indices of intra-industry specialization[a], 1970–84

	% of industries with index in range				
	1970	1973	1978	1979	1984
0–0.20	29	21	16	20	18
0.21–0.40	21	18	11	15	11
0.41–0.60	23	19	13	7	9
0.61–0.80	9	15	12	16	16
0.81–1.00	5	6	14	13	5
1.01–1.20	5	6	7	6	9
1.21–1.40	0	4	8	3	3
1.41–1.60	2	3	4	2	4
1.61–1.80	2	2	3	6	3
1.81–2.00	1	2	2	3	2
greater than 2	3	4	10	9	19
Overall average[b]	0.64	0.89	0.99	1.02	1.20

[a] $\dfrac{IIT_j}{Q_j}$ as described in text.

[b] Arithmetic average.

cent in almost two-thirds of manufacturing industries (see Table 10.6). Second, it should be emphasized that increases in the share of IIT in net production – it rose on average continuously over the period from 0.64 in 1970 to 1.20 in 1984 (see Table 10.8). – is compatible with increases in the share inter-industry (or net trade) in net production. As Table 10.8 shows, although the average level of inter-industry specialization fell somewhat between 1970 and 1973, over the period as a whole, average levels of inter-industry specialization increased. Third, average levels of inter-industry specialization, when measured at this level of disaggregation (i.e. at the level which approximates with an industry), are much higher than those reported by Hufbauer and Chilas (1974). In that study, specialization indices were indentified for the following six sectors – metals, chemicals, textiles and clothing, machinery, transport equipment, and other manufacturing. Given the reduction induced in more aggregate net trade balances by trade balances of opposite sign at lower levels of aggregation, it is hardly surprising that low and relatively constant (over time) indices were identified. The contention of this study is that changes in the relevant indices can only be appropriately interpreted if they are applied at the appropriate level of aggregation.

Let us consider the changes in industry indices summarized in Table 10.9. The post-Kennedy-Round period of multilateral-trade

Table 10.9 Changes in trade and specialization indices: UK manufacturing industries,[a] 1970–84

	Frequency of change in industry index					
	1970–3		1973–8		1979–84	
	Increase	Decrease	Increase	Decrease	Increase	Decrease
(1) $(X_j + M_j)$	99	1	100	0	91	5
(2) $|X_j - M_j|$ (of which change sign)	63	37 (4)	86	14 (4)	59	37 (10)
(3) IIT_j	99	1	97	3	89	7
(4) T_j	27	73	41	59	46	49
(5) B_j	73	27	59	41	49	46
$\dfrac{|X_j - M_j|}{Q_j}$						
(6) if $M > X$	18	13	13	18	32	8
(7) if $X > M$ (where sign changes)	11 (5)	47 (5)	35 (6)	16 (10)	11 (7)	28 (10)
$\dfrac{IIT_j}{Q_j}$						
(8) if $M > X$	20	12	28	2	25	15
(9) if $X > M$ (where sign changes)	52 (9)	6	44 (13)	8 (3)	32 (14)	7 (3)
	total no. of industries = 100		total no. of industries = 100		total no. of industries = 96	

[a]Industries defined as digit 3 of UK Standard Industrial Classification (SIC); SIC (1968) for 1970–3 and 1973–8 and SIC (1980) for 1979–84.

liberation (1970–3) is shown to be a period of predominantly *intra*-industry specialization. Although gross trade rose in nominal terms in all three periods (as would be expected over a period of real income and price increase) – in the case of the first period, net trade $(|X_j - M_j|)$ fell even in nominal terms for thirty-seven industries. By contrast, the absolute level of matched trade (IIT_j) rose in all but one industry, and, as a result, the share of intra- (inter-)industry trade in gross trade, $B_j(T_j)$ rose (fell) in seventy-three out of the 100 industries investigated. Thus, for seventy-two industries, the index of *intra*-industry specialization (IIT_j/Q_j) increased, and, for sixty industries, the *inter*-industry specialization index $(|X_j - M_j|/Q_j)$ fell.

198

After 1973 there is evidence of a slowing-down in the process of intra-industry specialization. The share of intra-industry trade in total trade, which had increased in 73 per cent of cases in the 1970–3 period, only increased in 59 per cent of cases over the period 1973–8 and for only 51 per cent of manufacturing industries over the final period. Indeed, net trade ($|X_j - M_j|$) decreased in only fourteen cases during 1973–8, although the more rapid growth in gross trade during this period than in the post-1979 period meant that T_j (the share of inter-industry trade in total trade) fell in more cases in the transition to EEC membership than in the post-Tokyo-Round period. The 1973–8 period, although displaying evidence of simultaneous inter- and intra-industry specialization, can be represented as one where intra-industry specialization still predominates somewhat. The share of intra-industry trade in gross trade (B_j) increased in 59 per cent of industries and in net output (IIT_j/Q_j) increased in 72 per cent of industries. By contrast, over the period 1979–84 the B_j index increased in only 51 per cent of cases and the intra-industry specialization index in only 59 per cent of cases. The post-Tokyo-Round period can be described in the case of the UK, therefore, as a period of further and approximately matched inter- and intra-industry specialization in manufactures.

How may this pattern of specialization relate to trade liberalization, and does it help us to distinguish between the alternative hypotheses on the specialization–trade-policy relationship outlined earlier? Of course, the methodology is crude. When making comparisons like this, over time, we are not holding other things constant, and changing non-policy influences may account to a significant degree for these different episodes of specialization – for the changes within and between periods. If, however, it is reasonable to believe that there were not substantial inter-industry changes in 'natural' influences in patterns of trade and specialization over this period, then cautious judgements about each episode of trade liberalization may be justified.[9]

The impact of multilateral liberalization

As we have seen, both the post-Kennedy and post-Tokyo periods were associated with some intra-industry specialization – in the case of the post-Kennedy period, intra-industry specialization clearly predominates. Neither episode gives any support for Case A (as set out in Table 10.4 on p. 190); therefore, liberalization does not appear to act as a constraint on intra-industry specialization. Table 10.10 records information on the extent to which the observed changes in trade and specialization indices in Table 10.6 are consistent with the

Table 10.10 Consistency of observed changes in trade and specialization indices with alternative hypotheses (in percentages)

	% of observed changes[a] consistent with alternative cases								
	1970–73			1973–78			1979–84		
	Case A	Case B	Case C	Case A	Case B	Case C	Case A	Case B	Case C
(1) $(X_j + M_j)$	99	99	99	100	100	100	95	95	95
(2) $|X_j - M_j|$	63	0[a]	63	86	0[a]	86	61	0[a]	61
(3) IIT_j	1	99	99	3	97	97	7	93	93
(4) T_j	27	73	0[a]	41	59	0[a]	48	51	0[a]
(5) B_j	27	73	0[a]	41	59	0[a]	48	51	0[a]
$\dfrac{|X_j - M_j|}{Q_j}$									
(6) if $M > X$	56	0[a]	56	42	0[a]	42	80	0[a]	80
(7) if $X > M$	81	0[a]	81	30	0[a]	30	72	0[a]	72
$\dfrac{IIT_j}{Q_j}$									
(8) if $M > X$	63	63	63	90	90	90	63	63	63
(9) if $X > M$	10	90	10	17	83	17	18	82	18

[a] denotes that constant values were predicted.

predicted effects of liberalization set out in Table 10.4. It shows that the absolute level of intra-industry trade (IIT_j) did not decrease as predicted by Case A. In fact, T_j (B_j) rose for a clear minority (majority) of industries, in particular in the first period, and contrary to the prediction of Case A. Given that indices (1) and (8) do not discriminate between the alternative hypotheses, Cases B and C clearly dominate Case A in all three periods.

From this evidence, it is more difficult to discriminate between Cases B and C. There is a problem of interpretation where no change in an index is predicted. Given the difficulties of defining constancy for the present purpose, any change (at the second decimal point) is recorded as an increase or decrease. Thus, Case C appears to predict poorly on the shares of intra- or inter-industry in gross trade, while Case B does the same for indices (2), (6), and (7). Although Case B dominates Case C, in terms of prediction for index (9), the evidence on balance supports the view that multilateral liberalization has encouraged both inter- and intra-industry specialization rather than intra-industry specialization alone. Indeed, in the post-Tokyo-Round period – after what is viewed as a particularly 'managed' liberalization – there is more evidence of inter-industry specialization than in the post-Kennedy-Round period. (The near equality of the frequency of industry increases and decreases in the B_j and T_j indices in the 1979–84 period may be interpreted as evidence of overall constancy of the shares of each type of trade, along the lines predicted by Case (or hypothesis) C.)

The impact of regional liberalization

The fact that more inter-industry specialization occurred in the transition to EEC membership than in the post-Kennedy-Round period might be cited as support for Case B. If the intra-industry specialization was more pronounced during an episode of multi-lateral than regional liberalization, especially given the regional liberalization of trade under conditions particularly conducive to the expansion of Linder-type or two-way trade, it might be argued that there has been a distinct GATT influence on specialization trends. But this argument is no longer supported if the comparison is between the 1973–8 and 1979–84 periods; intra-industry specialization is less pronounced in this later period of multilateral liberalization than in a period of regional liberalization. Although the summary information again does not clearly discriminate between Cases B and C for the period 1973–8, there is evidence of both intra- and inter-industry specialization during this period, and of consistency of the evidence with Case C. The results for net (inter-) and matched (intra-) trade, in absolute terms (indices (2) and (3)), are highly consistent with Case C. On *average*, the share indices (T_j and B_j) also remain relatively constant.

It would therefore be difficult to conclude that trade liberalization was, in general, a stimulus to inter-industry specialization alone (Case A) or to intra-industry specialization alone (Case B). The evidence examined for the UK is consistent with the view that there are concurrent natural sources of intra- and inter-industry specialization, and that trade liberalization, multilateral and regional, acts as a stimulus to both. Of course, it may well be the case that the manner in which commercial-policy reforms are negotiated and implemented, influences the pace of specialization, the direction of trade flows, and the commodity composition of each industry's imports and exports. The present analysis has not sought, and is not able, to identify such detailed policy influences. (It is unlikely that the 'antimonde' could be identified on a comprehensive basis at such a fine level of disaggreg-ation.) It is difficult to reject the view that trade policy matters in the short term and at the detailed level, given the growth in importance of non-tariff trade interventions by governments and quasi-official bodies. But this is quite consistent with the view that the post-war trend towards increased intra-industry specialization is not, in general, 'man-made' or policy-induced.

Specialization and structural adjustment

If prevailing industry trade and specialization patterns are not, in general, ultimately the result of policy-maker's resistance to the adjustment problems traditionally associated with increased inter-industry specialization, then it is legitimate to consider whether structural adjustment problems are, and adjustment policy responses should be, different – in the context of intra-industry specialization as opposed to inter-industry specialization.

Of course, the ensuing discussion presumes that, in general, trade (inter or intra-) is welfare-raising. In the case of intra-industry trade, it has been argued (e.g. Franko, 1979) that there may be welfare-loss if trade is the outcome of market-sharing by oligopolistic firms at non-optimal output levels. Similarly, it has been suggested that trade in differentiated goods could take product variety beyond the 'socially optimal' level, and could therefore under certain circumstances, and in particular for developing countries, reduce welfare (James and Stewart, 1981). Nevertheless, the possibilities for welfare-raising intra-industry trade are considerable, and the general consensus is that such trade is welfare-raising (see Greenaway, 1982, for a review of the factors influencing the magnitude of welfare gains). Indeed, there are potential additional gains in the context of intra-industry trade, associated with product variety and decreasing costs. But this does not mean that the gains from intra-industry trade are necessarily (in general) in excess of those from inter-industry trade. Since intra-industry trade is likely to be more intense in trade between countries with similar factor endowments and where pre-trade price differentials may be lower, then the scope for gains from price reduction may be lower in the context of intra-industry trade. The relative magnitude of the gains from inter- and intra-industry trade is ultimately an empirical issue, but there is evidence (e.g. Cox and Harris 1985) that considerable gains from liberalization may arise where industries are characterized by scale economies and imperfect competition.

Structural adjustment costs

Although there are no *a priori* grounds for expecting differential net gains from increased intra- and inter-industry specialization, it is frequently anticipated that structural adjustment costs will be lower (and therefore adjustment smoother) in the context of intra-industry specialization. Balassa (1967), for example, argues that increases in trade in differentiated goods can be achieved without changing production (at home and abroad) or with relatively minor adjustments in the within-industry commodity composition. Willmore (1979) similarly sees intra-industry trade leading to low adjustment costs where there is relatively high substitutability in production and the greater probability of within-firm or within-plant product variety. Finally, Helleiner (1979) argues that intra-industry trade that is the intra-firm trade of multinational enterprises may reduce adjustment problems. These commentators are therefore implicitly assuming that labour and capital markets are more likely to respond 'quickly' to price change, because the price changes are relatively small and /or because the mobility of factors (occupationally and/or geographically) is relatively great in the context of intra-industry specialization. In addition, Krugman (1981) has questioned whether the Stopler– Samuelson proposition necessarily holds in the context of intra-industry trade. In an H-O-S world, trade liberalization, and resulting inter-industry specialization, affects factor-rewards differentially – in a capital-abundant economy, trade benefits capital relative to labour. As a result, labour resistance to trade liberalization is explicable in this context. But Krugman (1981) shows that, if import substitutes and exports use similar factors in similar proportions and if trading partners have similar factor endowments, both capital and labour can gain from trade. Given that prices are likely to be less sticky in an upward direction, adjustment is likely to quicken for a further reason.

Despite these strong *a priori* arguments, some caution may be expressed. There is no strong empirical information to support the 'lower adjustment cost' hypothesis. Are, for instance, variations in factor intensities lower, and substitutabilities in production greater, within industries than between industries? In theory, we expect this to be so, but the results of empirical work by Finger (1975), Rayment (1976), and Lundberg and Hansson (1986) comparing intra- and inter-industry variations in factor intensities do *not necessarily* confirm this. It might be argued, therefore, that *observed* intra-industry and inter-industry trade are both explained by traditional factor proportions differences, and structural adjustment problems are identical in both cases. Given the depth of empirical support for non-H-O-S or Linder-type influences on two-way trade, it would seem more appropriate to interpret the evidence of *observed* heterogeneity within 'industries' as evidence of imperfect measurement of actual levels of genuine intra-industry trade. Significantly, Lundberg and Hansson (1986) find (Swedish) intra-industry trade levels to be *inversely* related to within-industry variance of various factor intensities. This gives support to the view that actual, if not observed, intra-industry trade is not explained by factor intensity and price differences and that it is likely in general to result in lower structural adjustment costs.

Structural adjustment policies

If for the moment we accept unquestioningly the economic rationale for structural adjustment policies – policies which ease shifts of factors of production within and between sectors and industries – then acceptance of the 'lower adjustment cost' hypothesis implies that industries subject to greater intra-industry specialization justify less assistance or compensation than those subject to greater inter-industry specialization. This implication may encourage governments to adopt more liberal trade policies or, at least, policies which encourage intra-industry at the expense of inter-industry specialization. (Our encouragement should be for the former rather than the latter.) In which case attention should focus on the nature, rather than amount, of structural adjustment policies. Adjustment problems, whether or not lower than in the case of inter-industry specialization, will exist in the context of intra-industry specialization. Given the apparent misuse of 'adjustment policies' in the past, it would be better to encourage governments to adopt optimal or appropriate adjustment policies for any type of specialization, rather than to encourage the adoption of specialization-restricting measures.

It is possible to draw a crude distinction between three alternative views of adjustment policy: a 'market-freeing' view; a 'market-argumenting' view; and a 'market-replacing' view. Proponents of the 'market-freeing' line rarely view adjustment problems as trade-created; they are the result of institutional and legislative constraints on the operation of efficient markets (see Blackhurst *et al.* 1978). While accepting the desirability of decentralized decision-making and of encouraging market efficiency, those who subscribe to the 'market-argumenting' view would question whether all distortions are government-induced and whether the political dimension of adjustment problems can be ignored. Although the 'market-argumenting' view recommends intervention to accelerate adjustment, it presumes that adjustment will occurs in the absence of intervention, albeit slowly. By contrast, the 'market-replacing' view tends to envisage that no adjustment will take place and that widespread interventions and direct controls are required.

If it is the case that adjustment is smoother under intra-industry trade expansion, then the possibility of complete market failure substantially disappears. Under increased inter- or intra-industry specialization, however, the argument that adjustment assistance is desirable to discourage defensive/restrictive action by sectional interests is persuasive. In which case, governments should be encouraged to employ the principles of optimal intervention analysis – to consistently and permanently assign specific adjustment policies to deal with specific aspects of the adjustment problem – rather than to use a blanket mixture of measures aimed at propping up industries or firms, in an *ad hoc* fashion over time as and when they come under pressure. Given that there is likely to be divergence between the private and social costs of scrapping capital and firing labour, then policies should be aimed at removing each particular distortion at source. Thus, the availablity of retraining grants, removal allowances, capital equipment grants, etc. could be used to accelerate the pace of adjustment in capital and labour markets in general. The amount of assistance given to industries facing differential increases in intra- and inter-industry specialization would then be endogenously determined by the extent to which particular market frictions were experienced. This is distinct from a situation in which policies of financial assistance and compensation are designed according to the specific requirements of individual sectors or industries. Governments have proved to be very keen, but very ineffective, in offering such selective support. As the earlier empirical analysis showed, this is due in no small part to the continuously changing pattern of specialization at the industry level.

Conclusions

Although there is scope for more formal and detailed empirical investigation of the impact of trade policy on patterns of trade and specialization, it is difficult to conclude, on the basis of the present study, other than that there are concurrent natural sources of both intra- and inter-industry specialization and that trade liberalization acts as a stimulus to both. *In general, and in the long term*, the post-war increases in intra-industry trade and specialization are not 'man-made' or policy-induced by the process of swapping tariff concessions or by discriminatory use of non-tariff interventions. Indeed, inter-industry specialization (when measured at the industry level) has been more extensive (in the case of the UK at least) than is suggested by the more recent literature on non-H-O-S trade flows between industrialized countries.

The management of tariff liberalization and of the 'new protectionism' clearly has an impact in the short term on the direction and detailed commodity composition of specific industry's exports and imports, but the ability of governments to resist specialization trends in the longer term (despite the evidence of considerable effort) is limited. Governments should, in fact, be encouraged to accelerate the process of structural adjustment, i.e. to augment market processes through active structural adjustment policies. It may well be the case that adjustment costs are lower in the context of intra-industry specialization than of inter-industry specialization, but they are still unlikely to be zero. Governments, therefore, should have continuous and uniform policies to deal with specific aspects of the adjustment process – the relocation of labour, retraining, the scrapping of capital, etc. – rather than seek to target trade-related assistance/compensation packages on a selective basis at specific sectors or industries. Finely targeted (trade-related) policies at the industry level are more likely in practice to discourage than to encourage structural change.

Acknowledgement

The author is grateful to Professor David Greenaway (University of Nottingham) for helpful comments on a first draft of this chapter.

Notes

1. The studies completed encompass developed market economies (Hesse 1974; Aquino 1978), less developed countries (Willmore 1974; Balassa 1979), small economies (Greenaway 1983), large economies (Hufbauer and Chilas 1974), and centrally planned economies (Pelzman 1978; Drabek and Greenaway 1984).
2. Bowden (1986), for instance, finds some support for both factor proportions (asymmetric influences on exports and imports) and Linder-type influences (symmetric influences on exports and imports) in explaining bilateral trade flows at the four-digit SIC level.
3. Deardorff and Stern (1981), for instance, suggest much smaller trade effects for the Tokyo Round than was estimated for the Kennedy Round by Finger (1976).
4. The index in the complete inter-industry case tends to X_j/Q_j as imports tend to zero; to M_j/Q_j as exports tend to zero and to M_j as total specialization occurs.
5. It is correct to conclude that intra-industry trade (in absolute terms) will increase if gross trade increases by more than net trade. In fact, Hufbauer and Chilas (1974) cite the absence of rises in aggregate specialization indices (of the form in indices 6 and 7) to justify their conclusion that little inter-industry specialization had taken place. The conclusion may be correct but the basis is unsatisfactory. The change in the index that corresponds with inter-industry specialization depends on the sign of the trade balance.
6. The implications for the share of intra-industry trade in gross trade (B_j) depend on the type of trade expansion. If $\Delta X_j = \Delta M_j$ then B_j increases as trade expands, but B_j is constant if proportional trade expansion $\Delta X_j/X_j = \Delta M_j/M_j$ takes place.

7. Arguably this might still represent the Hufbauer and Chilas argument, with reciprocal concessions resulting in a matched proportionate, rather than matched absolute, increase in both exports and imports. But Case B is a more accurate representation of the 'balanced trade' principle, since net trade balances are unaltered. In this case (Case C) net trade imbalance increases.
8. All three digit manufacturing categories were employed except for obvious 'remainder' categories, which are likely to be heterogeneous groupings.
9. Although the post-1979 period coincides with the UK's acquisition of oil-exporter status, which it can be argued accounted for the decline in the (aggregate) net trade balance on manufactures, the present analysis is not based on an evaluation of *average* levels of the relevant indices but of variations on an industry-by-industry basis.

References

Aquino, A. (1978) 'Intra-industry trade and intra-industry specialisation as concurrent sources of international trade in manufactures', *Weltwirtschaftliches Archiv* 114: 275–95.
Balassa, B. (1966) 'Tariff reductions and trade in manufactures among industrial countries', *American Economic Review* 56: 466–73.
—— (1967) *Trade Liberalisation among Industrial Countries: Objectives and Alternatives*, New York: McGraw-Hill.
—— (1979) 'Intra-industry trade and the integration of the developing countries in the world economy', *Staff Working Paper*, no. 312, Washington: World Bank.
—— (1986) 'Intra-industry trade among exporters of manufactured goods', in D. Greenaway and P. K. M. Tharakan (eds) *Imperfect Competition and International Trade*, Brighton: Wheatsheaf Books.
Bergstrand, J. H. (1983) 'Measurement and determinants of intra-industry international trade', in P. K. M. Tharakan *Intra-industry Trade: Empirical and Methodological Aspects*, Amsterdam: North-Holland.
Blackhurst, R., Marian, J., and Tumlir, J. (1978) *Adjustment, Trade and Growth in Developed and Developing Countries*, Geneva: GATT.
Bowden, R. J. (1986) 'An empirical model of bilateral trade (or its absence) in manufactured commodities', *Manchester School*, 54: 255–82.
Caves, R. E. (1981) 'Intra-industry trade and market structure in the industrial countries', *Oxford Economic Papers* 13: 203–23.
Cox, D. and Harris, R. (1985) 'Trade liberalisation and industrial organisation, some estimates for Canada', *Journal of Political Economy* 93: 115–45.
Deardoff, A. V. (1984) 'Testing trade theories and predicting trade flows' in R. W. Jones and P. B. Kenen (eds) *Handbook of International Economics*, vol. I, Amsterdam: North-Holland.
Deardoff, A. V. and Stern, R. M. (1981) 'A disaggregated model of world

production and trade: an estimate of the impact of the Tokyo Round', *Journal of Policy Modelling* 3: 127–5.

Drabek, Z. and Greenaway, D. (1984) 'Economic integration and intra-industry trade: the CMEA and EEC compared', *Kyklos* 37: 444–69.

Finger, J. M. (1975) 'Trade overlap and intra-industry trade', *Economic Enquiry* 13: 581–89.

────── (1976) 'Effects of the Kennedy Round tariff concessions', *Economic Journal* 86: 87–95.

Franko, L. G. (1979) 'Comments', in Giersch (ed.) (1979), *On the Economics of Intra-industry Trade*, Tübingen: J. C. B. Möhr.

Giersch, H. (ed.) (1974) *The International Division of Labour: Problems and Perspectives*, Tübingen: J. C. B. Möhr.

────── (ed.) (1979) *On the Economics of Intra-Industry Trade*, Tübingen: J. C. B. Möhr.

Greenaway, D. (1982) 'Identifying the gains from pure intra-industry exchange', *Journal of Economic Studies* 9: 40–56.

────── (1983) 'Inter-industry trade and intra-industry trade in Switzerland, 1965–77', *Weltwirtschaftliches Archiv* 119: 109–21.

Greenaway, D. and Milner, C. R. (1983) 'On the measurement of intra-industry trade', *Economic Journal* 93: 900–8.

────── (1984) 'A cross-section analysis of intra-industry trade in the UK', *European Economic Review* 25: 319–44.

────── (1985) 'Categorical aggregation and international trade: a reply', *Economic Journal* 95: 486–7.

──────(1986) *The Economics of Intra-Industry Trade*, Oxford: Blackwell.

──────(1989) 'The growth and significance of intra-industry trade' in J. Black and A. MacBean (eds) *Structural Change and Patterns of International Trade*,

Greenaway, D. and Tharakan, P. K. M. (eds) (1986) *Imperfect Competition and International Trade: Policy Aspects of Intra-Industry Trade*, Brighton: Wheatsheaf Books.

Grubel, H. G. and Lloyd, P. J. (1975) *Intra-Industry Trade*, London: Macmillan.

Havrylyshyn, O. (1983) 'The increasing integration of newly industrialised countries in world trade: a quantitative analysis of intra-industry trade', a paper presented to a Symposium on Intra-Industry Trade at the European Institute for Advanced Studies in Management, Brussels, May.

Havrylyshyn, O. and Civan, E. (1983) 'Intra-industry trade and the stage of development: a regression analysis of industrial and developing countries', in P. K. M. Tharakan (ed.) *Intra-industry Trade: Empirical and Methodological Aspects*, Amsterdam: North-Holland.

Helleiner, G. K. (1979) 'Transnational corporations and trade structure: the role of intra-firm trade', in H. Giersch (ed.) *On the Economics of Intra-industry Trade*, Tübingen: J. C. B. Möhr.

Hesse, H. (1974) 'Hypotheses for the explanation of trade between industrial countries 1953–70', in H. Giersch (ed.) *On the Economics of Intra-industry Trade*, Tübingen: J. C. B. Möhr.

Hufbauer, G. C. and Chilas, J. G. (1974) 'Specialisation by industrial countries: extent and consequences', in H. Giersch (ed.) *On the Economics of Intra-industry Trade*, Tübingen: J. C. B. Möhr.

James, J. and Stewart, F. (1981) 'New products: a discussion of the welfare effects of introduction of new products in developing countries', *Oxford Economic Papers* 33: 81–107.

Jones, C. D. (1987) 'Tariff and non-tariff barriers to trade', *Government Economic Service Working Paper*, No. 97, London: Department of Trade and Industry.

Jones, R. W. and Kenen, P. B. (eds) (1984) *Handbook of International Economics*, vol. I, Amsterdam: North-Holland.

Krugman, P. (1981) 'Intra-industry specialisation and the gains from trade', *Journal of Political Economy*, 89: 959–73.

Leamer, E. E. (1984) *Sources of International Comparative Advantage*, Cambridge, Mass: MIT Press.

Leamer, E. E. and Bowen, H. P. (1981) 'Cross section tests of the Heckscher–Ohlin theorem', *American Economic Review*, 71: 1040–3.

Loertscher, R. and Wolter, F. (1980) 'Determinants of intra-industry trade among countries and across industries', *Weltwirtschaftliches Archiv* 116: 281–93.

Lundberg, L. and Hansson, P. (1986) 'Intra-industry trade and its consequences for adjustment', in Greenaway and Tharakan (eds) *Imperfect Competition and International Trade: Policy Aspects of Intra-Industry Trade*, Brighton: Wheatsheaf Books.

Milner, C. R. (1988), 'Weighting effects in the measurement and modelling of intra-industry trade, *Applied Economics* 20: 295–302.

Pagoulatos, E. and Sorenson, R. (1975) 'Two-way international trade: an econometric analysis', *Weltwirtschaftliches Archiv* 111: 454–65.

Pelzman, J. (1978) 'Soviet–COMECON trade: the question of intra-industry specialisation', *Weltwirtschaftliches Archiv* 114: 297–304.

Pomfret, R. (1979) 'Intra-industry trade in intra-regional and international trade', in H. Giersch (ed.) *On the Economics of Intra-industry Trade*, pp. 115–31, Tübingen: J. C. B. Möhr.

——— (1985) 'Categorical aggregation and international trade', *Economic Journal* 95: 483–5.

Rayment, P. B. (1976) 'The homogeneity of manufacturing industries with respect to factor intensity: the case of the UK', *Oxford Bulletin of Economics and Statistics* 38: 203–9.

Robson, P. (1984) *The Economics of International Integration*, London: Allen & Unwin.

Tharakan, P. K. M. (ed.) (1983) *Intra-Industry Trade: Empirical and Methodological Aspects*, Amsterdam: North-Holland.

Toh, K. (1982) 'A cross-section analysis of intra-industry trade in the manufacturing industries', *Weltwirtschaftliches Archiv* 118: 281–300.

Tumlir, J. (1979) 'Comment' on paper by Finger and De Rosa in H. Giersch (ed.) *On the Economics of Intra-industry Trade*, Tübingen: J. C. B. Möhr.

Willmore, L. N. (1974) 'The pattern of trade and specialization in the

Central American Common Market', *Journal of Economic Studies*, November, pp. 113–34.

—— (1979) 'The industrial economics of intra-industry trade and specialisation', in H. Giersch (ed.) *On the Economics of Intra-industry Trade*, Tübingen: J. C. B. Möhr.

Winters, L. A. (1986) 'Britain in Europe: a survey of quantitative studies', Working Paper no. 110, London: Centre for Economic Policy Research.

—— (1987) 'Patterns of world trade in manufactures: does trade policy matter?', Discussion Paper no. 160, London: Centre for Economic Policy Research.

Chapter Eleven

Voluntary export restraints and lobbying: another example of the non-equivalence of equivalent restrictions

David Greenaway

Introduction

One of the most widely noted manifestations of structural change in the world economy over the last quarter of a century has been the emergence of the 'new protectionism'. The broad features of this phenomenon are reasonably clear – increasing use of non-tariff barriers, many of which are grey-area measures; increasing use of discriminatory instruments of intervention; an increasing tendency to target discriminatory measures against less-developed countries (LDCs) in general, and newly industrializing countries (NICs) in particular (see Nogues *et al.* 1986). Although the emphasis of commentators may vary, there is some measure of agreement to the effect that the growth of the new protectionism is related to shifting comparative advantage coupled with the success of GATT in binding tariffs. As a result, demands for 'emergency protection', or 'safeguard protection', or 'adjustment assistance', have been satisfied to an increasing extent by 'grey-area' measures such as voluntary export restraints, surveillance measures, source specific quotas, and so on (see Greenaway 1983).

The growth of the new protectionism has provided a fundamental threat to the credibility of the GATT system. Just how serious a threat this poses will become clearer with the outcome of the Uruguay Round of trade negotiations. The purpose of this contribution is not to focus on these wider issues but to concentrate on an aspect of one of the most prevalent forms of non-tariff intervention – the voluntary export restraint (VER). Despite the inefficiency of the instrument, it has been widely used. The forces behind its 'popularity' are explained by the application of simple public choice ideas. Using this framework one can demonstrate quite easily that although VERs may be suboptimal from an economic standpoint, from a political standpoint they are in fact optimal.

This chapter is organized as follows. The following section

summarizes the 'stylized facts' on VERs, the next section focuses on a neglected aspect of the instrument, namely the distinction between a volume and ratio VER. The penultimate section considers some political economy implications – in particular, some implications for lobbying activity – and the final section reviews the implications of the analyses for the future use of VERs.

Voluntary export restraints: some 'stylized facts'

VERs tend to be semi-formal arrangements whereby producers in one country consent to limit their exports to another country to a given volume, or market share, over a given period of time. They are therefore explicitly discriminatory and source-specific,[1] bilateral and specified for a given period of time.

The price and output effects of VERs are well known. In general, the potential for a higher domestic price exists, and with this the possibility of an expanded domestic supply of the import substitute (or an unchanged level of supply that is higher than would otherwise be the case). The exact magnitude of these price and output effects depends in the usual way on supply and demand elasticities. The effects, however, are known to differ from those of an equivalent tariff for several reasons. First, the fact that the restraint is source-specific allows exporters to extract rent from domestic consumers. The existence of this rent is largely responsible for the additional costs of VERs over equivalent tariffs. Second, the capacity of the restraint to eliminate competition at the margin, creates the possibility for domestic suppliers to raise prices towards monopolistic levels. Both of these effects ensure that the costs of a VER will exceed those of an equivalent tariff. These effects may, however, be moderated by a further by-product distortion of VERs, namely 'trade diversion'. Because the instrument is source-specific, it may permit unrestricted, higher-cost imports into the restricted market.[2]

Estimating the price and output effects of VERs is complicated. Essentially one is estimating a shadow price, invariably using indirect methods. Notwithstanding this, there are a number of studies which have now been published. For instance, Tarr and Morkre (1984) for five sectors in the USA; Greenaway and Hindley (1985) for four sectors in the UK; Silberston (1984) for textiles and clothing in the UK; and Hamilton (1985) for textiles and clothing in a number of countries. These and other studies identify positive price effects, and suggest that substantial rent transfers follow. Even where positive (domestic) output effects are identified, those studies which compare VERs with alternatives offer strong, convincing evidence to the effect that the VER is a relatively costly instrument of intervention (see, for instance,

Greenaway and Hindley 1985).

This theoretical and empirical work poses an interesting problem for analysts: if VERs are relatively costly instruments of intervention, why are they so widely used? To answer this question, one needs to understand the incentives facing all parties to the 'bargain'. The emerging theory of the political economy of protection does just this (see Frey 1985). In focusing attention on the incentives facing agents, it provides valuable insights into the way in which the political market for protection operates, and offers a credible and convincing explanation of the proliferation of VERs. A stylized version of that explanation is as follows. Domestic producers of import substitutes pressing for protection may not be indifferent to the form of protection; a revealed preference for protection by VER may result due to the fact that industry lobbies are involved in the negotiation of the VER (unlike with a tariff); the costs of the VER are not recorded in the public accounts (unlike with a production subsidy); and the VER can be regularly renegotiated. On the supply side there are several factors which make a VER more attractive to bureaucrats/ policy-makers than an equivalent tariff or subsidy. The costs of the instrument are not recorded in the public accounts; the instrument does not explicitly break any international undertakings; and ultimately the policy-maker can disclaim all responsibility for the instrument. What about those groups who bear the costs of VERs, namely foreign exporters and domestic consumers? The former group gain rents from a VER which do not accrue with a tariff or subsidy. Faced therefore with potential protection, exporters are likely to have a distinct preference for exclusion by VER over alternatives. Moreover, once the agreement is in force and the early market entrants have property rights on market shares or volumes, this can be used to exclude potential new entrants (as appears to be happening with the MFA). With regard to domestic consumers, in general they are badly informed with regard to the economic effects of VERs. As a result, resistance to their introduction is minimal. Moreover, consumers are a notoriously poorly organized lobby. Even given information on the costs of the intervention, effective anti-protection lobbying is therefore unlikely (see Jones 1984 and Hamilton 1986 for detailed comments).

Volume VERs, ratio VERs, and lobbying

It can be readily established from the existing literature why domestic producers, in lobbying for protection, may have a preference for VERs, and why foreign producers may be compliant in agreeing to VERs. One question which has not thus far been examined is whether

213

there will be any particular preference for one type of VER arrangement rather than another. VERs may constrain exporters by volume or by market share, and, in practice, both co-exist. Is the process of selection random? In this section we use simple partial equilibrium analysis to comment on the differences between volume and market share, or ratio, VERs.

In Figure 11.1 the market conditions for importables in a small open economy are presented. D_H represents domestic demand for importables; S_H, domestic supply of the import substitute; and S_W the world supply of the importable. It is assumed initially that even where imports originate from a single source, the suppliers are not in a position to exploit their latent market power, perhaps because the export industry cannot effectively cartelize. The purpose of making this assumption is to simplify the analysis; it does not affect the qualitative results which follow. Moreover, the economic effects of market concentration in the export market have been well explored by Takacs (1978), Murray *et al.* (1983), and Herander (1986). Our present interest lies primarily in the effects of differing *domestic* market structures.

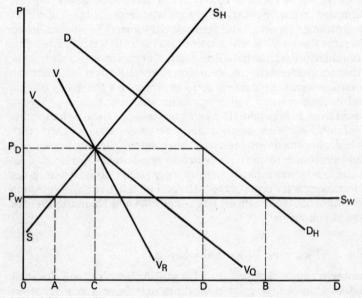

Figure 11.1 The market conditions for importables in a small open economy

214

When trade is unrestrained, total market demand is 0B. Of this, 0A is provided by domestic suppliers, AB by importers. Suppose now that the domestic industry successfully lobbies for import protection. It is decided to provide this protection by means of a VER and the objective of the intervention is to raise domestic output from 0A to 0C by restricting imports from AB to CD. This objective could be achieved by introducing a volume VER which restricts import volume to CD, or by means of a ratio VER which restricts the share of imports to CD/0D. If a volume VER is introduced, the residual demand curve facing the domestic industry is VV_Q, i.e. DD_H displaced horizontally by the distance CD. By contrast, if a ratio VER is imposed, the residual demand curve facing domestic suppliers is traced out by VV_R. This is steeper throughout its range than VV_Q, since clearly as total demand expands, the *volume* of imports expands (and vice versa with regard to market contraction). Thus, at all points along W_R, the ratio of imports to apparent consumption is CD/0D.[3]

The impact of either type of VER on price depends upon market structure at home and abroad. As noted above, the effects of alternative market structures on the export side have been extensively explored, and we will concentrate solely on the implications of the structure of the domestic market. Suppose initially that this were characterized by competition, such that all firms were price-takers. With a volume VER of VV_Q, domestic price rises from $0P_W$ to $0P_D$, the border price of imports increases accordingly, and the usual redistributions and net losses result. This is the standard case analyzed in the literature, and this result also holds for the ratio VER.

Suppose, however, that the domestic market were concentrated, being either monopolized or capable of effective cartelization. In this case, W_Q becomes the monopolist's average revenue curve. By eliminating competition at the margin, the VER enhances the monopolist's market power and allows price to rise above P_D. If SS_H is treated as the monopolist's marginal cost schedule, then clearly the intersection of MC and the MR schedule derived from W_Q will lie to the left of 0C, and, as a result, price will exceed P_D. This, of course, is not a new result. The ability of a VER to enhance the market power of a domestic monopolist has been identified by several commentators (e.g. Hindley 1980). What has not previously been recognized, however, is that this effect may differ as between the volume and ratio VER. Clearly, if the residual demand curve is VV_R and the marginal cost curve SS_H, the profit maximizing price with the ratio VER exceeds that for the volume VER. This is shown in Figure 11.2. The MR schedules for VV_Q and VV_R are QQ' and RR' respectively. In the case of the volume VER, output is restricted to 0F and price rises to $0P_Q$. By confining importers to a fixed share of the market, however,

215

the ratio VER permits the domestic monopolist to restrict output to
0G and raise price even further to $0P_R$.

From this simple piece of comparative statics one can see that in
circumstances where the domestic market is highly concentrated,
lobbying for protection may take the form not only of lobbying for a
VER in preference to other forms of intervention, but may even take
the form of lobbying for a particular type of VER, namely a ratio VER
rather than a volume VER. Since one observes reliance on both types
of VER, this proposition could be easily tested.

There are various ways in which this analysis could be expanded.
Perhaps the most obvious extension is to consider a more dynamic
setting to evaluate whether the results still hold when demand is
shifting.

Begin again with the case where the domestic industry is competitive. In Figure 11.3, assume that demand increases from DD_H to
$D'D'_H$. This will result in equivalent horizontal displacements of VV_Q
and VV_R to $V'V'_Q$ and $V'V'_R$ respectively. In the case of the volume
VER, pressure of excess demand at P_D drives price up to P'_Q. Imports

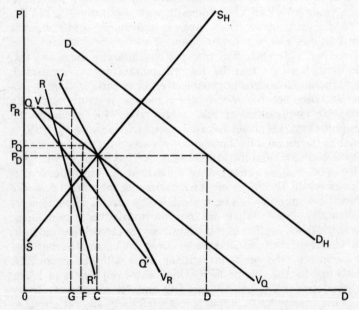

Figure 11.2. Market structure, volume, and ratio VERs

216

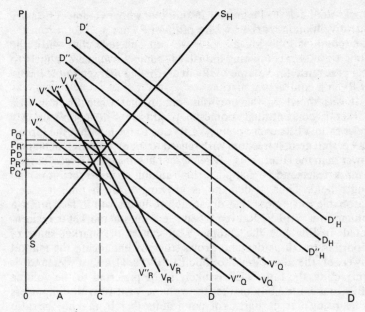

Figure 11.3. Demand shifts, volume, and ratio VERs

remain fixed at CD and marginal supplies are met from (relatively expensive) domestic producers. This is a well-known effect of quantitative restrictions in general, and it also holds for the volume VER. Note, however, that in the case of the ratio VER, domestic price increases from P_D not to $P_{Q'}$ but to $P_{R'}$. The extent of the price increase is ameliorated in the case of the ratio quota. This follows because part of the increase in demand is met by additional imports. The VER is still fully operative, but overseas suppliers now have the same share of a larger market.

These price effects are exactly symmetrical for a demand contraction. Thus when DD_H shifts to $D''D''_H$, price falls from P_D to $P_{Q''}$ in the case of the volume VER and from P_D to $P_{R''}$ in the case of the ratio VER. The price fall is less with the latter because demand contraction initiates a fall in the volume of imports. This does not occur with the volume VER and price therefore falls more quickly towards its free-trade level. This therefore provides a second, empirically testable proposition – namely, that price fluctuations associated with demand

217

shocks are likely to be greater in markets where volume VERs are operative than in markets where ratio VERs are in effect. From the standpoint of lobbying activity, we can conclude that when the domestic import competing industry is competitive, there is likely to be a preference for volume VERs in a growing market, but for ratio VERs in a contracting market.

It was shown in the previous section that when the domestic market is concentrated, domestic producers will unambiguously prefer ratio VERs over volume VERs due to the fact that the former may permit greater freedom with regard to the exploitation of market power than the latter. This, of course, applies *at a given level of output*. If market demand is changing, this ranking of preferences may no longer hold. Thus, if demand is growing through time it seems reasonable to suppose that domestic producers will in fact prefer a volume to a ratio VER, even when the domestic market is concentrated. In this case the volume VER causes the market share of importers to fall as demand grows, thereby enhancing the market power of the domestic monopolist. By contrast, if demand is contracting, the ratio VER is likely to be preferred to the volume VER. In a contracting market the volume VER provides importers with a rising market share as demand shifts, thereby making the ratio VER more attractive to the domestic monopolist. This, then, presents a third empirically testable proposition – namely, that when demand is growing, domestic producers will lobby for volume VERs rather than ratio VERs;[4] when demand is contracting, lobbying activity will be directed towards securing a ratio rather than a volume VER.

Political economy considerations

This simple piece of comparative statics suggests that the relative incidence of volume and ratio VERs may not be random. Instead it implies that the demand for a specific type of VER may be a function of domestic market structure, and in particular market concentration and the growth of demand. The capacity of VERs to exclude competition at the margin creates a non-equivalence between ratio and volume VERs which lead domestic producers to press for particular forms of protection. Moreover, once we think about the problem in a dynamic setting, it may be that foreign producers are not indifferent as between volume and ratio VERs. Specifically, the following testable propositions can be adduced:

a) Other things being equal, domestic producers will prefer a ratio to a volume VER, when the domestic market is highly concentrated.
b) If the domestic market is expanding (contracting), domestic producers will prefer a volume (ratio) to a ratio (volume) VER.

c) Price fluctuations associated with demand shocks are likely to be greater in a setting of volume VERs compared with ratio VERs.

In addition to these we can also deduce a fourth implication:

d) Foreign producers will prefer a ratio VER in a growing domestic market, but a volume VER in a contracting market.

As yet, no systematic analysis of the relative incidence of volume and ratio VERs has been undertaken, nor of the factors which influence this incidence. The purpose of this paper has been to suggest that this pattern is unlikely to be random but will be fashioned by various aspects of market structure.

Notes

1. Source-specific quotas (SSQs) are relatively common. Indeed, the MFA operates by relying on SSQs. In this paper SSQs and VERs will be treated as analytically equivalent. To all intents and purposes they are equivalent. The circumstances under which there may be non-equivalences are discussed by Herander (1986).
2. Note, of course, that although trade diversion may moderate price and output effects (and by implication reduce the costs of VERs, from the domestic economy's perspective), from a global perspective they are unambiguously welfare-reducing.
3. To simplify matters we are ignoring empirically relevant distortions associated with VERs, such as upgrading and trade diversion. Their inclusion makes the analysis more complicated, but leaves the qualitative results unaltered.
4. In the early 1960s an agreement was reached between Italian and Japanese automobile manufacturers to limit the flow of automobiles in either direction to a few thousand units. The pressure for the agreement came mainly from the Japanese, concerned about competition from Fiat. Given the rise to pre-eminence of Japanese automobile manufacturers in the 1970s and 1980s, together with the alleged difficulties of penetrating the Japanese market, it would be nice to conclude that the decision of the Italian car manufacturers to negotiate this source-specific quota was a piece of inspired judgement which illustrates this point perfectly. Unfortunately it probably had more to do with luck than judgement.

References

Frey, B. (1985) 'The political economy of protection', in D. Greenaway (ed.) *Current Issues in International Trade: Theory and Policy*, London Macmillan.

Greenaway, D. (ed.) (1985) *Current Issues in International Trade: Theory and Policy*, London: Macmillan.

—— (1986) 'Estimating the costs of voluntary export restraints and tariffs: an application to non-leather footwear in the UK', *Applied Economics* 18: xx.

Greenaway, D. and Hindley, E. V. (1985) *What Britain Pays for Voluntary Export Restraints*, Thames Essay 43, London: Trade Policy Research Centre.

Hamilton, C. (1985) Economic aspects of voluntary export restraints, in D. Greenaway, *Current Issues in International Trades*.

Herander, M. (1986) 'The (non)-equivalence of quantitative restrictions', *Journal of Economic Studies* XX: 64–73.

Hindley, B. V. (1980) 'Voluntary export restraints and article XIX of the GATT', in J. Black and B. V. Hindley (eds) *Current Issues in Commercial Policy and Diplomacy*, London: Macmillan.

Jones, K. (1984) 'The political economy of voluntary export restraints agreements', *Kyklos* 37: 82–101.

Murray, T., Schmidt, W., and Walter, I. (1978) 'Alternative forms of protection against market disruption', *Kyklos* 31: 624–37.

—— (1985) 'On the equivalence of import quotas and voluntary export restraints, *Journal of International Economics* 14: 191–4.

Nogues, J. J., Olechowski, A., and Winters, L. Alan (1985) 'The extent of non-tariff barriers to industrial countries imports, *The World Bank Economic Review* 1: 181–99.

Silberston, Z. A. (1984) *The Multi-Fibre Arrangement and the UK Economy*, London: HMSO.

Takacs, W. (1978) The non-equivalence of tariffs, import quotas, and voluntary export restraints, *Journal of International Economics* 8: 565–73.

Tarr, D. and Morkre, M. (1984) *Aggregate Costs to the United States of Tariffs and Quotas on Imports*, Washington, DC: Federal Trade Commission.

Chapter Twelve

Skills in international trade policy

Allan Webster

Introduction

Skills have long been argued to be a source of comparative advantage for developed countries. From the findings of Leontief (1953), the standard Heckscher–Ohlin framework of international trade theory has been subjected to the argument that the foundation for comparative advantage is human rather than physical capital. Findlay and Kierzkowski (1983) have derived a theoretical adaptation of the Heckscher–Ohlin model in which comparative advantage is based upon human capital. Their modification, in effect, argues that a capital-abundant country will tend to export skill-intensive goods and to import goods which are intensive in unskilled labour.

Recognition of the potential role of skills or 'human capital' in determining international trade flows has led some authors to suggest intervention either in markets for human capital or in markets for goods which are intensive in skills. Thus, Reich (1983) has argued:

> So now the new importance of skill-intensive production makes comparative advantage a matter of developing and deploying human capital. In a very real and immediate way, a nation chooses its comparative advantage. The flexibility of its institutions and the adaptability of its work force govern the scope of choice. Decisions on human capital development define a nation's competitive strategy.
>
> (Reich 1983: 773–804)

However, it is far from clear that such intervention is necessarily optimal. Indeed, if the domestic economy is already providing human capital at an optimal level there is little to be gained by inducing a distortion which would create a sub-optimal outcome. Thus, the argument of Reich is only likely to be of serious interest to international trade policy if distortions exist to the extent that there is under-provision of human capital in the domestic economy. This chapter argues in the following section that such under-provision is, indeed, a likely feature of markets in human capital.

Given the existence of market failure or market imperfections there is a clear case to be made for the type of policy that Reich advocates. However, it is not immediately clear whether such a policy is likely to improve trade performance in all possible cases. For the modified Heckscher–Ohlin framework of Findlay and Kierzkowski, the likely outcome of, say, subsidies to human capital is reasonably straightforward – such interventions would be likely to increase the endowment of human capital and, therefore, re-inforce the specialization of the skill-abundant country in skill-intensive goods. Indeed, the Rybczynski (1955) theorem could be invoked to provide fairly standard results in this case.

It is not the purpose of this chapter to pursue such a line of argument further, as the workings of the Heckscher–Ohlin framework are sufficiently well-developed to render trivial any analysis of the workings of such a policy. It is, however, the purpose of this paper to consider how human capital subsidies may work under different theoretical explanations of trade. In the third section, therefore, the role of a skill subsidy in a model of the type developed by Falvey (1981) is discussed. This is still very close to the basic neo-classical trade model, in that trade is still determined by comparative advantage which, in turn, is determined by relative factor endowments. However, the main distinction between this model and a standard Heckscher–Ohlin model is that international exchange occurs between different qualities of the same commodity rather than between different commodities. Indeed, it is argued here that quality is likely to be intensive in skills and, therefore, skill subsidies can enhance comparative advantage when such advantage is manifested in trade between different qualities rather than different goods.

From the perfectly competitive framework of Falvey's model, the fourth section of this chapter moves on to consider a skill subsidy in the framework of the duopolistic model of Brander and Spencer (1985). This, in effect, synthesizes two strands of strategic trade policy. A number of authors have suggested that trade policy should target certain 'strategic' industries which confer special benefits to the domestic economy. Some, such as Spencer (1986), have advocated a policy to seek increased monopoly rent from the world economy whereas others have advocated the promotion of human capital-intensive activities. This section argues, in effect, that these two approaches are not mutually exclusive and that under plausible circumstances a rent-seeking policy could be better pursued by human capital rather than export or production subsidies.

Under-provision of human capital

For the purposes of this chapter it is assumed that goods are produced by using any or all of three factors of production–capital, labour, and human capital. In contrast to the neo-classical trade model, capital is assumed to be capable of being perfectly traded internationally and the economy in question is assumed to be small in terms of world capital markets. This means that the economy faces a given world rate of return to capital (r) and that domestic firms face a perfectly elastic supply of capital at this rate of return. Similarly, if there is excess supply of domestic capital, given r, this excess is absorbed by world markets. The consequence, therefore, is that domestic endowments of capital cannot affect the capital intensities of domestic industries or the industrial or trading structure of the domestic economy directly.

Assume also that the domestic endowment of labour is fixed. The endowment in this sense is the total potential work force. Workers can be induced to enter or leave the work force by the prevailing incentives or to offer more or less labour, but the total amount of labour upon which the economy can call is dependent only upon the number of healthy adults in the domestic economy of working age. It is assumed that labour cannot be internationally traded and that the government is unable to influence the domestic endowment of labour. If so, the domestic endowment of labour is capable of influencing the domestic structure of production and trade as the wage rate (w) is domestically determined. However, the government is unable to influence the structure of the domestic economy by changing the endowment of labour.

Human capital, as it is embodied in people, is also assumed to be incapable of being internationally traded. As the rate of return on human capital (z) is, therefore, domestically determined, it is capable of influencing the structure of production and trade. Moreover, the total endowment of human capital is assumed to be capable of being changed by investments in human capital. The government can, therefore, alter the endowment of human capital by adopting policies which make investment in it more or less attractive to agents in the economy.

Arguments of this type have led authors such as Reich (1983) to advocate policies to develop human capital, but this view has been criticized by Schultze (1983) and by Dixit and Grossman (1986) principally upon the grounds that human capital is likely to be highly inelastic in supply. However, as Dixit and Grossman recognize, the endowment of human capital is capable of being increased by the structure of incentives – in short, if new investment in human capital is encouraged, then the supply curve is shifted outwards. Thus, the efficacy of a policy to develop human capital depends more on its ability to stimulate new investment in skills than to stimulate existing skilled workers to supply additional effort.

To treat human capital as an investment, it is assumed that there is a base period cost incurred by both the worker and the firm of $C_0{}^a$ and $C_0{}^b$ respectively. The net return to human capital in each time period is given as $(z_t - w_t)$ for the worker and $(MVP_t - z_t)$ for the firm, where MVP_t is the marginal value product of human capital in period t. Net present values for the worker and the firm can, therefore, be written as:

$$NPV_a = -C_0{}^a + \sum_{t=1}^{T_a} \{z_t/(1+d)^t\} - \sum_{t=1}^{T_a} \{w_t/(1+d)^t\} \qquad [12.1]$$

$$NPV = -C_0{}^b + \sum_{t=1}^{T_b} \{MVP_t/(1+r)^t\} - \sum_{t=1}^{T_b} \{z_t/(1+r)^t\} \qquad [12.2]$$

where d is the worker's discount rate.

As Equation 12.2, in effect, argues that the firm recoups the cost of its initial investment at the expense of the gross return to human capital, Equation 12.1 can be written as:

$$NPV_a = -C_0{}^a - C_0{}^b + \sum_{t=1}^{T_a} \{MVP_t/(1+d)^t\}$$

$$- \sum_{t=1}^{T_a} \{w_t/(1+d)^t\} - NPV_b \qquad [12.3]$$

Consider first the base period costs. Other things being equal, training subsidies to either the worker or the firm reduce either $C_0{}^a$ or $C_0{}^b$ and, therefore, tend to render investment more profitable to the worker. Similarly, a factor subsidy to the firm lowers the cost of human capital which, for the same present value to the firm, increases the present value for the worker. A factor subsidy to the worker achieves the same effect by raising the net return to human capital. Indeed, it is possible, using Equation 12.1, to express training subsidies to the worker in terms of a factor subsidy (to the worker) equivalent and using Equation 12.2 to express training and factor subsidies to the firm in equivalent terms.

Thus, the conclusion of this is to suggest that policies do exist which would increase the desired level of investment in human capital and, thereby, the stock of human capital. This is not, however, to suggest that it would necessarily be desirable to do so. Indeed, if markets already provide a socially optimal level of human capital, welfare could not be improved by further increasing it. The case for human capital subsidies is, therefore, not one of 'could' but one of 'should' such policies be used.

This case rests principally upon the existence of market failure and/or market imperfections which would lead to under-provision of human capital. First, the existence of positive externalities would imply that the social marginal value product is greater than the private marginal value product and, therefore, that the level of investment was less than the socially optimal. Suppose, for example, that skills facilitate innovation and that innovation generates external benefits. It therefore follows that skills must generate external benefits.

Second, the social marginal value product is likely to exceed the private in the presence of imperfect competition. Whilst a competition policy would clearly be more appropriate, this may not be possible if a monopoly or oligopoly is 'natural'. A more commonly invoked form of market failure for human capital is financing constraints (see, for example, Siebert 1985). The argument here is that as human capital is embodied in the individual it cannot serve as collateral for a loan. Thus, it is possible that either the firm or the individual or both will be unable to incur the initial costs necessary for investment to occur.

Lastly, as Dixit (1986) argues, the prospect of predatory firms bidding away trained workers from the investing firm could lower the incentive to invest. This alone will not necessarily lower investiment as the investing firm can, in effect, shorten its time horizon (T_b) such that it recovers the initial cost within the expected duration of employment. From Equation 12.2 this would imply a lower value of Z_t in the first T_b time periods to yield the same net present value, taking C_0^b as fixed. If financing constraints also exist for the worker and if Z_t is pushed below some subsistence value for the first few time periods the worker may be unable to undertake a potentially profitable investment. This is more likely the shorter the firm's expected duration of employment, the higher the value of C_0^b, and the lower the marginal value product (through, say, learning-by-doing effects) in the initial time periods.

Thus, it is possible to invoke a variety of arguments that human capital endowments will be below the socially optimal level. However, the main assessment of whether such issues are worthy of the attention of policy-makers must be an empirical one. Siebert (1985) reviews a number of studies which have estimated the private rates of return to education for the UK and the USA. In general these are higher than the rates of return on similarly risky investments in physical capital and higher than market interest rates. This would tend to suggest that there is an empirical case for under-provision of human capital.

Comparative advantage in quality

The basis of this section is the model of Falvey (1981). A broadly similar model is discussed by Kierzkoski (1985). Both, in essence, adapt the Heckscher–Ohlin trade model to the case of a vertically differentiated product. Falvey considers a perfectly competitive industry producing a single good which is capable of being produced at any point on a continuous spectrum of quality. Whilst Falvey assumes two factors (labour and capital), it is here assumed that the good is produced using also human capital as a third factor. The assumptions made in the second section of this chapter – that capital is perfectly traded and that the country is small in world capital markets–are retained. Two countries are assumed.

Following Falvey, units of quality are chosen such that production of one unit of quality β requires one unit of labour, α units of capital, and β units of human capital. As quality is, therefore, indexed with human capital, higher quality requires more human capital-intensive techniques. The costs of producing one unit of quality β are defined

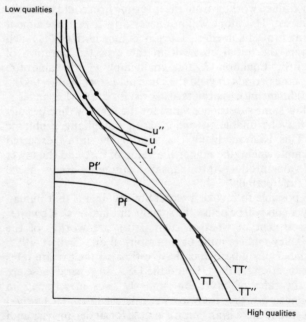

Figure 12.1   Quality and a human capital subsidy

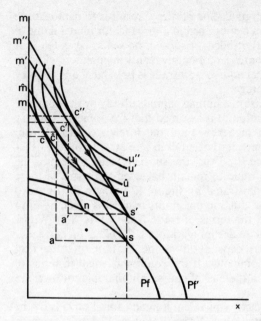

Figure 12.2 Human capital subsidies as a stratgic policy

for the domestic and foreign country as:

$$C(\beta) = w + \alpha r + \beta z \qquad [12.4]$$

and

$$c^*(\beta) = w^* + \alpha r^* + \beta z^* \qquad [12.5]$$

Consider the marginal quality (β_1) for which the unit costs are the same in both countries. As r is exactly equal to r^*, this implies:

$$\beta_1 = (w - w^*)/(z^* - z) \qquad [12.6]$$

For any other quality this implies:

$$c(\beta) - c^*(\beta) = (\beta_1 - \beta)(\{w - w^*\}/\beta_1) \qquad [12.7]$$
$$= (\beta_1 - \beta)(z^* - z)$$

Thus, in a parallel fashion to Falvey's model, the country with the lower wage will tend to export qualities below the marginal quality and the country with the lower return to human capital will export

227

qualities above the marginal. The principal result is to demonstrate that a similar result can be obtained in a three-factor model if one of these factors is perfectly traded. It should, however, be noted that although this model shares factor endowments in common with the Heckscher–Ohlin model no two-way trade is possible if one country has an absolute advantage.

Now consider the case of a human capital subsidy by the domestic country without retaliation. It is assumed that the domestic country has a lower z and a higher w than the foreign country. From Equation 12.6 it can be seen that a fall in z relative to all the other variables would reduce β_1. Thus, the subsidy tends to reduce the marginal quality. For trade to remain balanced the terms of trade must decline. This is illustrated by Figure 12.1 where the outward shift in the domestic production possibility frontier is given by Pf to Pf′ and the change in the terms of trade from TT to TT′. Whilst Figure 12.2 shows welfare declining (u to u′), the effect on consumer welfare is ambiguous as it depends on whether the terms of trade effect or the growth effect dominates. If the country is small in terms of world trade in the good there is, of course, an unambiguous welfare gain.

Consider now an exactly equivalent human capital subsidy by the foreign country as retaliation. From Equation 12.6 this tends to increase the marginal quality. Thus, the range of qualities produced by both countries is shifted up the quality spectrum. Although, for the qualities previously exported by the domestic country, prices have fallen relative to the lower qualities, this is now offset by a move 'up-market'. The terms of trade, therefore, if they decline at all, decline by less than if there is no retaliation. The scope for welfare gains is, therefore, greater. This is illustrated in Figure 12.1 by the shifts from TT′ to TT″ and from u′ to u″.

In conclusion, then, human capital subsidies are not likely to yield significant welfare gains if the country is large in world trade and if there is no retaliation. If, however, the policy is reciprocated by the foreign country then gains are indeed likely whether the country is small or not. These gains are, at least in part, gains in consumer welfare in both countries through the consumption of higher quality products.

Skill subsidies in a duopolistic model

Brander and Spencer (1985) construct a model in which a single domestic firm competes with a single foreign rival to supply an export market. Domestic consumption of the export good is assumed to be negligible. Both the domestic and the foreign duopolist behave according to Cournot conjectures (each firm acts on the assumption that its rival will not change its output). As both firms earn monopoly rent they show that shifting output from the foreign to the domestic firm can increase domestic welfare. This shift in market share is achieved by an export subsidy.

Figure 12.3 reproduces Brander and Spencer's diagram. The reaction functions of the domestic firm (A) and of the foreign firm (B) give an initial equilibrium at point n. The export subsidy lowers the marginal cost to the domestic firm and, therefore, shifts out its reaction function. From the foreign firm's viewpoint this is a credible strategy in the absence of retaliation and its optimal strategy is to contract its output. Thus, a new equilibrium is achieved at point s, where domestic output (X) is increased and the foreign rival's output (Y) is decreased. Monopoly rent is, therefore, shifted to the domestic economy.

Brander and Spencer also show that welfare gains are still possible even if the government of the foreign rival retaliates. Thus, the subsidy to firms A and B tends to lower prices to consumers on the (third) export market. This provides an incentive for the third country to import more of the duopolistic good and to export more of a composite competitive good. Production of the rent-conferring activity can, therefore, increase for both A and B at the expense of competitive production which confers no rent.

This model has led some authors – Krugman (1987) and Spencer (1986) – to advocate a strategic trade policy in which export subsidies are targeted upon industries capable of earning monopoly rent. The question of interest here is whether human capital subsidies can better

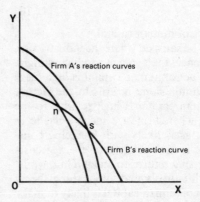

Figure 12.3 The basic Brander and Spencer case

achieve similar effects. It is assumed that either the competitive good uses no human capital and a constant per unit subsidy is available to all firms or that such subsidies are targeted upon the duopolistic industry. The condition for the human capital subsidy paid to the firm (s') to achieve the same output effect as the export subsidy (s per unit of output), is that marginal cost is reduced by the same amount(s). Note that, with negligible domestic consumption of the duopolistic good, the export subsidy could be equally treated as a production subsidy.

It is shown in Webster (1988) that the per unit of human capital subsidy that achieves the same effect on output as the export/ production subsidy per unit of output is given by:

$$s = \{ MC \cdot [MP_h(MC/C \cdot \beta - 1/X) + \theta_3/z] \} \cdot (dz/ds') \qquad [12.8]$$
$$= \Omega \cdot (dz/ds')$$

where MC is marginal cost, MP_h is the marginal product of human capital, C is total cost, β is a positive coefficient measuring the curvature of the logarithmic cost function, X is output, and θ_3 is the marginal share of human capital in the total product.

The total subsidy costs under the export subsidy (TC_s) and under the human capital subsidy ($TC_{s'}$) are given by:

$$TC_s = s \cdot X = - \Omega \cdot X \cdot (dz/ds') \qquad [12.9a]$$

$$TC_{s'} = s' \cdot H \qquad [12.9b]$$

where H is human capital.

For the total subsidy cost to be less with the factor subsidy requires:

$$TC_s/TC_{s'} > 1 \text{ or, equivalently, } \{ - (dz/ds')/s') \cdot \Omega \cdot AP_h \} > 1$$
$$[12.10]$$

where AP_h is the average product of human capital.

This condition is more likely to be satisfied where the industry uses human capital intensively (and hence, the average product is high), where the marginal physical product of human capital is high (as is likely with under-provision and diminishing returns to the factor), where the marginal share of human capital is high relative to the return to human capital (in effect, where firms are 'income elastic' in their demand for human capital, as is likely with financing constraints), and where marginal cost is high relative to average costs (where there are not sharply increasing returns to scale). Thus, whilst it is impossible to be conclusive, it is likely that, other things being equal, substantial under-provision of human capital is likely to make the cost to taxpayers of using a human capital subsidy to achieve the

230

same gains (in terms of rent) less than that for a production/export subsidy. Thus, under these circumstances, net welfare gains are likely to be greater.

The distribution of the gains from increased rent is also of consequence, as one factor of production (capital) is capable of being held by foreign residents. As gains in domestic welfare are the net gains to domestic residents, the two policies need to be compared on the basis of their distributional effects. As capital is assumed to be the only factor capable of being held by foreign residents, changes in the share of capital are equivalent to changes in the share of total product for foreign residents. Thus, the policy which tends to increase the share of capital tends to distribute relatively more rent to foreign residents than does the one which tends to decrease the share of capital.

In Webster (1988) it is shown that, for a linearly homogeneous production function, the change in the share of capital in the total product of the industry is given by:

$$dk = \{(K/L) \cdot (\varepsilon_{LK} + 1)\} d(r/w) + \{(K/H) \cdot (\varepsilon_{HK} + 1)\} d(r/z)$$
[12.11]

where ε_{LK} and ε_{HK} are the elasticities of substitution of capital for labour and capital for human capital. Both elasticities are negative such that a rise in the price of capital relative to labour lowers the capital to labour ratio. Similar expressions can be derived for the change in the share of labour and the change in the share of human capital.

An export subsidy does not have a neutral effect on the shares of factors in total product. This is because, whilst the increase in output results in increased demand for each factor, the rate of return on capital is fixed on world markets. Thus, the consequence of this increased factor demand is to lower the price of capital relative to both the wage and the return on human capital. In Equation 12.7 both $d(r/w)$ and $d(r/z)$ will, therefore, be negative. If both elasticities of substitution are inelastic this will reduce the share of capital and, therefore, increase the share of domestic residents. However, if both substitutions are elastic, the result of the export/production subsidy is to increase the share of foreign residents in total domestic product of the industry. Similarly, as elasticities of substitution can be expected to become more elastic over time, the export subsidy will tend to erode gains in the share of domestic residents over time.

In the case of the human capital subsidy, the elasticity of substitution of capital for human capital must become positive – provided the rise in the price of human capital induced by the subsidy is less than the subsidy itself. If so, the effective price paid by the firm per unit of human capital is $(z - s')$, which is lowered despite the increase in z. Thus, the subsidy causes the capital to human capital ratio to fall, with a fall in the relative price of capital. As a result, some of the share of capital is shifted to human capital irrespective of whether the elasticity of substitution is elastic or not.

However, whether the net effect is to reduce the share of capital also depends on transfers of share between capital and labour. This principally depends on whether the wage falls or rises as a result of the subsidy to human capital. Reduced demand for labour as a result of substitution of human capital for labour will tend to reduce the wage whilst the increase in output will tend to raise the wage. With falling wages, the effect on the share of capital (if the elasticity of substitution of capital for labour is inelastic) is ambiguous, and the share of capital falls if this substitution is elastic. If, however, wages rise, the effect on the share of capital is ambiguous with elastic substitution, and is reduced with inelastic substitution.

If it were possible for policy-makers to know all the relevant parameters, the best policy according to the share of total product criterion could be selected. In the absence of such detailed knowledge it could be argued that a human capital subsidy is preferable to an export subsidy as:

(i) the worst outcome for the export subsidy policy is a decrease in the share of total product for domestic residents, whereas the worst outcome for the factor subsidy is ambiguous. Even if this results in a decrease in share for domestic residents, it must be strictly less (from Equation 12.7) than that which would occur under the worst outcome for the export subsidy.

(ii) it is the only policy which unambiguously raises the share of a domestically held factor (human capital) irrespective of the values of the elasticities of substitution.

(iii) if elasticities of substitution are elastic in the long run, it is less likely to result in a long-run decrease in the share of domestic residents.

As the model is of imperfect competition, if the production function is not linearly homogeneous than this analysis requires adjustment as the total product is not directly shared amongst the factors of production – in short, some of the rent is retained by the firm. For the purposes of this chapter it is assumed that any such excess accrues to the owners of the firm. This excess, therefore, is attributed to capital.

So far, the partial equilibrium and distributional effects of human capital in the Brander and Spencer model have been analyzed.

232

Following Brander and Spencer, the simple general equilibrium effects also require analysis. As it is necessary to introduce domestic consumption of good x at this stage, the export/production subsidy is now solely a production subsidy. This necessarily requires that the subsidy rate and that for the (output) equivalent human capital subsidy must be greater to achieve the same effect in the export market. In addition, it is now assumed that both the duopolistic firm and the competitive industry use human capital but the duopolist uses it more intensively. The human capital subsidy is assumed to be paid only to the duopolist.

To abstract from the distributional effects discussed earlier, both the production and the human capital subsidy are presumed to have an identical effect on the rent accruing to domestic residents. The human capital subsidy is, again, set to achieve the same output effect as the production subsidy. Figure 12.3, which is based upon Brander and Spencer's diagram, illustrates the analysis. Production and consumption of the duopolistic export good (x) are measured on the horizontal axis and the competitive import good is measured on the vertical axis (m).

In the absence of a human capital subsidy, the production possibility frontier is given by Pf. In the absence of any intervention, the terms of trade are given by the line mn. Given these terms of trade, consumption is determined at point c and production is given at point n. The effect of the Brander and Spencer production subsidy is to shift production to point s. The terms of trade worsen from mn to ms, but, in spite of this, there is a net gain in welfare (from u' to û) due to the transfer of rent to domestic residents.

Now consider the effect of the human capital subsidy. As this increases, the endowments of one factor of production (the production possibility frontier) is moved outward to Pf'. As good x is relatively more intensive in human capital, the shift is greater in terms of x than in terms of m. As the effect on the output of x is, by assumption, the same as the Brander and Spencer case, production is therefore at point s'. Note that exports are less under this policy, as the resulting increase in domestic income increases domestic consumption by more.

The effect on the terms of trade depends on whether the country is small in terms of world trade in the competitive good (m). If so, its price cannot be changed by either policy. As the change in output is the same under both policies, the change in the price of the export good must be the same if trade is frictionless. The terms of trade are therefore unchanged, if the domestic country is small in m. To reflect this, the terms of trade are represented by m's', which has the same slope as ms. The gain in welfare is greater (u to u') for the factor subsidy than for the production subsidy. Both imports and exports are increased by less than the production subsidy case, the trade triangle being c'a's' against cas. This is because the growth effect increases potential domestic production of both goods. The factor subsidy is, therefore, less predatory than the production subsidy, as the welfare gains are (in part) provided by domestic growth.

If, however, the domestic country is not small in terms of world trade in m, the terms of trade can diverge from the Brander and Spencer case. As the domestic production of m is decreased by less at the same terms of trade, the effect of allowing its price to vary can only mean that it will fall by less. In this case, the deterioration in the terms of trade will be less than the Brander and Spencer case (this is shown by the line m"s'). If so, a yet higher level of welfare is obtainable at u".

Thus, in terms of simple general equilibrium effects, the human capital subsidy performs better than the production subsidy. This is because it stimulates domestic growth. In turn, this means that pursuing rent through the factor subsidy has two beneficial effects – it is less predatory and it yields greater gains in domestic welfare for the same increase in the output of x.

Conclusions

The second section of this chapter argued that human capital subsidies can increase investment in skills both by individual workers and by firms and, therefore, increase the total endowment of skills in an economy. This is only an optimal policy if the social returns to such an investment are greater than for other forms of investment. It has been argued that there are plausible reasons and there is some empirical evidence to suggest that this is the case.

The implications of such a policy for the structure of international trade have then been sought. For the duopolistic model of Brander and Spencer (1985) it was shown that a skill subsidy can achieve the same goal of increasing domestic rent generating activity as a production subsidy. Moreover, subsidizing human capital offered a better prospect of the additional rent being retained by domestic residents and reduced the adverse general equilibrium effects.

For a good produced by a competitive industry but differentiated by quality, human capital subsidies tend to move export industries 'down-market' in the absence of retaliation. Moreover, if the country is not small in terms of world trade, they can lead to adverse trade effects. However, an equivalent retaliation can lead to gains for both countries, in the form of increased income and increased quality to consumers. Thus, from the discussion of vertical-product differenti-ation, there are grounds to believe that human capital subsidies perform best as a multilateral rather than a unilateral policy. If, then, inadequacies in the provision of human capital occur in a number of countries there are clear potential gains to agreeing to use human capital subsidies as an instrument of trade policy.

However, the discussion here is of an exploratory nature, as there are considerably more representations of market structure than have been discussed here. For example, the introduction of Bertrand rather than Cournot conjectures substantially alters the results of the Brander and Spencer model as Grossman (1986) notes. Comparison with other policies designed to increase the provision of human capital is, however, less difficult. As is noted in the second section of this chapter, it is possible, for example, to express training assistance to either workers or firms in terms of a subsidy equivalent; and their effect on the structure of trade can therefore be derived by an analagous process.

References

Brander, James A. and Spencer, Barbara J. (1985) 'Export subsidies and international market share rivalry', *Journal of International Economics* 18: 83–100.

Dixit, Avinash, K. (1986) 'Trade policy: an agenda for research', in Paul R. Krugman (ed.), *Strategic Trade Policy and the New International Economics*, Cambridge, Mass.: MIT Press.

Dixit, Avinash K. and Grossman, Gene M. (1986) 'Targeted export promotion with several oligopolistic industries', *Journal of International Economics* 21: 233–49.

Falvey, Rodney, E. (1981) 'Commercial policy and intra-industry trade', *Journal of International Economics* 11: 495–511.

Findlay, Ronald and Kierzkowski, Henryk (1983) 'International trade and human capital: a simple general equilibrium model', *Journal of Political Economy* 91 (6): 957–78.

Greenaway, David and Milner, Chris (1986) *The Economics of Intra-Industry Trade*, Oxford: Basil Blackwell.

Grossman, Gene M. (1986) Strategic export promotion: a critique, in Paul R. Krugman (ed.) *Strategic Trade Policy and the New International Economics*, Cambridge, Mass.: MIT Press.

Kierzkowski, Henryk (1985) 'Models of international trade in differentiated goods', in David Greenaway (ed.) *Current Issues in International Trade*, London: Macmillan.

Krugman, Paul R. (1987) 'Strategic sectors and international competition', in Robert M. Stern (ed.) *US Trade Policies in a Changing World Economy*, Cambridge Mass.: MIT Press.

Leontief, Wassily W. (1953) 'Domestic production and foreign trade: the American capital position re-examined', *Proceedings of the American Philosophical Society* 97: 332–49.

Reich, Robert B. (1983) 'Beyond free trade', *Foreign Affairs*, Spring, 773–804.

Rybczynski, T. M. (1955) 'Factor endowment and relative commodity prices', *Economica* 336.

Schultze, Charles L. (1983) 'Industrial policy: a dissent', *The Brookings Review* 2 (1): 3–12.

Siebert, W. Stanley (1985) 'Developments in the economics of human capital', in Derek Carline, Christopher A. Pissarides, W. Stanley Siebert, and Peter J. Sloane, *Labour Economics*, London: Longman.

Spencer, Barbara J. (1986) 'What should trade policy target?', in Paul R. Krugman (ed.) *Strategic Trade Policy and the New International Economics*, Cambridge, Mass.: MIT Press.

Webster, Allan (1988) *Human Capital Subsidies as a Strategic Trade Policy*, Discussion Paper, University of Reading.

Index

Abbreviations used in the index are consistent with those in the text.

adjustment, structural 4–5, 10, 34
  costs of 202–4
  policies 204–5, 205–6
  specialization and 202
  trade-induced de-
    industrialization 40–4
Advisory Council on Science and
  Technology (ACOST) 64
aerospace industry 149, 150
agricultural/industrial chemical
  industry 148, 150, 151, 152
Alps Electric 179
Anglo-Japanese Economic Journal
  181
Aquino, A. 183, 206
asset advantages *see* ownership
  advantages

Bacon, R. 30
Balassa, B. 183, 188, 202, 206
Baldwin, R. E. 38
Bank of England *Quarterly Bulletin*
  18
Bank for International Settlements
  82
bargaining power 98
Belgium 185
Bergstrand, J. H. 188, 189
Bhagwati, J. N. 72, 84
Blackhurst, R. 204
booming-sector models 40–4
Bowden, R. J. 206
Bowen, H. P. 190

Brander, J. A. 222, 227, 228–9,
  232–3, 234
'British disease' 4
Bryant, R. C. 83
Buckley, P. J. 92, 116
building materials 158, 159
business enterprises R&D 58
Butcher, J. 14

Canada 13, 20, 39–40
  investment: domestic 18; foreign
    128–9, 130, 132, 136
  services 71, 72, 79
Cantwell, J. A. 92, 94, 95, 97, 120
Casson, M. C. 92, 97, 116, 121,
  122
catching up effect 96–7, 100–1,
  104, 107–8, 111, 112
Caterpillar Tractor 170
Caves, R. E. 38, 117, 118, 189
centralization of MNE
  management 83–4
Chambers, E. J. 39–40
chemical industries 148–52 *passim*,
  177
Cherry, H. 14
Chilas, J. G. 183, 191, 197, 206
Civan, E. 188
Clegg, L. J. 140
coal 5, 44
Coates, J. H. 31
Cole, W. A. 35
Colts 167

consumer chemical industry 149, 150, 152
competitiveness 75
  Japan 170–5
  UK 21–3
containerization 76
Contractor, F. J. 172
controlled delivery systems 78–9
co-operative R&D 64–5
Corden, M. 4, 16, 40
costs
  labour 21–3, 51
  structural adjustment 202–4
Cowling, K. 98
Cox, D. 202
Crafts, N. F. R. 36–7

data flows, transborder 76–7
David, P. 37–8
Deane, P. 35
Deardorff, A. V. 186, 206
debt 81, 88
decline 5, 33–44
  UK 4, 12, 13–14, 43–4; causes 14–23
defence R&D 58, 62
degree of internationalization 99, 102–4, 108–9
de-industrialization 12, 30, 40, 41–2, 43–4
  see also decline
delivery systems, controlled 78–9
demand, VERs and 216–18, 219
Denmark 185
distribution, human capital and 231–2
diversification 8, 143–62
  exports 157–60
  geographical 118, 153–6, 160–1
  industrial 144–53, 160–1
division of labour 79–80
Dixit, A. K. 223, 225
Drabek, Z. 206
Drucker, P. F. 175
Dunning, J. H. 163, 170, 181
  foreign direct investment 92, 114, 116, 126; economies of the firm 119–20; intra-industry

trade 123, 125; ownership advantages 115, 118
internationalization 91, 93, 98, 106
Japanese competitiveness 171
research intensity 23, 31
UK pharmaceutical industry 177
duopolistic trade model 222, 228–34
'Dutch disease' 40

ecletic theory 116
economies, firm-specific 8, 117, 119–21, 122–3
Economist, The 181
electronics/electrical appliances industry 152
Eltis, W. 30
employment
  OECD countries 12–13
  services 67, 86–7
  UK 13, 24, 28, 86
endowment of labour 223
Erdilek, A. 126
Ergas, H. 61, 62, 63
Europe 170, 174
  internationalization of firms 7, 91, 112, 156
  see also European Economic Community; *individual countries*
European Economic Commission 181
European Economic Community (EEC) 28
  co-operative R&D 64
  foreign direct investment: intra-industry 132, 134, 136, 137; Japan and 168, 172, 179, 180; US and 128–9, 130, 173
  services 79, 88
  UK membership and trade liberalization 10, 194, 199
exchange rate adjustment 23
export subsidies 229–32
exports, diversification and 157–60
  see also trade

Falvey, R. E. 222, 226–7

farm/industrial equipment industry 149–52 *passim*, 158, 159, 160
Fiat 170, 219
Financial Times 21
Findlay, R. 221, 222
Finger, J. M. 183, 203, 206
firm-specific economies 8, 117, 119–21, 122–3
Fishlow, A. 34
food industry 148, 150, 152, 158, 159, 160
Ford 27, 170, 176
foreign content ratio 98–9
foreign direct investment (FDI) 92
    inter-industry 116
    intra-industry *see* intra-industry FDI
    import-substituting 123–4
    services 84–5, 89
foreign production ratio
    diversification 153–6, 160–1
    internationalization 98–9, 104, 105–7
Forsyth, P. J. 41
France 20, 91, 185
    internationalization 107–12 *passim*
    investment: domestic 18; German 135
    R&D 55, 62
Franko, L. G. 143, 181, 202
Freeman, C. 62, 97

General Agreement on Tariffs and Trade (GATT) 10, 68, 78–9, 191, 211
    see also Kennedy Round; Tokyo Round; Uruguay Round
General Motors 27, 176
geographical diversification 118, 153–6, 160–1
Germany, Federal Republic of 185
    innovation 49–63 *passim*
    internationalization 91, 94, 107–12 *passim*
    investment: domestic 18; intra-industry foreign 127, 130, 133–5, 136–7, 138–9

labour costs 22, 51
    productivity 20, 51
    services 71, 72, 73
Gerschenkron, A. 34, 35
Giersch, H. 68
Goodhart, C. 16
Gordon, D. F. 39–40
government-funded R&D 56–8
government policy *see* policy
Graham, E. M. 121–2
Gray, H. P. 76, 79, 83, 88
Gray, J. M. 83
Greenaway, D. 127
    intra-industry trade 183, 187, 202, 206
    VERs 211, 212, 213
Griliches, Z. 52
Grossman, G. M. 223, 235
growth
    investment and 17–18
    rate of firm's main activity 146, 147
    stage model 34–5
Grubel, H. G. 72, 75, 127

Hamilton, C. 212, 213
Hansson, P. 203
Harris, R. 202
Havrylyshyn, O. 188
Heckser-Ohlin model 221, 222, 226
Helleiner, G. K. 203
Herander, M. 214, 219
Hesse, H. 206
high research-intensity (HRI) industries 31, 52–5
    UK 24–8, 30, 52–5 *passim*
Hindley, B. V. 88, 212, 213
Honda 176
Honeywell 170
House of Lords *Report from the Select Committee on Overseas Trade* 14, 23, 31
Hufbauer, G. C. 183, 191, 197, 206
Hughes, K. 52
human capital 10–11, 221–35
Hymer, S. H. 116, 117, 121, 140

IBM 168, 170
ICI 170
import-substituting FDI 123–4
industrial/agricultural chemical
    industry 148, 150, 151, 152
industrial diversification 144–53,
    160–1
industrial/farm equipment industry
    149–52 *passim*, 158, 159, 160
industrial organization approach
    to FDI 116–17
industrial strategy 178–9
industrialization 35–7
    see also de-industrialization
inflation 41, 43
information-intensive services 72,
    78
Innis, H. A. 38
innovation 5–6, 49–65
    differences across countries 60–4
    internationalization 94–5
    performance and 5–6, 50–60, 61
    services 67–8, 75–7, 79–80, 88
    see also research and
        development
instability 80–3
insurance industry 88
integration
    effects on trade 188
    global financial markets 80–3
inter-industry FDI 116
inter-industry trade 9, 183, 184
    liberalization and specialization
        192, 195–7 *passim*, 200–2
        passim, 205
internalization 116
internationalization 7, 65, 91–112
    decomposition of changes in
        degrees of 102–4
    evidence on recent trends 105–
        12
    measures of determinants of 98–
        101
    theory of process 93–8
intra-industry FDI 7–8, 75, 114–
    39, 140
    definition and measurement
        126–7

estimates of 127–37
    industrial impact 125–6
    intra-industry trade and 123–5,
        137
    review of theory 115–23
intra-industry trade 183, 187
    intra-industry FDI and 123–5,
        137
    liberalization and specialization
        9–10, 184–6, 188–92 *passim*,
        195–205 *passim*
intrusion hypothesis 6–7, 68, 85–6
Invest in Britain Bureau 169
investment
    foreign direct *see* foreign direct
        investment; intra-industry FDI
    human capital as 224–5
Ireland 185
Italy 18, 20, 185, 219
    internationalization 91, 107–12
        passim
ITT 168

James, J. 202
Japan 71, 128–9, 185
    domestic investment 18
    employment 13
    innovation 5, 49–63 *passim*
    internationalization 7, 91, 94,
        107–12 *passim*
    investment in UK 9, 167–81;
        competitive advantages 170–3;
        presence in UK 168–70
    Italian car industry 219
    productivity 20
Japan Technology Transfer
    Association 63
JETRO 179
Jones, C. D. 195
Jones, D. T. 19–20
Jones, K. 213
Juhl, P. 125
JVC 181

Kennedy Round 10, 194, 197–8
Kidd, J. B. 171
Kierzkowski, H. 221, 222, 226

Kindleberger, C. P. 77
Knickerbocker, F. T. 121
Kogut, B. 119, 120
Komatsu 167
Krugman, P. 203

labour
  costs 21–3, 51
  endowment of 223
  international division of 80
Leamer, E. E 186, 190
learning-by-doing 37–8
Leontief, W. W. 221
Levich, R. A. 88
liberalization of trade 9–10, 184,
  205
  as constraint 190–1
  episodes of 193–5
  impact of multilateral 199–201
  impact of regional 201–2
  as stimulus 191–2
  UK 193–9
Lloyd, P. J. 127
lobbying 213, 216, 218
location advantages 95–6
  internationalization and 101,
    104, 107–8, 110–11
  of the UK for Japan 175–7
Loertscher, R. 188
Lorange, P. 172
low research-intensity (LRI)
  industries 28–9, 31
Lundberg, L. 203
Luxemburg 185

Maddison, A. 14, 33
Maddock, R. 40
management, centralization of 83–
  4
market structure 214–19
Marsh, F. 171
Matsushita 181
McCarty, J. 38
McCloskey, D. 35–6
McCulloch, R. 67
McCullough, A. 31
McLean, I. 40
medium research-intensity (MRI)

industries 28, 31, 53, 55
Medium-Term Financial Strategy
  16
Mendis 20
Merck Sharpe and Dohme 170
metal manufacturing/products 152,
  158, 159–60
Mexico 84
'microchip' hypothesis 20, 24
Milner, C. R. 127, 183, 187, 188
Ministry of International Trade
  and Industry (MITI) 63, 174
Morkre, M. 212
motor vehicle industry 149, 150,
  152, 158, 159, 160
  Japan and Italy 219
  UK 27, 176–7
Muellbauer, J. 20, 21, 31
Multifibre Arrangement (MFA)
  213
multilateral liberalization 194, 199–
  201
multinational enterprises (MNEs)
  centralization of management
    83–4
  diversification *see* diversification
  internationalization *see*
    internationalization
  profits 87
  UK manufacturing 27–8, 30
  see also intra-industry FDI
Murray, T. 214

National Health Service 177
Neary, J. P. 4, 16, 40
NEC 178, 179
Nelson, R. 61, 63, 64, 65
Netherlands 185
newly industrializing countries
  (NICs) 115
Nicholas, S. 38, 41
Nissan 167, 176, 178
Nogues, J. J. 211
Norman, G. 119, 123, 125, 126
North, D. C. 38
North British Rubber 167
North/North trade 6, 79, 80
North Sea oil 14, 40

effect on manufacturing 4, 5, 16–17, 43, 44
North–South trade 6, 79–80

Office of Technology Assessment 70, 73, 88
Ohmae, K. 181
oligopolistic rivalry 8, 117, 121–2, 124, 125
Organization for Economic Co-operation and Development (OECD) 12–13, 52, 56, 61, 143
output
    UK manufacturing 24–9 *passim*
    VERs and 212, 215–16
overseas production ratio *see* foreign production ratio
'owned' subsidiaries 88
ownership advantages 115
    internationalization 93–5, 95–6, 97, 107–8, 109–10, 112; measurement 99–100, 104
    intra-industry FDI 8, 117–18, 122, 137
Ozawa, T. 181

Pagoulatos, E. 188, 189
paper/wood products 148, 150, 151, 155, 156
parent export ratio 157–60
Patel, P. 61, 62
Pavitt, K. 61, 62
Pearce, R. D. 23, 31, 98, 106, 163
Pelzman, J. 206
Perez, C. 97
Performance, innovation and 5–6, 50–60, 61
petroleum industry 148, 150, 151–2, 152–3
    see also North Sea oil
pharmaceutical industry 149, 150, 152, 177
Philip II of Spain 42
Philips 168, 170
policy 9
    economic restructuring 177–9, 181, 204–5, 205–6

human capital development 223–5
intra-industry FDI 121, 125, 137
R&D 63–4
Spain's de-industrialization 43
trade 187–8; specialization and 188–205
Pomfret, R. 183
Pratten, C. F. 21
prices 87
    VER effects 212, 215–18, 219
product development 27, 30
production
    internationalization of 92; *see also* foreign production ratio
    location of 175–6
production subsidies 230, 231, 233–4
productivity
    innovation and 51–2
    UK 19–21, 22–3
protectionism, new 195, 211
    see also voluntary export restraints
Pugel, T. A. 125

quality 222, 226–8

ratio VERs 10, 215–19 *passim*
rationalized FDI 119–21, 123–4, 125–6, 137
Ray, G. F. 21, 22
Rayment, P. B. 203
Reagan administration 81
reciprocity 180–1
regional liberalization 194, 201–2
Reich, R. B. 221, 222, 223
research and development (R&D) 61–4, 178, 179
    co-operative 64–5
    costs 172
    performance and 5–6, 52–60
research intensity 23–9, 31, 52–5
resource movement effect 42
rivalry, oligopolistic 8, 117, 121–2, 124, 125
Robinson, B. 31

Robson, P. 188
Rostow, W. W. 34–5
Royal Dutch Shell 168
rubber industry 149, 150, 151
Rugman, A. M. 87, 92, 118, 121, 125
Rybczynski, T. M. 222

Sauvant, K. P. 77, 87, 88
scale, economies of 120
Schlesinger, J. R. 81
Schultze, C.L. 223
scope, economies of 8, 119
services 6–7, 12, 14–15, 67–86
Sharp Electronics 167, 178
Shelp, R. K. 88
Siebert, W. S. 225
Siemens 170
Silberston, Z. A. 212
silver 41
Sinclair, W. A. 38
Singer 167
Singh, A. 30
skill subsidies 10–11, 222, 234–5
    duopolistic model 228–34
    quality 226–8
skills 221–35
    under-provision 221–2, 223–5
Smith, M. 15–16, 31
Sony 178, 179, 181
Sorenson, R. 188, 189
source-specific quotas (SSQs) 219
    see also voluntary export restraints
sourcing ratio 99
Spain 5, 40–1, 42–3
specialization of trade 183–6
    liberalization and 187–205
Spencer, B. J. 222, 227, 228–9, 232–3, 234
spending effect 41
splintering 72
staple vent-for-surplus model 38–40
Stern, R. M. 206
Stewart, F. 202
Stopford, J. M. 119, 120, 123
strengths, firm-level 146–7, 150

structural adjustment *see* adjustment
Sugden, R. 98
Sumitomo Rubber Company 169

Takacs, W. 214
take-offs 34–5
Talbot 176
tariffs 37–8
    see also liberalization of trade
Tarr, D. 212
technology
    internationalization and 97–8
    sophistication of services 75–6
Technopolis programme 63
Teece, D. J. 119
Temperton, P. 16
Teremato 171
textile tariffs 37–8
Thirlwall, A. P. 12, 15, 27, 30
Thompson, G. 60
tobacco industry 158, 160
Toh, K. 189
Tokyo Round 10, 195, 199, 200
Toshiba 179
Toyota 176
trade
    industrialization and 35–8
    innovation and performance 53–5
    intra-industry FDI and 123–5, 137–8
    liberalization *see* liberalization
    reciprocity 180–1
    services 72–5, 86; direct implications of growth 75–80; indirect implications of growth 80–5
    skills 10–11, 221–2, 226–35
    specialization *see* specialization
    theory of international 15
    UK manufactures 26–9 *passim*
    vent-for-surplus models 38–40
    see also voluntary export restraints
trade diversion 212
trade unions 98